RETHINKING CYBER SECURITY

GENE LLOYD

Cover image © Shutterstock.com

Kendall Hunt
publishing company

www.kendallhunt.com
Send all inquiries to:
4050 Westmark Drive
Dubuque, IA 52004-1840

Copyright © 2022 by Gene Lloyd

ISBN 979-8-7657-0543-8

Kendall Hunt Publishing Company has the exclusive rights to reproduce this work,
to prepare derivative works from this work, to publicly distribute this work,
to publicly perform this work and to publicly display this work.

All rights reserved. No part of this publication may be reproduced,
stored in a retrieval system, or transmitted, in any form or by any
means, electronic, mechanical, photocopying, recording, or otherwise,
without the prior written permission of the copyright owner.

Published in the United States of America

CONTENTS

CHAPTER 1: History 1

CHAPTER 2: Paradigm Shift 15

CHAPTER 3: Traffic Analysis 33

CHAPTER 4: Vulnerability Assessment 51

CHAPTER 5: Penetration Testing 67

CHAPTER 6: Incident Response Evidence Collection 85

CHAPTER 7: Incident Response Evidence Analysis 99

CHAPTER 8: Hardening Windows 113

CHAPTER 9: Hardening Linux 127

CHAPTER 10: Hardening Network 141

CHAPTER 11: Cloud Security 155

CHAPTER 12: Cryptography 169

APPENDIX 1: Linux Commands 185

APPENDIX 2: Meterpreter Commands 187

APPENDIX 3: Common Ports and Protocols 193

History

CHAPTER 1

Cyber security is loosely defined as techniques and measures used to protect computer systems from unauthorized access. Cyber security is made up of physical and technical controls specifically designed to allow authorized users to operate unimpeded on systems and networks while blocking any activity deemed unallowable (by the person or organization whose authority determines the level of security in place). Simply put, cyber security keeps bad actors out, lets good actors in, and ensures all services are available for secure use. It has existed in some form for several decades—previously known as computer security—but was not a real consideration when the internet was first created.

The early days of computing was focused more on connectivity and communication. There was very little consideration for the possibility of individuals attempting to break into or manipulate systems, at least not at the level we see today, so the concepts of cyber security available for networks today was born significantly later… as hacking became more of a serious threat.

Hacking has a colorful history that actually started long before the Internet was born – when the first small packets of data were transmitted between interconnected computers. Curious people who have an interest in how technology works tend to stumble upon ways technology can be modified or manipulated to accomplish different goals. This is a natural knack for some who like to tinker with devices – to figure out how they work, how they can be modified, and in some cases, how they can be manipulated to function in a way different from their original design. That curiosity can easily cross the line into questionable or illegal activity, which is exactly what eventually started happening when people started looking at ways to manipulate communication systems. The role of cyber security has broadened alongside the growth of hacking and taken on much more responsibility than protecting a handful of computers in an office. The daily dependance on computing devices has raised the stake, requiring a significant level of vigilance to keep hackers out of systems.

Hacking has taken on a few different meanings in society. It has become a synonym for making a product or idea better such as waterproofing a pair of shoes or more safely storing Christmas ornaments. Clearly, this is not the same as breaking into a computer. Hacking, for the purposes of this book, is gaining unauthorized access to a computer or network through the manipulation of protocols or applications. This includes all forms of computing devices—smartphones, tablets, satellites, televisions, and even internet-connected appliances to name a few. If a device can connect to the internet, it has the ability to communicate with other devices, and could potentially be broken into by an unauthorized user. Keep this definition in mind as you work through each chapter. To be fair, it is also important to note, not all hackers consider themselves criminals, requiring the hacker definition be a little more nuanced.

Some hackers see their actions as political statements. Some are fighting for a free internet where no one's activity is monitored. Some use their skills to blast their ideas across the internet in the hopes of starting a digital revolution. And some are actively looking for ways to make money through theft and manipulation. All of these categories pose a threat. The security world has even tried to redefine terms by referring to hackers as people who break into systems for good intentions, and creating a new term, crackers, to identify users who break into systems for bad intentions. This was an attempt to delineate between those who use their skills to test the security of systems and subsequently secure vulnerable devices from attack, and those who look for ways to gain something out of there hacking exploits.

The terms white hat, grey hat, and black hat were also created to form similar delineations. White hats are the good hackers, black hats are the bad hackers, and grey hats are… you guessed it, somewhere in between. These terms were borrowed from old Western movies where the good guy often wore a white hat while the bad guy wore a black hat. And so, we have yet another set of terms to consider.

The reality in the security world is that professional security experts need to learn to think like a bad actor in order to provide a greater level of protection. Police officers are often trained to think like criminals, so they can guess at what the criminal's next action will be, and more easily catch them before a new crime is committed. Taking that same approach in cyber security has helped to secure many networks. But it has also muddied the definition waters and forced the creation of these new terms. It is important to know the variations, and in this book, the hacker term will exclusively be used as someone with bad intentions to eliminate confusion.

Where did hacking originally begin? One of the earliest forms of hacking, coined phone phreaking, took advantage of the technology used to manage phone networks, with the goal of making free phone calls. Phone phreaking was the process of gaining access by mimicking the tone used on analog phone lines. A tone at just the right frequency, 2600 hertz, would allow users to place free phone calls to anywhere in the world. This was possible because the signal was used internally by telephone companies to control trunk lines. The process was relatively simple once you knew it was possible. Anyone wanting to take advantage would simply dial a 1-800 number, which would cause the phone system to connect the user to an unused trunk line. Next, the caller would send the 2600 hertz signal through the phone, tricking the distant exchange into thinking the call was completed, while making the local exchange think a call was still in place. All that was left was to dial a number they wanted to call anywhere in the world. Phone phreakers were able to use this simple trick to make all the free phone calls they wanted.

Many different methods were used to create the 2600 hertz tone. Most phreakers constructed small electronic boxes, originally called blue boxes, that would generate the tone on demand. Others tried to mimic the tone with organs or similar instruments. One convenient coincidence for phone phreakers popped up as a toy prize in the Captain Crunch line of cereal. A small plastic toy whistle was distributed in the cereal starting in the mid-1960's as a gimmick for kids to signal mealtime. This was a convenient coincidence for phone phreakers because it was accidentally discovered in 1971 by John Draper that this whistle blew at a perfect 2600 hertz. Yes, a toy whistle was capable of taking control of telephone trunk lines and making free phone calls. You did not need an engineering degree, electrical soldering skills, or an understanding of the pitches of different frequencies. You just needed enough money for a box of cereal. You can watch a video of John Draper demonstrating this whistle here:

https://www.youtube.com/watch?v=3Dgs0oTe2M8

This capability died in the 1980's when phone networks upgraded their systems with newer technologies, effectively ending the phone phreaking craze. Phone phreaking did something many hacking exploits also do today—it took advantage of a technology that did not include security measures to keep unauthorized users out of the network. Security was an afterthought in that era. The engineers creating technologies for the world to communicate were not thinking about nefarious actors attempting to exploit these systems. And that is exactly what opened up the door of possibility for phone phreakers to continue their activity for approximately fifteen years. Many varieties of hackers have used this same simple ideology of exploiting weaknesses, from the early days of phone phreaking all the way up to current time. Vulnerabilities in systems create the opportunities hackers crave.

The biggest phone threats we have today come in the form of malicious apps camouflaged as something fun or useful. Smartphones have given users capabilities once thought futuristic and out of reach. The old rotary dial phones gave way to push button phones, then flip phones were all the rage, and now powerful computers sit in the pockets and purses of billions of users around the world, showing digital technology has advanced very quickly. The advancement brought new security risks, not just in the form of vulnerable applications, but also vulnerable people. People themselves have weaknesses that can be exploited without the use of keyboards, codes, and commands. Social engineering techniques convinced people to give up access to systems long before the art of hacking solidified into what it is today.

Social engineering is the method of tricking people into believing something that is not true. It has historically been used in the hacking world to gain access to systems or data by pretending to be an authorized user. Social engineering was much easier to employ in the early days of computing because many users were unaware of potential security risks. For example, an individual could call an unsuspecting secretary pretending to be a system administrator working on a problem. With the right script they could easily acquire a username and password that could later be used to access internal company systems. This straightforward approach is not as effective today because most users have now had enough basic training to know the importance of not providing these details to anyone. But in the early days, social engineering was the easiest way to gain access.

This is possible because with the right scenario, people tend to naturally believe what they are told, within reason, and if they are not trained to be on the lookout for someone actively trying to manipulate them into divulging information, they can easily fall prey to such an attack. It is a simple enough idea that has taken many years of training for users to recognize when someone is trying to 'socially engineer' them into giving up access or information. Most people today know passwords should not be shared, not everyone should not be allowed in a building, and just because someone is wearing a maintenance uniform does not mean they are authorized to wander the hallways alone. Crafting emails with malicious links was one way to catch users off guard, but even that method is becoming less successful today. There are many famous social engineering feats that have been pulled off over the years.

The breach into Yahoo's email servers in 2014 started from social engineering. Three billion user accounts were ultimately impacted after someone gained unauthorized access using a concept known as spear phishing. Phishing is a technique where a crafted email is sent to a mass number of users within a company with the hopes at least one person will click on a malicious link included in the email. These messages mimic what may be received from a system administrator mandating passwords be reset, a bank claiming your account is about to be closed, or similar messaging that evokes an emotional response. Waiting at the other end of the link is a system housing some form of malware which is automatically downloaded onto a user's computer and provides backdoor access into the system. All it takes is for one user to be fooled by the phishing email to make the attack successful.

Spear phishing is essentially the same methodology (as phishing) with one minor difference. These forms of attacks target specific users instead of a large number of employees. The spear phishing messages tend to be more crafted for a specific user based on information the hacker may have previously obtained. A well-crafted email appearing to come from your child's school stating that your child is in trouble for cheating on an exam will quickly get your attention. Including a link in that email purporting to be a photograph of the exam in question is very likely to be clicked. This is how spear phishing works. The type of spear phishing message that worked against Yahoo is unknown, but the attack targeted a user with some level of privileged access and, as history shows, was ultimately successful. One email, worded in a specific way, to a targeted user, can provide access to a hacker without the need for scanning, assessments, or exploits.

Another successful social engineering feat was Kane Gamble's attack against senior U.S. Government officials in 2015, a feat that landed him a prison sentence. Gamble impersonated the director of the CIA in phone calls to Verizon and AOL giving him access to phone numbers and accounts he then used to harass other senior leaders in the FBI, Department of Homeland Security, Department of Justice and several advisors to the President. At one point, the CIA director's outgoing calls on his personal home phone line were automatically forwarded to a Palestinian political movement number. The really crazy part is Gamble was only 15 years old at the time. The face of this attack shows a lot of embarrassment for those involved in being duped by a teenager. It also shows how difficult it is to get away with public criminal activity against powerful people. Anyone can end up a target of phishing, so everyone needs to be aware of these attacks take place.

These types of activities highlight the need for a greater level of user training to more easily recognize email phishing attempts. Sometimes it is obvious, when the message has very poor English grammar and is clearly not from any legitimate person needing you to take action on a situation. Other times, these messages are so well crafted even the most experienced professional may think it is real and consider clicking the link. Many attacks do not specifically target users, so they do not need to have detailed knowledge of how to defend vulnerable systems. But training to recognize and report attacks directed at users, such as phishing, and the broader social engineering methods, is one of the best ways to keep these activities from being successful. It was once proposed, and implemented for a time in some organizations, that stripping all HTML content out of emails before they arrive in the user's mailbox was the best method to combat this tactic. It certainly works. A link cannot be clicked on if it does not exist. But this also removed many other capabilities. Properly training users became the balanced approach.

The first known internet worm was created by Robert Morris in 1988, as an experiment to determine the size of the ARPANET, the precursor to the internet. It is estimated that the worm propagated through 10% of the 60,000 systems connected at the time, wreaking havoc on college and U.S. Government systems. Infected systems slowed to a crawl as the worm worked its way in and out of the network sucking up the available bandwidth and computing power. Morris claimed the damage was unintentional and was caused by a programming error, but that did not keep him out of hot water. He was convicted of violating the relatively new U.S. Computer Fraud and Abuse Act and sentenced to a lengthy probation period along with fines and community service. The Morris worm showed hackers the possibility of creating large scale denial-of-service attacks by exploiting the same unpatched vulnerability on thousands of systems. This was the first worm, but certainly not the worst.

Fifteen years after the Morris worm, a new worm slammed the internet with much greater consequences. Other worms existed between this time, but the impact of the SQL slammer worm lit up intrusion detection systems around the world. This attack took advantage of a vulnerability in unpatched Microsoft SQL servers, infecting vulnerable systems and turning each one into a propagation machine, spreading the virus further across the internet. Its rapid spread caused a 'denial of service' on internet hosts as the amount of traffic quickly increased, overwhelming routers around the world. Fortunately, for home users, the SQL slammer worm was not a threat because SQL servers are rarely run in someone's home. This worm had more impact on businesses and ultimately network bandwidth. The internet slowdown persisted until systems could be cleaned and blocks put in place to end the propagation.

Online criminal activity has steadily increased since the advent of computing and creation of the internet. For a season of time, the criminals had the upper hand in running rough shod over networks in systems. Each new application brought the possibility of a new vulnerability which could be exploited and very few people understood the importance of plugging those holes before someone else found out how the software could be manipulated. Most hackers in the early days were focused more on the challenge of breaking in and less on the disruption of services or theft of information. Some of that was certainly of interest, but the larger element of hacking was for fun and to gain a better reputation amongst peers. The balance of power has shifted to security professionals as most of society has become aware of the importance of maintaining security over systems and data. But there is still a lot of work to do.

Technology has a way of providing capabilities without always including the best security as part of the package. The creation of wireless internet access brought about an explosion of Wi-Fi networks in the early 2000's, and almost every one of them were installed with numerous inherent security problems. The wireless equivalency protocol (WEP)—designed to provide a measure of security when clients requested access to a Wi-Fi network—was so flawed it was easily broken, allowing anyone to connect to a Wi-Fi router. Once this access was gained, malicious actors could begin scanning for vulnerabilities on the internal side of the network and quickly gain access to user systems. This was a major problem for home users, where most Wi-Fi devices were being installed. It spawned such ideas as wardriving, where someone would drive through neighborhoods looking for open or vulnerable Wi-Fi networks, and warchalking, where marks would be left on sidewalks or walls identifying potential Wi-Fi targets. It was relatively easy to drive down a street while a laptop scanned the area for potential connections.

War chalking to identify a Wi-Fi access point without a password.

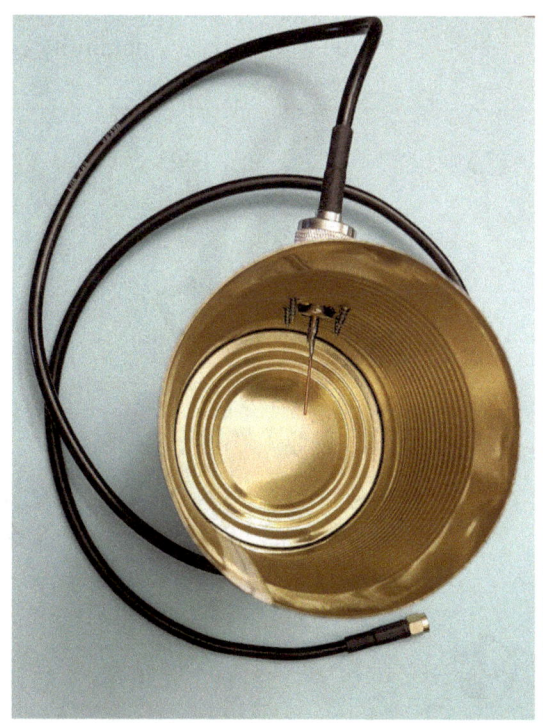

The business world had its own challenges with Wi-Fi as allowing this level of access to users essentially created backdoors into networks where Wi-Fi networks sat behind a firewall. The ease of gaining access to a Wi-Fi network put many companies at risk and eventually resulted in the best practice of using logon servers, in combination with Wi-Fi access points, to force users to authenticate to the network after establishing a wireless connection. Free wireless access still exists in many places today where customers can use the internet while shopping, eating, or meeting with friends. The difference in this public capability is the access point is isolated away from other systems offering only a gateway to the internet and nothing else. Securing Wi-Fi access will be discussed further in chapter 10 along with other network hardening techniques.

Web applications became the top target in the past decade with so many companies transitioning from traditional HTML designs with embedded scripting languages to full-blown applications. Store fronts became much more functional and user friendly. Navigating and making purchases became much more intuitive using an application designed with programming languages that increased capabilities within a web environment. This was a good thing, right? Yes. The challenge though, is that many of these applications were designed in-house without any real security testing to make sure they were not serving up the server on a silver platter. The two most common things hackers would previously do with a website was (1) deface it for some street cred or political motivation, or (2) use it as a way into a network. Web applications gave additional opportunities to gain direct access to backend customer and sales databases allowing for modification of product data and theft of personal information.

Many large organizations started offering bug bounties to anyone who discovered a potential vulnerability on their website. It was cheaper and easier to pay a third-party expert for vulnerability information than pay the cost of cleaning up after an incident. The catch is the expert needed to register for the program, participate by a set of rules, and not reveal the vulnerability to anyone else. Not a bad set of rules to practice vulnerability assessments and make some extra money at the same time. This process continues today as more and more applications continue to increase on websites. Companies learned the value of providing incentives for approved operators to actively look for vulnerabilities. It is cheaper than the alternatives and cheaper than higher, large penetration testing organizations to run an operation against the network. It never hurts to have a second set of eyes to catch a small mistake that could turn into a big problem.

© Art studio G/Shutterstock.com

A nice side effect of malicious network activity is that it spawned the growth of security technologies at a very accelerated rate. The need for better controls in a variety of areas caused some concepts – which already existed – to become common necessities for everyday use of computers. Malware, such as the worms already mentioned along with other viruses, increased so dramatically it required every system to run some form of antivirus software. This was great for users and the organizations that provided the software. Antivirus became a big business and continues to be a necessity today. Antivirus also increased in its capability to recognize and stop most viruses before any damage can be done. That should always be the goal of a security technology. Stop activity before harm can be done. If it does not perform that function, it is not doing its job!

Email spam filters also showed dramatic improvement. Email boxes used to be littered with so many unwanted spam messages that it was hard to weed out the bad and find the good. These messages were mostly mass advertising campaign for products and services 99% of the recipients had no interest in. They were a result of organizations selling email addresses and email servers being poorly configured to allow the relaying of messages. We see very little spam today as multiple organizations worked to filter out the garbage, eliminate the weaknesses in email servers, update protocols, and drive the spammers mostly out of business. That junk mail folder you have in your email account is the result of this work and today's methods catch nearly all spam before it hits your real inbox. Now the form of advertising on the internet is more targeted through websites and social media, though there are ways to limit that content as well.

More recent history has brought about the craze of using Virtual Private Network (VPN) services to give users greater privacy online. Users are recognizing that the level of tracking internet activity has increased dramatically in the past decade. Some may think this is paranoia of government's monitoring everything they do, which is certainly true in communist nations, but it is the social network, search engine, and advertising arenas who are siphoning up most of the everyday user activity. It is not difficult to collect information on an individual who freely uses a platform designed for information searching or sharing. Google catalogs everything their search engine is used for and attaches it to a user profile if the individual is logged into their services. Social networks leverage user activity into targeted advertising and large advertising organizations correlate internet traffic to render specific ads a user may be interested in seeing. The data generated from internet activity has become a big business.

This can feel like invasion of privacy, but that is a hard claim to make when the information is being freely give to the organizations through using their services. Consider how much personal information the average person places on social media platforms. Over time, someone with access to all the user's information could conceivably build a profile of where the individual lives, works, vacations, and how they spend most of their time. And all of the information is provided up on a virtual silver platter while interacting with other online users. A VPN service, which will be covered more in depth in a later chapter, creates an encrypted communication stream between the user and the location of the VPN provider's server, and all subsequent internet activity appears to originate at the point of that server. This masks a user's true location. Many people have taken to this practice to create at least a small level of privacy when using some internet services.

Future Concerns

The history of this field eventually advanced to the point where experts began to tout the importance of a layered security approach providing a level of security throughout an entire network, not just at the perimeter. This is still a sound idea today, though other methodologies should also be adopted to make it even more difficult for attackers. Hacking may not ever cease to be a problem, but if we make systems virtually impenetrable, the criminal activity associated with hacking will greatly lessen. Security professionals need to be willing to use every potential technology to keep online criminal activity at bay. There needs to be more out-of-the-box thinking to develop creative solutions for the challenge that has been staring networks in the face for several decades. Security is not difficult if leaders in this field are willing to make the tough decisions between allowing any device to service to participate on a network or restricting the network to only what is necessary.

The Internet of Things (IoT) has and is bringing more everyday devices onto the internet. Some kitchen appliances are now able to connect to the internet, thermostats and lighting controls can hook into your local network and be controlled by voice commands, and of course, the personal assistants, such as Amazon Alexa, allow a person to listen to music, purchase products, and a myriad of other things while these

devices pull information from an internet connection. But are they secure? Is there a vulnerability lurking in the code a hacker can exploit? Can a malicious actor make changes to your thermostat in the middle of the night? Can someone hack the speaker on Alexa and listen to your private conversations? These may sound like paranoid fears, but if history has taught us anything, a vulnerability in one device can wreak havoc. Time will tell if security was a priority when these types of devices were developed.

Is it nice to have a refrigerator list out the prices for the produce you are running short on? Sure! Is it beneficial to have a pseudo-intelligent digital assistant answer questions instead of manually searching for the answer in a browser? Definitely. But what is the cost? The security professional always needs to think about the potential cost. What is the cost for allowing a device with little to no inherent security to communicate on the network? What other communication is taking place? These are the questions experts need to ask and users need to be trained to think about. Here is a little secret – these are the questions hackers like to ask. What is going on behind the scenes that I can use to manipulate the system and gain some level of access? At the very least, any IoT device added to a network should have a full penetration test run against it before allowing it to operate with internet access. Like web applications, security has not been the number one priority in IoT product development.

Security was mostly an afterthought for many years in software production and is now a much more solidified part of the coding process in more traditional arenas, but not in every arena. The computer science field has come a long way to make security a priority instead of a knee-jerk response when something negative occurs. Our networks are more secure today than ever before in history, or they at least have the capability to be more secure, and that trend will continue into the future as more technologies are developed to provide security on every device we use. Networks do not need to be vulnerable. The technology exists today to keep anyone out of a network if the correct measures are put in place and users are willing to accept less capabilities in return for greater security. It is often a balancing act between these two desires with a little bit of lackadaisical attitude peppered in.

It has been said many times that those who do not learn from history are doomed to repeat it. Every cyber security professional needs to be aware of the different elements of attacks which have occurred in the past and use that information to bolster security and train users of potential threats. Some historical activity continues today as it still works on occasion. Phishing emails can still be effective; it only takes one user to click on a link. Social engineering can still be effective. One tired employee working long hours can easily fall for a well-crafted script. Wars tend to result in the development of new technologies and capabilities which provide a greater level of protection for society. War itself is destructive, but the technological advancements could help to keep other wars from ever starting.

The variety of hacking methodologies which have occurred have also spawned many great security tools in use today. The ReCAPTCHA tools developed by Google to discern the difference between humans at the keyboard and digital bots attempting to submit data on websites has eliminated a lot of unnecessary spam messages.

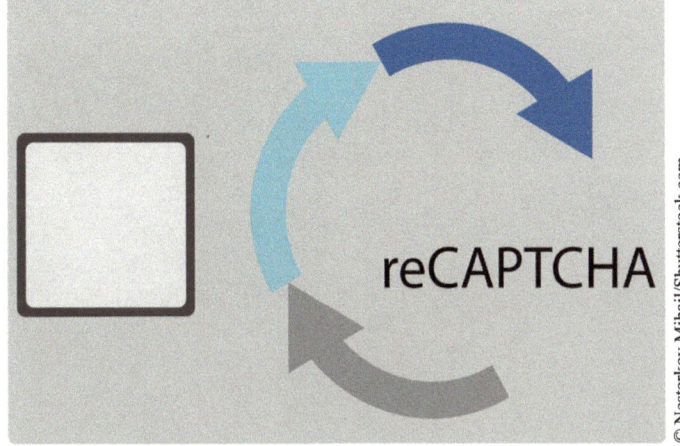

Newer strategies for network security and advanced antivirus algorithms have further slowed the propagation of attacks that suck away needed bandwidth. Many more technologies will invariably be developed as hackers change their modus operandi and look for more creative ways to penetrate systems. What we, as cyber security professionals, cannot allow to happen is a lackadaisical attitude towards security once again giving digital criminals the upper hand. We have the high ground in this battle, and as long as we maintain a vigilant posture, we are much more likely to win each new skirmish.

Chapter 1: Review Questions

1. Cyber security keeps _____.
   a. Good actors out
   b. Bad actors in
   c. Bad actors out
   d. Good actors safe

2. _____ people like to figure out how technology works.
   a. Curious
   b. Crazy
   c. Manipulative
   d. Malicious

3. If a device is connected to the internet, it has the ability to _____.
   a. Hack other systems
   b. Communicate with other systems
   c. Protect other systems
   d. Manage other systems

4. Some hacking is an extension of _____ statements.
   a. Divisive
   b. Paranoid
   c. Political
   d. Educational

5. A white hat is _____.
   a. A hacker with bad intentions
   b. A hacker with good intentions
   c. A former bad hacker turned good
   d. A government hacker

6. A black hat is _____.
   a. A hacker with bad intentions
   b. A hacker with good intentions
   c. A former bad hacker turned good
   d. A government hacker

7. Phone phreaking used a tone at _____ to gain access to phone networks.
   a. 2600 MHz
   b. 2500 Hertz
   c. 3600 MHz
   d. 2600 Hertz

8. What toy was used to break into phone networks?
   a. Legos
   b. Wheaties figurine
   c. Model train whistle
   d. Captain Crunch whistle

9. Today's biggest phone threats are ___.
   a. Malicious apps
   b. Unaware users
   c. Insecure networks
   d. Wi-Fi

10. _____ tricks people into providing information or access.
    a. Societal engineering
    b. Social mechanics
    c. Social engineering
    d. Social manipulation

11. People tend to _____ what they are told when a scenario makes sense.
    a. Believe
    b. Refute
    c. Ignore
    d. Challenge

12. The Yahoo breach was a result of _____.
    a. Spear fishing
    b. Spear phishing
    c. Phishing
    d. Fishing

13. Kane Gamble's attack was the result of _____.
    a. Spear fishing
    b. Spear phishing
    c. Phishing
    d. Fishing

14. User _____ is the best way to combat phishing attempts.
    a. Emails
    b. Reluctance
    c. Punishment
    d. Training

15. The first known internet worm was _____.
    a. SQL Slammer worm
    b. Morris worm
    c. Mason worm
    d. Malevolent worm

16. War _____ scanned neighborhoods for open Wi-Fi networks.
    a. Chalking
    b. Driving
    c. Scanning
    d. Pinging
17. War _____ marked locations of open Wi-Fi networks.
    a. Chalking
    b. Driving
    c. Scanning
    d. Pinging
18. _____ applications are one of the top web-based targets today.
    a. Email
    b. Server
    c. User
    d. Web
19. _____ bounties pay users to find vulnerabilities.
    a. Vulnerability
    b. Spider
    c. Bug
    d. Incentive
20. _____ services provide greater privacy when using the internet.
    a. Firewall
    b. VPN
    c. Router
    d. Masking

Paradigm Shift

CHAPTER 2

Cyber security is a definitive necessity in today's world of interconnected devices, as perpetual online users aggressively consume internet bandwidth 24 hours a day. Security is what keeps us safe. We lock the doors of our homes each night to ensure no unauthorized individual gains access. We set alarms to add a secondary level of protection just in case someone attempts to push past those physical barriers, and in some cases, put additional layers of security in place to ensure we can protect what is important to us. Cyber security was mostly ignored in the early days of the internet, but as more users plugged into cyberspace, and nefarious actors found ways to manipulate protocols, the need for effective layers of security became abundantly clear. The problem was simple to define. People had a need to protect their data from criminals who were constantly on the prowl for a target that could be easily manipulated.

The same need continues to exist today, and in many different formats, as many electronic devices have the ability to connect to the internet. If the device can connect to the internet, someone can connect to the device. Controlling access for who is allowed to connect is the challenge in this field. But every situation is not the same. The mega corporation with thousands of servers and worldwide users will require a much more in-depth security solution than a small business with a single laptop and a Wi-Fi router. Networks that allow external connections to digital services will need software and devices that filter access requests while isolated networks can simply keep the door closed to any form of external connections. It is easy to preach on paper about in-depth security measures, but the deployment and management of those measures is much more nuanced in the real world.

As a professional in this field, or someone just dipping your toes into the waters, it is important for you to understand this nuance, and not go full bore with all available security mechanisms in every situation. There is always a level of assumed risk when operating on the internet. There is also always a method of over-engineering a security solution to simply comply with past perspectives on best security practices. Cyber security should not be approached as a cookie cutter solution. There are methods and capabilities that all networks should have in place, such as antivirus software, and there are those which are only needed when specific services are provided to users, such as a virtual private network (VPN) server. The methods we put into place should be tailored to the needs of the network and capabilities required by the users; no more, and no less. This requires a paradigm shift.

As in any other field, there must be a willingness in the realm of cyber security to update and modify standard practices. Consider some of the major hacking events of the past decade—Target, Home Depot, the U.S. Government Office of Personnel Management (OPM), and Colonial Pipeline were all attacked in some measure by hackers. None of these organizations have publicly revealed the totality of security devices or protocols in place on their networks, but the fact that hackers were able to gain access reveals that the security was not tailored to their particular needs. In the case of Colonial Pipeline, the attack likely came from hackers in Eastern Europe (a). Why would a company operating on U.S. soil allow connections from Eastern Europe into their oil pipeline operation? Similarly, the consensus among experts is that state sponsored hackers in China were responsible for the attack on OPM that resulted in the theft of millions of federal employee personnel records (b). The question is the same as with Colonial Pipeline. Why would OPM ever allow connections from China into their network?

These examples, of course, can extend to many other successful hacking attempts of the past, and they all point to the reality that either our current approach to security is not as effective as it needs to be, or organizations ignore best security practices and make themselves vulnerable to attack as a result. It is likely a combination of both issues. In the cases mentioned above, a simple block of all activity from nations outside of the United States could have completely eliminated, or greatly increased the difficulty of, hacking into Colonial Pipeline and OPM. Other more complex methods could have also been used to repel attacks of this nature, but the security mechanisms in place failed to protect the networks. These events are a great reminder for everyone involved in cyber security that the cookie cutter approaches employed over the past decade are not the perfect solution for every organization.

New leaders in this field need to take a look at the complex solutions we often put in place and consider if there are simpler, more effective solutions. It is very common to put expensive solutions into place, which need to be managed by highly skilled professionals in order to be effective and then be lured into a sense of false security because a particular device is attached to a network. Shifting our perspective to focus on tailored solutions for the networks we manage is a much more cost-effective, security-effective, and manageable practice. This often requires out-of-the-box thinking to implement solutions that hackers cannot effectively attack. A combination of traditional cyber security methods and out-of-the-box thinking can often give even the smallest of networks a robust security framework that hackers will have great difficulty penetrating.

Take for example, the placement of web servers on a network. The web server, as the public-facing connection to an organization, has long been an easy avenue of attack into a network because if hackers could gain access to the web server, they could then pivot into other systems on the network and continue to wreak greater havoc. The typical network had the web server connected to the same switch or hub as other devices and this configuration allowed for an easy hopping point for other more critical systems (see figure 2.1a). Hackers were not only focused on defacing a web page to bring embarrassment to the organization, but they were also looking for a deeper level of access and the web server connection made it all the more possible. Experts had to creatively consider a methodology that allowed for the web server to continue to serve its function and at the same time eliminate this large security risk.

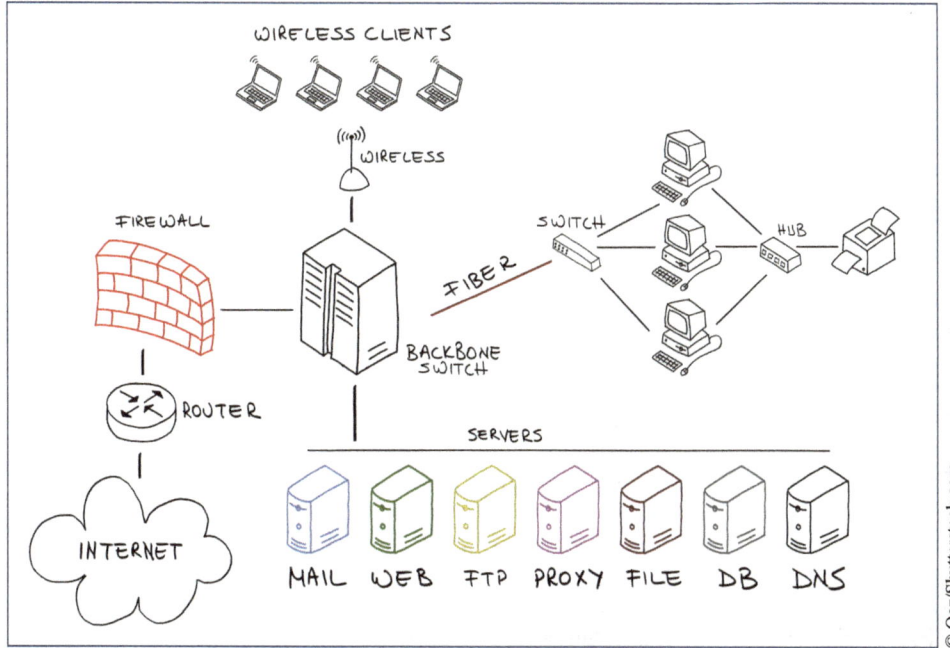

FIGURE 2.1A: Network diagram without DMZ

The first big fix action for this problem was to relocate the web server to another portion of the network where it could be isolated from other systems. This was coined the demilitarized zone, or DMZ for short, borrowing from military terminology where a strip of land is used as a buffer between nations that establishes a separation between opposing military forces. The DMZ in computer networks serves a similar purpose by creating an intentional network segment logically isolated away from all other production systems. The design is very simple, as you can see in figure 2.1b, where the devices located in the DMZ are sandwiched between two firewalls that contains web traffic and controls the other types of traffic allowed to flow into the internal network. This solution was not developed just for web servers, but for any other device or service that required to be available to outside connections. Email and domain name system (DNS) servers are also commonly located in the DMZ.

A simpler method to eliminate these specific risks with public-facing services is to outsource some (or all) of those services to a 3rd party, eliminating the need for associated traffic to traverse the organization's network. Hosting a web server with a web hosting provider does not eliminate the possibility of the website being hacked, but it does eliminate the potential hopping point into the organization's internal network. It also outsources the requirement of all associated patching, upgrading, and securing of software and services. Within risk management, this is known as risk transference, and within cyber security it eliminates a possible avenue of attack. Both are necessary elements in securing a network. This solution may not be practical for an organization with large on-site databases interconnected with web services. But for a small business with a simple web store, this solution eliminates a lot of overhead and unnecessary equipment.

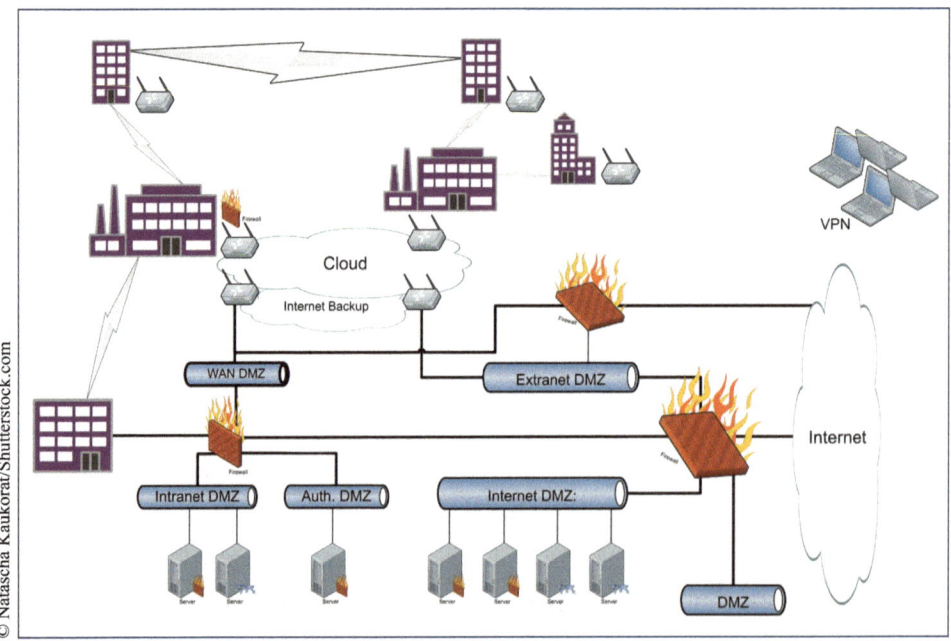

FIGURE 2.1B: Network diagram with DMZ

So, the need to look at cyber security with fresh eyes is glaringly apparent in light of the systemic failures seen in government and industry over the past decade. Are the threats not being taken seriously enough to put the right measures in place? Or do we need to develop better strategies that can more effectively stop a hacker in their tracks? Historically, experts in this field have favored a layered security approach to provide an in-depth security architecture, covering every conceivable path of attack. This approach works very well so long as all devices are properly configured, systems are immediately patched when updates are available, and analysts vigorously monitor network traffic 24/7/365. This method is very effective at keeping bad actors out of the network. The reality is that, in most cases, this is not how security operations are actually approached on a day-to-day basis, for several reasons.

First, except for large organizations holding plenty of capital, most business operations cannot afford the cost of maintaining such a rigorous security posture. Security devices, especially the high-end ones, are incredibly expensive. The number of required devices to hit maximum protection in a layered defense posture can put a lot of stress on the operations budget. We also have hardware repair, maintenance fees, and upgrades which add another layer of repetitive costs to be factored into the equation. Second, all this equipment needs to be managed a highly trained staff. Maintaining manpower for a high-level security posture is relatively easy in the short-term but very difficult in perpetuity. Complacency tends to creep in over time when there is very little nefarious activity, causing employees to pay less attention to detail, which increase the risk of a successful attack. And the risk we were trying to avoid comes right back into play.

This is why blending cyber security best practices with real world expectations is incredibly important. The overall need for security will always exist, but the specific measures required will be different in every organization. Forcing a one-size-fits-all approach does not serve anyone's best interest. The network in question should first be analyzed to determine which capabilities are needed, what services are offered, and common day to day usage of internal systems. This analysis can easily help to determine the type of security appliances and software the organization needs to put in place. Every network does not need armed human guards at the door, attack dogs roaming the property, and auto destruct sequences built into the servers. Many smaller networks with a minimal web presence can deploy a scaled-down methodology with some added tightening of restricted source connections, resulting in a very strong security posture.

Even with scaled down measures, security is still an inconvenient necessity. Users need access to specific capabilities in order to successfully accomplish their tasks. The mission of the organization cannot bow to heightened security methods. If the users are unable to work, the mission fails. Security must be adapted for mission accomplishment. And then there is the employee morale factor. Many company networks allow access to news, sports, social media, and other similar internet content for employee consumption. Should this even be allowed? Is there any reason within a normal business environment where employees would need access to this type of information? Of course, the answer is typically no, but managers often allow some web surfing to boost morale, accepting a level of risk as a result.

Sometimes cyber security professionals need to be the bad guy and recommend access to certain types of activity should be restricted or blocked.

You need to have the courage to inform management of potentially dangerous practices and the necessary fix actions to eliminate security risks. It does not need to be doom and gloom, but as the expert protecting the network, part of your job is to make sure management is aware of activities that can lead to a hacking incident. It is then their job to determine which risks are acceptable for the organization. Managers need to balance mission accomplishment with budgetary allowances, and security is only one piece of the puzzle. Is it an important piece? Definitely! But keep in mind that your fix actions typically come with a price tag. Security can be a drain on the budget, causing quick request denials, so always come with a creative solution that can solve the problem without budgetary strain or sinking employee morale. This is especially true as we continue to move towards more mobile capabilities.

Accessing internet capabilities used to require physically sitting in a home or office with wired connections to route data to and from connection points around the world. That has changed dramatically in the past decade. Wireless and mobile connectivity is the name of the game today. Users consume mobile data at an incredible rate accessing entertainment and social media on smart phones virtually everywhere they go. The advancement of technology providing this level of access also provides an incredible capability to remotely access large network capabilities from remote locations. Employees do not even need to go into the office to work on their daily tasks. It can be done from anywhere an internet connection is available, which is pretty much everywhere in first-world nations today. These remote connections need to be established securely, which is relatively simple to do. Hardware and software solutions for encrypted connections are readily available but are not always used. Some of the necessary actions, such as this one, are easily enforceable while others are more difficult to implement.

It is difficult to achieve 100% perfect security when using mobile devices for several reasons. First, the operating systems on smartphones and tablets are not set up with the same level of user access permissions found on more traditional systems. This creates the possibility that a stolen device could establish a trusted connection without administrators being aware of the untrusted individual using the device. The same is true for stolen laptops with weak user login credentials. Second, these devices cannot always be controlled in the same manner as something physically connected to a network. Administrators typically have full control over systems attached to the network, providing a greater granularity of access control. The limits in mobile devices make this much more difficult. Third, users love to install third-party apps on their smartphones and tablets. Those apps can come from anywhere and have any number of hidden capabilities that allow hackers some level of access. Mobile capabilities are incredibly important today. Minimizing access and limiting the devices allowed to establish remote connections is also important and needs to be taken seriously.

Social media access is another simple paradigm shift. It is everywhere, and everyone has something to share, even if it should never be shared. Allowing access to social media from a business environment can be a huge security risk. It is incredibly easy for an employee to copy data and upload it to their social media platform of choice. If it is juicy enough, it could rapidly spread across the world causing harm to an organization's reputation, destroying profit margins, or giving competitors an unfair advantage. People overshare personal information on these platforms with the goal of going viral and attaining a level of fame or influence. A disgruntled employee could see the release of private company information as an opportunity to become famous, and possibly make a profit as well. These can be big motivators. Edward Snowden had to physically sneak out his stolen data! Allowing social media access on a network makes it so much easier to push this data into the public arena.

In some areas, we have replaced good security principles with the convenience of access. Convenience is never a good excuse to eliminate a layer of security. It is convenient to stay logged into an investment application on a smartphone to buy and sell stocks quickly. But what happens if that phone is lost or stolen? Someone instantly will have access to your investments without the need for any type of password. It is inconvenient to log out when walking away from a computer for a period of time. Staying logged in allows a user to instantly pick up where they left off and eliminates the time needed to prepare the operating system for use. What happens when a disgruntled employee walks past that computer and uses it to send emails or steal data? Convenience can become a very dangerous thing, which is why security should never be sacrificed to make something more convenient.

This is advantageous for hackers who are looking for easy targets. In most cases, hackers are looking for weak targets that can easily be manipulated. Anyone working in this field needs to learn to think like a nefarious actor when determining the best security mechanisms for a particular system, network, or project. What data is the most important to the attacker? What is the easiest path of attack? What can someone accomplish if they gain access? Thinking from this perspective will force you to think outside of the box. Hackers know the common security practices touted by security professionals for many years, and in some cases, may understand those practices better than the people putting them into place. This reality makes it especially important to include hacker motivations in your thought process when reviewing policies or procedures that have been in place for a long time. It can be a creative way of staying one step ahead of hackers.

A creative security professional can develop a methodology that does not perfectly mirror what is typically expected, forcing hackers to change their methodology or convincing them to look for an easier target. Hackers only need to be perfect one time to gain access, while cyber security professionals need to be perfect 100% of the time. Blending in some non-standard creative methodologies rarely used in other places can create enough of a headache for an attacker to move on to another target and leave your network alone. One simple method is to change the port numbers used for some common protocols. Hackers know that the secure shell (SSH) service default configuration utilizes TCP port 22. When port 22 is open on a firewall, they expect it to be SSH. Changing this service to run on a different port number commonly used for services less susceptible to attack could create enough obfuscation that keeps an unexperienced hacker from noticing the difference. There are some common ways we allow security to be limited, and if we correct those limitations, we can start moving in the right direction. Appendix 3 contains a listing of the commonly used protocols and their associated port numbers.

Limiting Factors

Most open-source software is banned from use in many organizations because management perceives them to be insecure, less capable, and impractical. All of these concerns are fair and are certainly true with some applications, but in the security arena, many of the best applications are developed as freely distributable and include the original source code allowing users to examine and modify as needed. It is important to note at this point that hackers rarely use commercial software. They use a combination of open-source tools and their own programming skills to accomplish their goals. Using these same tools to test the security of a network is great way to think like a hacker and save an organization a significant number of financial resources that would normally be spent on commercial software alternatives, turning those resources into profits or freeing them for other uses. Immediately balking at this potential capability, due to preconceived notions, reduces available tools and makes the job of security more difficult.

Capability	Open Source	Capability	Open Source
Firewall	PFSense	Virtualization	Virtual Box
IDS/IPS	Snort	Wireless IDS/IPS	Vistumbler
VPN	OpenVPN	SSL Certificates	Let's Encrypt
Pen Testing	NMAP, Nessus	Log Management	Fluentd
Encryption	TrueCrypt	Reverse Proxy	Nginx
Backups	Bacula	Honeypots	Honeynet

Common open-source security tools

One freely available methodology that can stop hackers in their tracks is the use of encryption. It is relatively easy to configure, incredibly strong, and is available as open-source or included in the most commonly used operating systems. There is no good reason not to utilize some form of encryption capabilities. Sensitive data should be stored in an encrypted state as much as possible. A variety of freely-available tools allow for the creation of encrypted containers that hold sensitive data in an encrypted state and only decrypt when that data needs to be accessed or modified. When used correctly, even the most powerful supercomputers on the planet cannot easily break the algorithms currently available. One thing easily recognized from the earlier mentioned successful hacking attempts is that the stolen data was stored in an unencrypted state. If it was encrypted, the data would have been of no value to the attackers and the plethora of personal data would never have been released. One simple method could have saved millions of dollars in government fines and legal fees. Perhaps a change in the legal requirements for how companies store and protect data would be beneficial to everyone.

Companies have been held liable when it was clear they did not implement the appropriate level of security, but not to a level that provides pressure to make significant changes. Target, for example, was ordered to pay $18.5 million in fines to state governments for the attack against their systems. They also settled a class-action lawsuit by agreeing to pay a maximum of $10,000 dollars to each customer who provided evidence of a loss resulting from the data breach (b). The $10 million limit on this settlement only allowed for 4,100 of the 41,000,000 affected customers to receive the maximum allowed amount. Other companies have orchestrated similar settlements, but the legal landscape of security requirements, apart from HIPPA related data, remains unclear (c). The best way to change a decision maker's focus on cyber security is to show who the real victim is when a massive data breach occurs.

Who is most affected by cybercrime against large organization? Yes, those organizations are typically required to pay some type of settlement or fine to the government, but the real victims are all the people whose personal data was stolen. Identity theft spawning from stolen records can easily empty someone's bank account, destroy their credit, and cause other secondary and tertiary results that take years to unravel. The real victims rarely receive any form of compensation because their personal data was leaked. Free access to some sort of identity theft monitoring service is often the only thing they receive. This does not undo the damage, restore lost resources, or cover the costs of the time and effort required to deal with the aftermath. Companies must consider the damage caused to true victims when allowing weaknesses within their security infrastructure and laws should establish minimum requirements when personal data is stored or processed by an organization.

Security has historically been a secondary thought as managers and leaders juggle the requirement of running a successful organization. This is true in for-profit operations, charities, and government entities. Finite resources are often the big factor and when a choice needs to be made between purchasing a firewall or investing in something that has a financial return, the firewall tends to lose the battle. Security can be seen as a financial black hole that creates an endless drain on the budget—as emerging threats and technological advances seemingly require constant upgrades or strategy adjustments. This leads to ignoring risks in favor of focusing on business operations that create a profit. Profit is the primary goal of a for-profit business, so it is very logical for business leaders to think from this perspective. The often-unconsidered reality is that security is a major element that allows continuous operation of an organization. This is becoming more evident as large data breaches capture public attention. Unfortunately, it has taken the loss of data and capabilities to prove the point. Adding security to the focus of high-level leaders can help to avert these types of losses and point the rest of the organization in the same direction.

Everyday users tend to see security as a set of rules restricting their actions, removing capabilities, and limiting their productivity. Like managers, their perspective is slightly skewed. This can be easily corrected with training that provides a greater degree of awareness for existing threats and the potential targets within the organization that hold interest for attackers. For example, email phishing attempts were very popular for several years because they proved to be incredibly effective. It was known that if you sent a crafted email with a malicious link to enough people in the same organization, at least one person would click on the link. Just one click is enough to gain access! Two common tactics employed to curb this particular threat were to disable HTML in all emails so links could not be clicked and train users on phishing methods. Consistent training over a period of time caused this threat to be less successful. It still exists today, but well-trained users now recognize and delete these emails without giving them a second thought; training users needs to be part of the overall process.

Security is more about process than it is about hardware. Hardware devices are part of the overall equation, but the entire cyber security mechanism within an organization starts with the intentional creation of policies and procedures that establish an overarching process. Well written policies that define all requirements related to the security of the network creates a top-down approach to ensuring a rigorous and effective process. This will be different for every organization, depending on some of their needs, but every organization has some level of commonality in the use of common services such as email, internet access, sensitive data, and physical security.

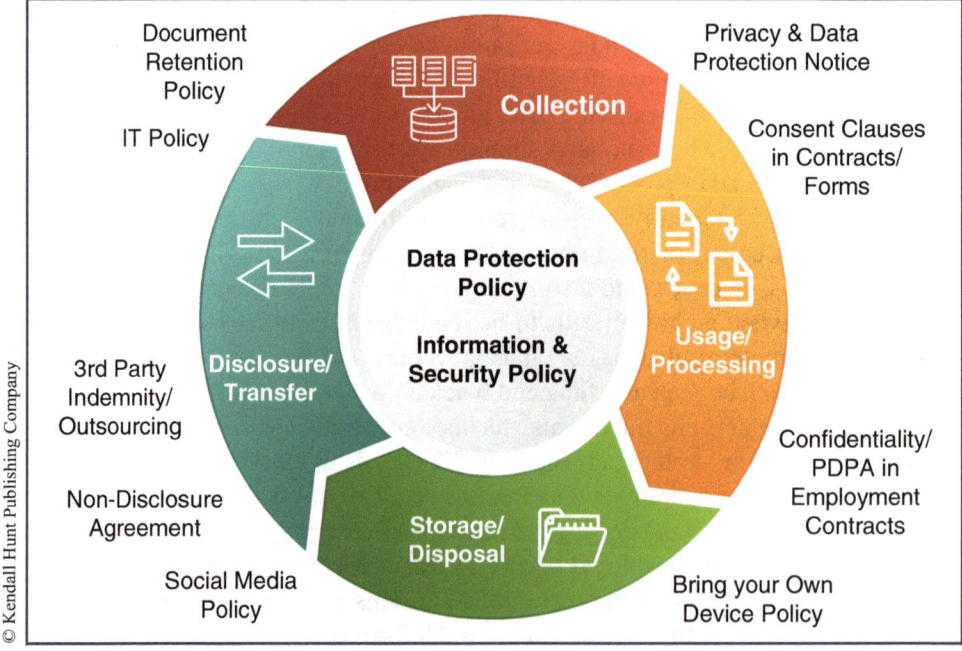

Common policy list

People lock their front doors to keep out anyone who has not been given access to their homes. How many keys do you give out to your front door? How many people have unfettered access to walk into your home at any time? Typically, only the people who live in the home have a key. Everyone else must knock, and then be provided or denied access, based on their request for entry. Access is restricted to maintain privacy, secure valuables, and protect the people within the home. Some homes have additional measures in place to provide greater levels of security such as alarm systems or guard dogs. Criminals tend to look for weak targets and, unless they are highly skilled at their craft and highly motivated to attack a particular target, they will often bypass secure buildings. This is simply common sense, and the same concepts apply in the digital world.

So, here's the big question: can this same concept be applied to networks? The answer is yes! And the best part is that it is an easier method to manage. There are two general approaches to controlling traffic at the perimeter of a network. The most commonly used method, known as blacklisting, is one where access is allowed by default and denied by exception. This allows for connectivity from any IP address not explicitly blocked, providing the maximum amount of connectivity to the world. This approach is reactive in that it usually only blocks addresses that have previously attempted nefarious activity. This does not mean the network is wide open for access, it means the services provided by the network are accessible to anyone who is not explicitly blocked.

The opposite method, known as whitelisting, blocks by default and allows by exception. In this model, the only IP addresses allowed connectivity to a network are those that are explicitly trusted. This method could limit connections from the majority of the world, greatly limiting the potential for being attacked. An organization with zero international business has no need for the entire world to connect to its network. And even those who do conduct international business likely only need to provide international access to their website and associated web applications. Think back to the earlier example of the Colonial Pipeline incident. A whitelisting model could have easily prevented this attack from ever occurring. But whitelisting can be controversial because it also limits employee access to external websites. Employees like the ability to read the news, check sports scores, or conduct other non-business-related web activity and most organizations allow this activity as long as it does not interfere with work-related duties.

Whitelisting models can be tailored to provide access to common websites and still maintain a very secure posture. It is highly unlikely a hacking attempt will originate from a well know news website. Even if the whitelist included 200 websites and all external IP addresses of other trusted locations, it would still eliminate more than 99% of all web traffic. This has the added benefit of lessening the workload of analysts who monitor network traffic and administrators who maintain perimeter security devices. Whitelisting is a simple and rarely used concept that incredibly effective at eliminating threats simply by denying access.

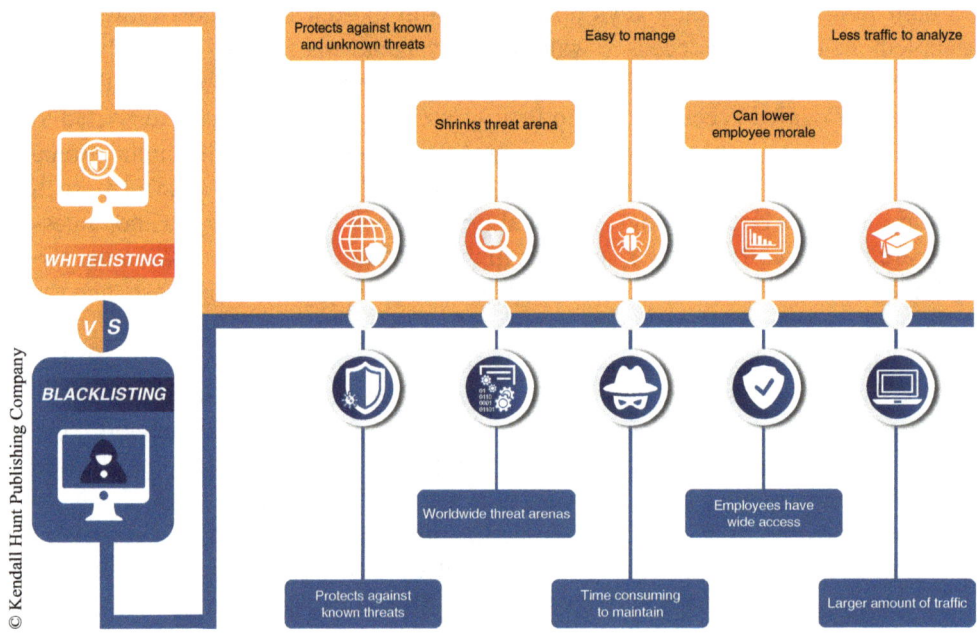

Whitelisting vs. Blacklisting

Cyber Security Positions

The field of cyber security continues to grow and morph into many different arenas. This has required the creation of specialized positions to focus primarily on security disciplines. You should be aware of each of these, the role they play, and how they fit together as part of an overall team. These positions have interconnecting duties, so it is essential to have great teamwork and communication in order to create an overall, solid security posture. The titles or position names may not be the same in every organization, but the function and roles are similar to these eight positions:

- Network Analyst: Network analysts monitor the traffic traversing the network to look for anomalies and potentially malicious activity. They are often the first human line of defense in recognizing and identifying potential attacks. They alert the incident response team when there is evidence of a successful attack and coordinate with the security engineers for updated alerts.
- Malware Analyst: Malware analysts are extremely specialized in analyzing viruses and other forms of malware to see how it affects systems and networks. Their work involves reverse engineering malware applications and typically leads to the creation or modification of antivirus signatures and intrusion detection system (IDS) alerts.
- Security Engineer: The security engineer is responsible for maintaining configurations on perimeter devices, such as firewalls, routers, and IDS. They work closely with network analysts to implement blocks on suspect IP addresses, update IDS alerts, and manage the overall flow of network traffic.

- System Administrator: System administrators manage many of the services available on a network as well as servers and user workstations. They are not typically listed among other security professionals, but they play a crucial role in managing access controls for users and systems, installing patches, and monitoring internal network activity.
- Vulnerability Assessor: A vulnerability assessor researches the latest vulnerabilities announced by software manufactures, determines which ones apply to current capabilities and services, and scans the network to see if any system needs to be updated or patched. They coordinate with system administrators who act on the required updates.
- Penetration Tester: Penetration testers take vulnerability assessments to the next level by attempting to exploit discovered vulnerabilities with the ultimate goal of gaining access to systems or data. Their work mimics that of a hacker and reveals the holes most susceptible to attack.
- Incident Responder: The incident response team is responsible for conducting a full investigation of any security incident on the network. Their job is to determine how the attacker gained access, which systems were affected, if anything was stolen or damaged, and actions needed to secure and recover the affected systems. Their reports drive updates and changes made by system administrators and security engineers.
- Chief Information Security Officer (CISO): The CISO is the top security manager in charge of all security operations in an organization. They establish policies ensuring the network is secure and maintain oversight of all security positions within an organization.

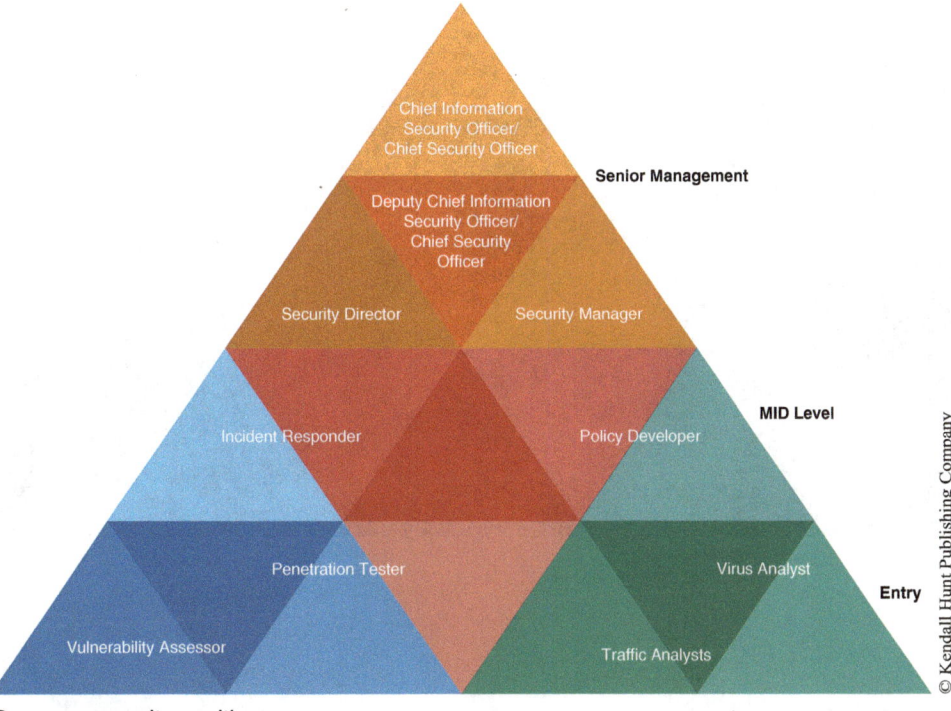

Common security positions

Practical Application – Tools of the Trade

Every chapter in this textbook will end with a section on practical application giving you an opportunity to practice what you are learning. It is good to have a basic knowledge of concepts, but practical application takes it to the next level to provide you with applied knowledge. Hands-on experience is a fundamental requirement in actively defending a network or conducting a penetration test to exploit weaknesses. Many of the concepts you learn can be legally practiced at home in a safe environment, so take time after each chapter to practice, practice, and practice some more.

Kali Linux – Kali Linux is the go-to penetration testing configuration of Linux. It is a free distribution which can be downloaded and installed on many hardware platforms. Kali includes hundreds of tools penetration testers, network defenders, and even bad actors can use to accomplish their work and to practice their skills in safe environments. One of the nice things about Linux operating systems is they do not use as many resources as Windows which eliminates the need for a high-end computer. You can use an old laptop laying around your house or pick up a cheap one somewhere and that is usually enough to get started. Make sure it has WiFi capabilities or you will not be able to run any tests against WiFi networks. It is highly suggested that you install a copy and use it regularly to familiarize yourself with its capabilities and practice using the tools of the trade.

Download location: www.kali.org
Installation instructions: www.kali.org/docs/installation/

Kali Linux

VirtualBox – VirtualBox is a free virtualization application that allows you to run multiple operating systems and configurations within a virtual environment. This is an excellent tool for practicing exploits, testing responses to malware, monitoring network traffic, and anything else you could do in a real-world environment. Virtualization allows us to practice in a safe environment. If your Kali system has enough juice, you can install and run it on the same system, otherwise you will need to install it on a different system connected to the same network. You can also run Kali as a virtual system on your everyday computer.

Download location: www.virtualbox.org
User manual: www.virtualbox.org/manual/UserManual.html

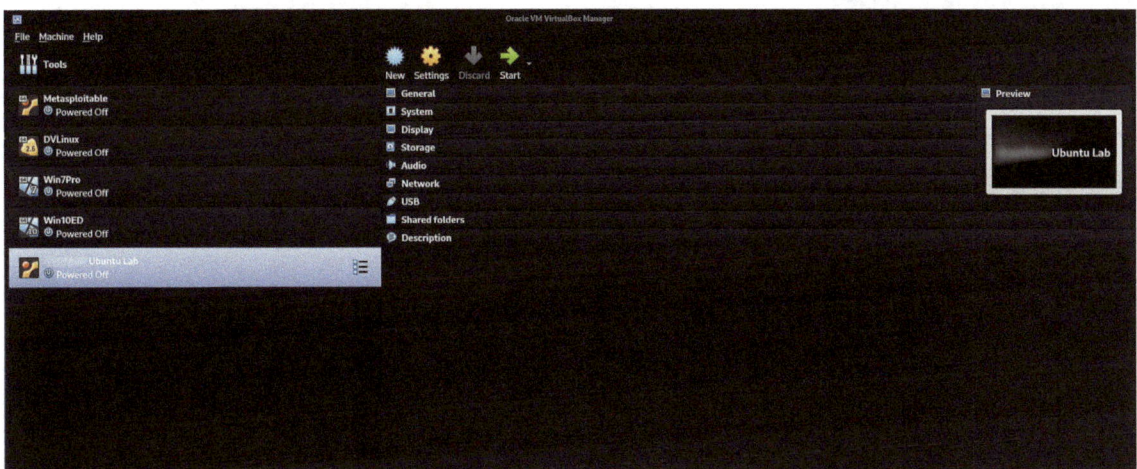

VirtualBox

External Wi-Fi Adapter – Effective testing of Wi-Fi networks requires multiple Wi-Fi adapters allowing one to connect to a network while the other sniffs packets or conducts other operations. There are many USB Wi-Fi adapters available on the market for around $20. Make sure you get one that is compatible with Kali Linux and can be put into monitor mode. A quick search of the internet will yield a good list of options and they can sometimes be found on secondhand websites as well. Connecting one of these devices along with VirtualBox could prove more challenging as there is another layer in the process. It is not impossible, but if you go that route, be prepared to do some troubleshooting to get everything working correctly.

It is best to run your penetration testing system on true hardware as you have more options and flexibility. VirtualBox is good for internal testing and training but is not great as a long-term penetration testing machine. The options are too limited to make it work perfectly for these types of operations. Some users also set up a dual-boot environment where they are prompted to select between Windows or

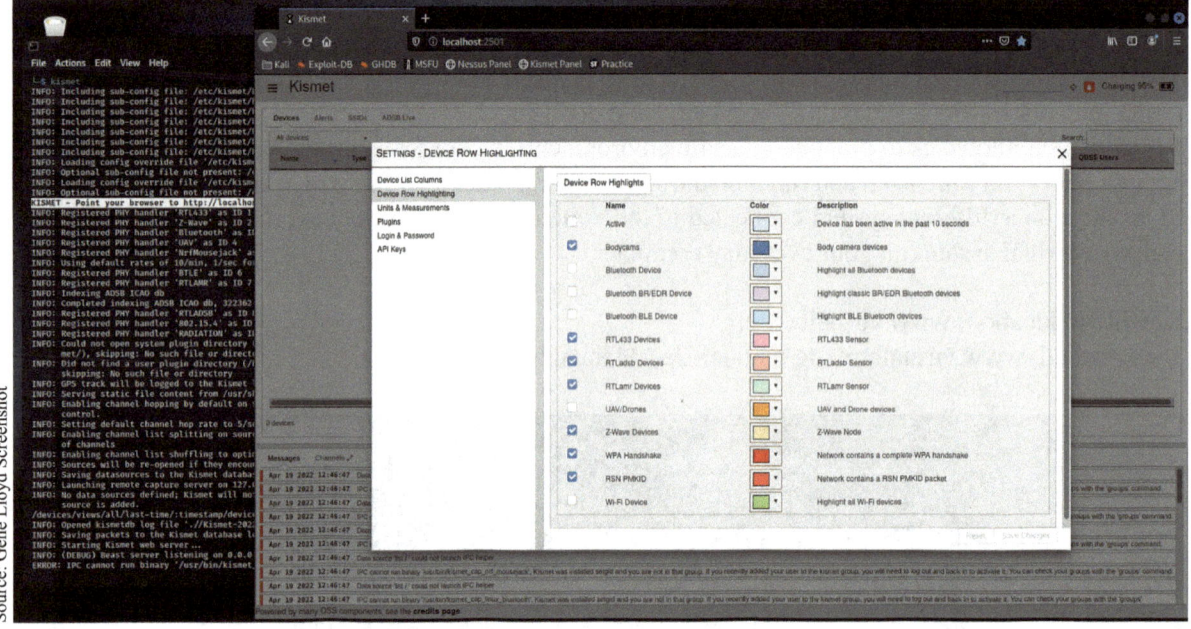

Kismet

Linux when they turn on their computer. This can be a great option if you do not need to use multiple computers at the same time. Keep in mind, if you take this route, anything on your Windows partition is usually accessible in Linux so you could still have access to files and folders while working from Linux.

Practice cannot be overstated. The more you practice, the more you will become familiar with the available tools. Do not dive into every tool all at once, trying to master the operating system in one fell swoop. Pick a particular piece of methodology and work on that until you have a good grasp of how it works and then move onto another. Build your skills in layers, just like you would on a musical instrument, and you will become more proficient over time. Every portion of the field of computer science takes a long time to master. Hacking, penetration testing, and defending against attacks is no different. There is a lot to learn in the field and, if you stay for a while, you will find that you can learn something new every day.

References

a. https://www.washingtonpost.com/world/national-security/chinese-hackers-breach-federal-governments-personnel-office/2015/06/04/889c0e52-0af7-11e5-95fd-d580f1c5d44e_story.html

b. https://www.usatoday.com/story/money/2017/05/23/target-pay-185m-2013-data-breach-affected-consumers/102063932/

c. https://www.washingtonpost.com/technology/2021/07/25/ransomware-class-action-lawsuit/

Chapter 2: Review Questions

1. There is always a level of _____ risk when operating on the internet.
   a. assumed
   b. low
   c. high
   d. intense
2. The attack on Colonial pipeline likely came from hackers located in _____.
   a. California
   b. China
   c. Mexico
   d. Eastern Europe
3. Organizations that ignore best security practices make their networks _____.
   a. hidden
   b. vulnerable
   c. irrelevant
   d. functional
4. Leaders in cyber security need to look for _____ solutions.
   a. more difficult
   b. simpler
   c. streamlined
   d. paranoid
5. The _____ server was a historically common target.
   a. web
   b. cloud
   c. file
   d. secret
6. The _____ creates an isolated network segment for public-facing devices.
   a. DMZ
   b. cloud
   c. file server
   d. switch
7. _____ can transfer some risk off your network.
   a. deleting
   b. hiding
   c. outsourcing
   d. spoofing
8. Cyber security professionals need to look at methodologies with _____.
   a. fear
   b. fresh eyes
   c. love
   d. intensity
9. Most organizations cannot afford a fully _____ security approach.
   a. layered
   b. automated
   c. specialized
   d. scaled down
10. Real-world _____ must be considered in security best practices.
    a. expectations
    b. tragedies
    c. hacks
    d. fears
11. Security is an _____ necessity.
    a. irrelevant
    b. unlikely
    c. inconvenient
    d. outdated
12. One job of a cyber security professional is to _____ risks.
    a. reveal
    b. hide
    c. ignore
    d. create
13. Accessing social media from a corporate network is a _____ risk.
    a. giant
    b. tiny
    c. security
    d. insignificant
14. Some have replaced security with _____.
    a. convenience
    b. games
    c. appeasement
    d. secrecy
15. Hackers typically look for _____ targets.
    a. difficult
    b. easy
    c. distant
    d. close

16. Many of the best security applications are _____.
    a. commercial
    b. expensive
    c. open-source
    d. difficult
17. _____ can protect data even if a hacker gains access.
    a. sunscreen
    b. enclaves
    c. antivirus
    d. encryption
18. _____ are most affected by cybercrime.
    a. individuals
    b. companies
    c. government
    d. manufacturers
19. Security has historically been a _____ thought.
    a. primary
    b. ignored
    c. secondary
    d. after
20. Whitelisting _____ by default.
    a. blocks
    b. allows
    c. trusts
    d. ignores

Traffic Analysis

CHAPTER 3

A core function of cyber security is monitoring network traffic for potentially nefarious activity and shutting it down before it can do any harm. Every network environment should have an employee, or a team of employees depending on the size of the network, dedicated to the work of analyzing traffic flowing in and out of the network. This may sound mundane, and it can feel that way at times, but it is one of the most important functions of cyber security. It is much easier to stop an attacker than it is to clean up the mess left in one's wake. Stopping an attack before it happens is always better than investigating how an attacker gained access, clearing out malware they left behind, restoring systems to a known good state, and plugging the holes that allowed them to gain access. Prevention is the top priority; monitoring the traffic is how we achieve that goal.

Everyone loves the idea of penetration testing because the job of actively hacking into systems, manipulating protocols, and sneaking past defensive mechanisms is exhilarating. It is the sexy side of cyber security. But the core element in this arena is the job of the analyst working to detect traffic successfully squeezing past defenses or hammering at the front door with the hopes of being successful. Many of the skills in system administration, penetration testing, and traffic analysis have a symbiotic relationship. Great system administrators can more easily detect unauthorized traffic because they have a strong familiarity with the behavior of normal traffic. They also make great attackers because they know how to manipulate a system once they gain access. Similarly, penetration testers can easily recognize nefarious actions because they are skilled in using hacking methods to break into networks. The best system administrator makes a great attacker, and the best penetration tester makes a great defender.

Traffic analysis is often an entry-level position in cyber security. It can be the first step towards becoming an incident investigator or can be a lifelong career on its own. This is an incredibly important function because a great analyst can detect an attack in progress and quickly get others involved to stop the attack before it causes any real damage. Most beginning analysts have at least a basic understanding of networking which provides a good foundation for learning greater details about packet-level analysis. Each packet that moves through the network has a function. It could be a small chunk of an email message, a piece of encrypted communication, a portion of a web page, or anything else for which the internet is commonly used. Recognizing the packets that are good—and the ones that are evil—is the job of the traffic analyst. It is not easy at first and takes some getting used to as many lines of data scroll past the screen in front of you. It may even seem like a foreign language but over time analysts learn to recognize what normal everyday traffic looks like on their particular network which makes the uncommon traffic stand out.

The first step to being a good traffic analyst is to understand how traffic flows through a network and what ports and protocols are most commonly used for services and applications. You should become very familiar with ports and protocols listed in Appendix 3 and practice looking at network traffic for each of these services so you will be able to differentiate between normal and abnormal traffic. Bank employees do not study counterfeit money. They handle real money so often that they can recognize when something fake comes across their desk. It looks a little different, has a different texture, and may even have a different smell. The same should be true for a traffic analyst. You should analyze normal traffic so often that abnormal traffic will stand out like a flashing set of lights. It may take time to gain this level of experience, but it is a valuable skill in this field.

Closely associated with ports and protocols are the known vulnerabilities that exist in different applications. Security experts routinely test software looking for ways to exploit an application and manipulate it into functioning for an unintended purpose—usually to gain some level of surreptitious access. New discoveries are announced and posted in multiple, publicly searchable security databases providing the world with data they can use to protect their infrastructures. These databases are also used by attackers as they look for weak networks with unpatched, vulnerable software. Microsoft has become famous for issuing patches for their operating systems and software on the second Tuesday of every month, known as "patch Tuesday." Several organizations also post their top 10 style listing of the most common vulnerabilities every year. All of these lists and databases serve as a tool to provide you, the security professional, the information you need to protect your systems more effectively. You should review these at least every week.

Analyzing traffic takes a lot of focus and some creative thinking, especially when you are first starting to learn what normal everyday network traffic looks like and the common traffic on your particular network. It is a good idea to start by letting the tool you use show you everything—so you can gain an understanding of the wealth of data that comes across the network every minute. The image below provides a screenshot of Wireshark, which is discussed in this chapter's practical application section, and the way it displays packets waiting to be analyzed. It is easy to see from this one image that a significant number of packets cross the network in just a few seconds. As you watch traffic in a live environment, take note of reoccurring ports and protocols being used and familiarize yourself with common activity on your network. Knowing the common activity makes the uncommon stand out like a sore thumb.

You will quickly realize watching all traffic in a live environment is impossible for a single individual. An average size network can easily generate more traffic than one person could even consider trying to analyze. Web browsing traffic is overwhelming by itself, and when we add in email, file transfers, database connections, and underlying communication protocols, it becomes evident that it is virtually impossible to thoroughly review every bit of traffic data. To make it manageable, filters are put in place to monitor specific types of traffic or to look for specific pieces of activity. For example, since it is not practical to look at all web traffic, a filter for abnormal web traffic attempting to issue specific commands would allow for in-depth analysis of specific connections while ignoring the rest of the benign web surfing data. The goal of traffic analysis is not to look at everything but to specifically look for traffic attempting to gain unauthorized access or exploit a vulnerability.

Some organizations have 24/7 operations where analysts work around the clock to monitor live traffic. This is an expensive operation and typically only affordable by larger companies with budgets that can sustain this level of manpower. Other organizations take the approach of having an analyst conduct a postmortem review of old traffic, typically from the previous day or weekend. This is certainly not as effective as a live operation capable of catching the criminal in the act, but it is the next best thing and a lot better than doing nothing at all. This type of analysis can yield the same investigative information and lead to the same defensive actions. Though, if a successful attack occurs, the actions will be after the fact and additional cleanup measures will be required. It is also good to keep in mind even live monitoring of a network does not guarantee 100% effectiveness in catching every bad act. This type of analysis is only one piece of the puzzle.

Traffic analysis should also include the review of logs from network devices. It is common to have some form of intrusion detection system (IDS) or software that helps with the monitoring process and streamlines what needs to be reviewed. Other network devices, such as firewalls, routers, and virtual private networks

(VPN), have logs showing connections the IDS may miss. Reviewing these logs is important when conducting incident investigations, as they may show exact points of connection and the devices involved. Many monitoring tools are focused on traffic at a specific point on the network, so augmenting that data with devices in other locations can provide a fuller picture of activity. It is also important to configure these devices for longer log retention times and to back the logs up regularly to maintain long-term historical and investigative data. Most network devices are set to overwrite the logs, sometimes as often as every day, which is great for storage space but horrible for an investigation.

As you become more experienced in reviewing logs and network traffic for attempting exploits, you will eventually come to recognize the difference between a skilled attacker and what is commonly referred to as a script kiddie. Script kiddies are people who download penetration scripts and run them indiscriminately against systems. They are easily recognized because their attempts lack sophistication and quite often attempt an exploit against an operating system or service the exploit does not affect. For example, running an exploit script designed to attack a Windows service against a Linux machine is obviously the work of an extreme amateur. The more you see this, the more you will recognize they pose no real threat. Alternatively, skilled hackers show a great degree of sophistication in how they weave through defenses with little or no detection. These are the ones you really need to look out for and are the most interesting to investigate if their attacks are successful.

An analyst working through this process also needs to consider what motivates a hacker to attack a system or network. Public notoriety used to be a major motivation for hackers, especially in the early days when it was very fringe, and few people had an understanding of how to break into computers or networks. Defacing a famous website with your handle was a popular way to gain credibility in the hacker community. In today's environment, the financial incentive is near the top of the list, as stolen data can be sold for significant sums and ransoms can be placed on penetrated systems threatening operations until the fee is paid. Many of the recently discovered incidents fall into this category. At a higher level, within governments, many intelligence operations have developed teams of experts who look for vulnerabilities on foreign networks to gain access and extract data. It is often cheaper and easier to break into a network halfway around the world than it is to use human assets.

A network IDS (NIDS) is the primary device used to monitor network traffic. The location of this device determines the type and amount of traffic it can process. Placing it at the perimeter, just inside of the firewall, will provide visibility of traffic the firewall did not block while placing it outside of the firewall will show all traffic coming into the network. You may think that outside of the firewall is a better location, but this will significantly increase the amount of data needing analysis. If the firewall is properly configured, the NIDS can be placed inside of the firewall, focusing only on the traffic that made it through the gatekeeper. Firewall logs can then be reviewed separately. The NIDS uses a process known as sniffing which, in a perfect scenario, pulls in a copy of every packet, compares it with a preconfigured set of rules, and then records an alert if the packet matches those rules.

There are multiple variables involved in a NIDS's ability to sniff traffic at an effective rate. The processing power of the system, the throughput speeds of the network interface card, available memory, and the configuration of the software all

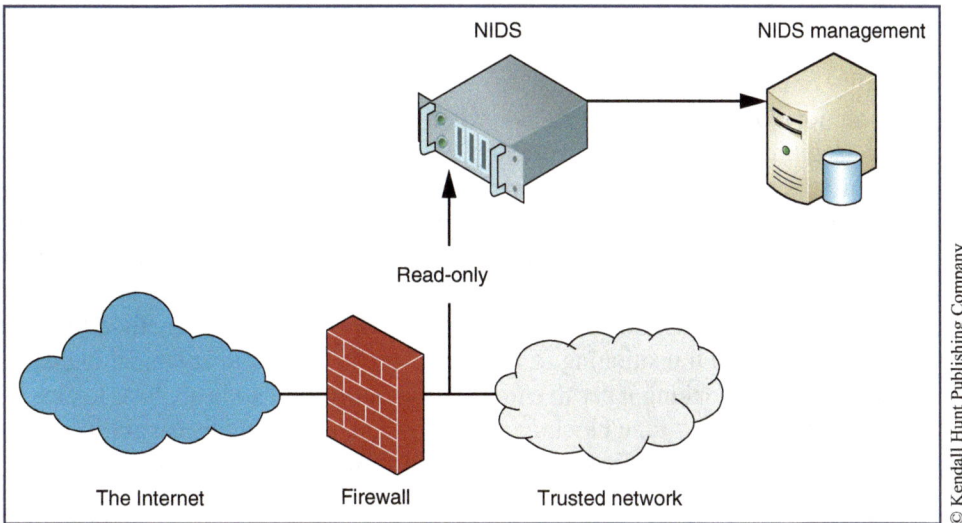

determine how much traffic the NIDS can actually process. The amount of data coming across the network can also affect this process. Can a NIDS reliably capture 100% of all network traffic at all times? It is possible but unlikely in most scenarios. Some packets will inevitably sneak past without ever being sniffed simply because the NIDS was not able to keep up with the flow. On large networks with large amounts of data throughput, it is a good idea to connect multiple NIDS devices to a load balancer which will allow the incoming traffic to be divided among multiple NIDS lessening the burden on each individual device and allowing for greater traffic visibility.

The NIDS is not the only type of IDS available for this process. The host-based IDS (HIDS) is another methodology placing IDS software directly onto the computers of a network to monitor traffic coming in and out of that specific system. This methodology typically installs HIDS software on every computer attached to the network but could be scaled back to only placing it on servers or highly sensitive systems. HIDS works in a very similar way to NIDS, creating alerts on any triggered data, and then sending those alerts to a centralized server for human analysis. A system running a HIDS will need some additional processing power and memory to function smoothly, otherwise, the user may see a decrease in performance. We do not want security tools to limit operational effectiveness. So, if a HIDS is used, the remaining functions of the system need to go unhindered. Of course, as you have likely already considered, monitoring alerts from these host-based versions require an increase in cyber security manpower.

Intrusion detection systems (IDS) are passive by nature. They do not take any direct action against traffic. Their job is solely focused on sniffing and reporting. A variation to this methodology is the intrusion protection system (IPS) which functions the same as an IDS with an additional automated capability. IPS devices are placed at the perimeter in line with the flow of traffic—requiring all traffic to flow through it before continuing into the network. This is significantly different from passive sniffing. The IPS compares each packet with the rules and triggers alerts in the same fashion as an IDS. Because the IPS is in line with the traffic, it has an additional capability to proactively take action. Rules can be configured allowing the IDS to block particular types of traffic instead of singularly notifying an analyst. This can be a good configuration for networks that do not have 24/7 monitoring capability or have limited staff capable of verifying illegitimate traffic.

A major downside to an IPS is—when a false positive triggers a blocking action—legitimate data can inadvertently be stopped from traversing the network. This can be a major problem for operational activity and may go unnoticed until a user initiates a trouble ticket to find out why their particular activity is no longer able to communicate with the network. These false positives are most common with new applications or services, so coordination with the cyber security team is incredibly important when new capabilities are added to the network. A good method to avoid false positives when transitioning to an IPS device is to disable any blocking capabilities, effectively making it passive for a period of time allowing analysts to closely monitor traffic and fine-tune blocking actions before enabling this capability. Host-based IPS (HIPS) devices also exist and function similarly as a HIDS.

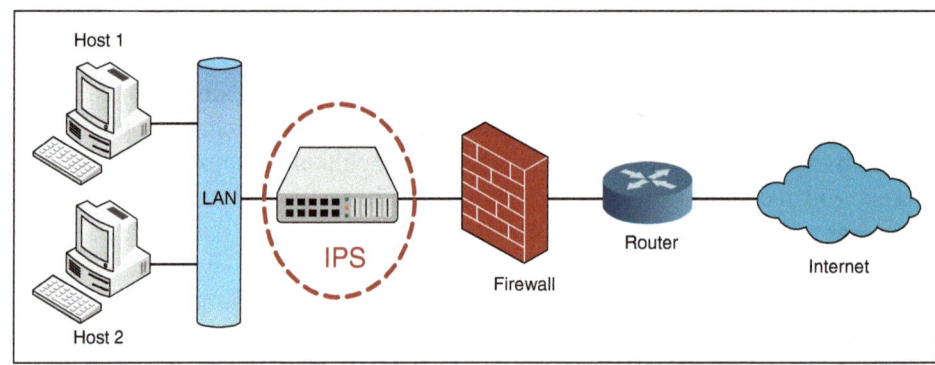

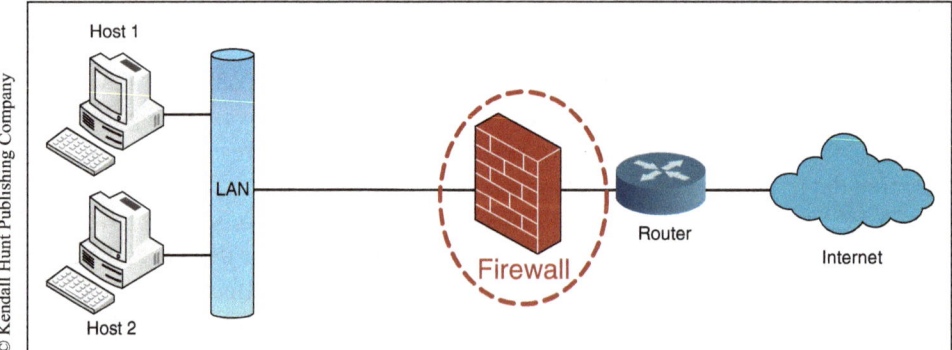

One other thing to consider when using an IDS or IPS is you are not limited to placing these devices at the perimeter. They can also be placed at different locations within the internal network. A device at the perimeter only sees traffic coming across that single point and is blind to all activity on the internal portion of the network. Host-based software can help fill that gap, creating greater traffic analysis coverage, which is very adept at catching potential insider activity but comes at the cost of higher system utilization. An alternative is to segment the network into multiple sections and place the IDS or IPS at the perimeter of each of those segments. Organizations with particularly sensitive data should segment in this way to provide secondary levels of protection against attackers who successfully breach the perimeter as well as the personnel who attempt to surreptitiously access that data.

At this point, you may be wondering what to look for when analyzing network traffic. When using an IDS or IPS, those systems or software applications will provide you with a specific alert whenever network activity matches its configuration. Analysts review those alerts to determine if any additional action is required or if the alert is benign. Every alert does not need to have an associated action, and in fact, many alerts are triggered on common everyday traffic. You will need to learn to recognize the difference between traffic common to your specific network, so you can more easily recognize potentially dangerous connections. There is always the possibility of false positives when working in a defensive role, but it is better to err on the side of caution than risk the possibility of an incident allowing an attacker to gain access or steal data.

Great analysts take the time to learn about which ports are open on the firewall, the services offered to external and internal users, and the most common attacks exploiting these services. Being armed with this data makes the job a lot easier—ignoring irrelevant traffic and focusing on the packets posing the greatest threats. For example, if you know port 22 is closed on the firewall and you see someone repeatedly attempting a secure shell exploit, which typically runs on port 22, you can be reasonably sure that their actions are a very low threat. This type of situation would not warrant any additional action other than to block the offending IP address to keep them from attempting other exploits. It is clear in this type of situation someone is trying to gain access, but they are likely less sophisticated if they are attempting an attack for something that does not exist on your network.

The most common action to take against malicious traffic coming across a network is to block the offending IP address. This is also the easiest action because it immediately stops that individual from attempting any further connections. In some organizations, the analyst can immediately implement blocking action, and in others, some coordination is required with other personnel. The big question that arises is, how long do we keep the block in place? Over time the block list can become large enough that it slows down the router's ability to process traffic. Every packet needs to be compared with the block list to see if it is authorized, and the longer the list, the more time the comparison takes. This is not a difficult challenge to overcome, it simply requires a policy that sets a timeline for when blocks should be removed. A 30-day timeline is usually easy to manage, and a month of no access will send low-level attackers off to look for a new target. The bottom line is that blocks are great for attempted access, but what do we do when analysis reveals someone already gained access?

Successful attacks require a completely different response, and a slew of variables will need to be considered to determine the best action. This is rarely a one size fits all scenario. Similar to blocking, organizations will need to have a policy in place that specifies the goals of what is desired when responding to these situations. The ultimate goals are to remove the hacker from the network, clean up their actions, patch the vulnerability that allowed them to gain access, and restore the system to an operational state. How we accomplish those goals is based on how much we want to learn and whether any legal retribution is desired. There are a lot of questions to consider, which is why having an incident response checklist is so important. We will cover this in more detail in chapters six and seven, but for now, consider the following questions that need to be answered when an incident occurs:

- How was access gained?
- Why was the system vulnerable?
- Were there any malicious actions?
- Was any data stolen?
- What is the current state of the victim system?
- How does this affect operations?
- Should law enforcement be involved?
- What needs to be accomplished to restore the system to operational status?

This is just a short list to get you thinking about the investigative process and it should further highlight the importance of establishing a solid defense. Sadly, weaknesses in many organizations go unnoticed until a major incident occurs. It is never beneficial to wait until after an attack to secure a network. It is never beneficial to wait until your house is robbed before you start locking the front door. An active defense requires proactive actions before an attack occurs, reducing the likelihood of an attack to as close to zero percent as possible. There will always be some chance of an attack. We can never eliminate that completely, but we can greatly limit the possibility by putting the correct measures in place. The role of the analyst should be to look for potentially dangerous activity within a very narrow set of possibilities because all known security holes have already been plugged.

Patching a system for known vulnerabilities is one of the easiest actions to minimize network attacks. A vulnerable service connected to the internet is like a beacon for an attacker. Awareness of vulnerabilities and the associated attack vector makes the job of defense incredibly easy. All it requires is taking the time to keep systems and applications updated with the latest patches. Many successful network incidents are completely preventable with these types of simple actions. Your organization should have a list of all operating systems and applications in use along with their associated patch version and information on where new patches can be obtained. A simple check every week is often enough to ensure known vulnerabilities are dealt with, reducing the workload of the analysts. Cyber security is not conducted within a silo, it includes a lot of interconnected pieces working together to provide the best possible security solution.

Common Attacks

As the internet has grown and expanded into virtually every sector of business, government, and personal activity, organizations have started to develop lists of the most common vulnerabilities targeted by malicious actors. These lists change slightly every year depending on current trends and new technologies and should be part of any cyber security professional's normal reading and research. Some vulnerabilities tend to stay on this list because they are highly prevalent across the internet and their exploit can cause significant damage. The majority are related to errors in the coding of software applications that can sometimes be manipulated if the flaw is discovered.

One example is a buffer overflow, which exploits memory buffers within programs that have been incorrectly coded. Buffer overflows occur when a program attempts to store more data in a buffer than it is designed to hold. Memory buffers are designed with specific parameters when the program is written. If not coded correctly, the data within the buffer can overflow into another portion of memory causing unexpected and potentially disastrous results. Successful attacks can allow for command execution and other nefarious actions. One of the more famous buffer overflows is the SQL Slammer worm which exploited this type of vulnerability in Microsoft's SQL Server causing a widescale denial of service. In this instance, the overflow was used to propagate the worm to other vulnerable servers across the internet in a very short amount of time. Analysts initially recognized the problem because a mass amount of traffic started flooding the internet on port 1434, commonly used for this service, and further investigation led to understanding the nature of the attack. Using a form of bounds checking within the programming code often solves this problem, but that is outside the scope of a cyber security analyst and is handled by software engineers.

Many websites today include web-based applications that provide most of the functionality for users. Those applications are commonly created in-house and, as a result, do not always go through a rigorous security review process. Because they are so prevalent, web apps have become a very common point of attack. Larger companies have even created bounty programs that allow approved professionals to test the security of their applications and receive a financial payout if they discover a flaw. Analysts should study how the web apps are used on their network function and learn about the network traffic generated in normal interaction. This makes it a lot easier to recognize attempts at exploiting the capabilities of the application.

What you will find as you continue to learn more about vulnerabilities is that the majority of them are caused by a programming or configuration flaw. It is highly likely that any modern program with thousands of lines of code is going to contain a flaw. Software manufacturers hope these flaws are discovered by their own teams so patches can be issued before any damage is caused. That would be a perfect scenario, but this is not always the case. Maintaining awareness of the latest vulnerabilities affecting your specific network is the best way for an analyst to stay ahead of the power curve. Knowing what to look for is the key to being a great analyst, and the only way you can prepare is by vigilantly researching the newest vulnerabilities regularly.

Another common attack today is SQL injection, which attempts to inject commands to a website to manipulate data. SQL, short for Structured Query Language, is a programming language used to manage data within a database and manage the structure of the database. Attackers can attempt to gain access to a database by using customized search queries on web applications connected to a backend database. If successful, this methodology can provide the criminal with all the information contained within a specific database table, which could include usernames and passwords, private customer information, bank account balances, or anything else that may be stored as data within a database. The possibility of what an attacker can gain is only limited to what someone would store in the system. It is also possible to modify and delete data using these techniques. We correct the problem by, you guessed it, modifying the code used in the web app to filter and restrict particular symbols and commands.

There are many more vulnerabilities than any one book can ever cover, but there is good news. Tens of thousands of known vulnerabilities are stored in publicly accessible databases for anyone to review. Many analysts use these databases to search for potential vulnerabilities contained in applications in use on their networks. These are valuable tools you should familiarize yourself with, as teams of professionals have provided in-depth analysis of how an attack works, what systems or applications are vulnerable to the attack, and the available patches. In some cases, code that can be used to test the attack is also available. This is great for conducting vulnerability assessments or penetration tests, which will be covered in a later chapter. Some of the most commonly used databases are available below:

- CVE Database – www.cve.mitre.org
- Rapid7 Database – www.rapid7.com
- Vuln Database – www.vuldb.com
- National Vulnerability Database – www.nvd.nist.gov

Proactive vs. Reactive

What you have likely discovered as you read through this chapter is that it is more important to be proactive than reactive. A reactive security posture waits for something bad to happen and then reacts to that singular event without considering how it may affect the rest of network operations. Reactive approaches are dangerous because employees are forced to play catch up and are rarely prepared for the nefarious activity that may occur. A proactive security posture is different in that it places devices, applications, tools, and personnel in place with an expectation that an attack will eventually happen. This method can eliminate the majority of known threats before they ever happen—saving time, money, and resources. Every possible negative thing that can occur in life points to the reality it is always better to be prepared. This is certainly true in cyber security. Hackers tend to look for soft targets. Hardening your network is one of the best methods to avoid dealing with a security incident.

One great method to be proactive is to never allow the installation of any software on the network without first performing a vulnerability analysis. It is a great idea to have a system, or completely separate network if financially possible, for testing new applications. Installing new software on non-production systems and conducting a simple scan can point out any glaringly obvious vulnerabilities that need to be corrected before allowing the software on the real network. This could also be conducted within virtual environments. These types of proactive actions provide peace of mind and eliminate potential headaches further down the road. How does this relate to monitoring network traffic? Easy; the more work we do ahead of time limits the amount and type of activity that may come across the network and allows network analysts to focus their attention on bigger threats. The avoidable ones should be avoided early on.

Practical Application – Tools of the Trade

You can practice monitoring network traffic in your own home with a few simple and freely available tools. The practical application section at the end of this chapter provides details on how to use some of the available tools and you should use it as a guide to get hands-on practice. The focus is on using tools available in Kali Linux, so make sure you have that installed using one of the methods from chapter 2. Some of these tools are already installed within Kali and others may need to be installed manually.

Kali is set up using repositories to update and install software. The following commands will keep your software up to date and install new applications as needed:

apt-get update	Downloads the latest version of the repository
apt-get upgrade	Upgrades installed applications
apt-get install [application-name]	Installs specific applications

Wireshark – Wireshark is a network protocol analyzer that allows you to see the intimate details of every packet it captures. It enables you to capture live traffic from a variety of networking mediums, perform offline analysis, and even import data captured using other tools. Wireshark is known and used throughout the cyber security field and is a tool you should be very familiar with using. It can be intimidating at first as it lists out all the packets coming across a network as you can see in. It takes a lot of practice to learn the nuances of this tool The secret is in the filters which allow for eliminating specific content or narrowing the focus to only see traffic related to a current task.

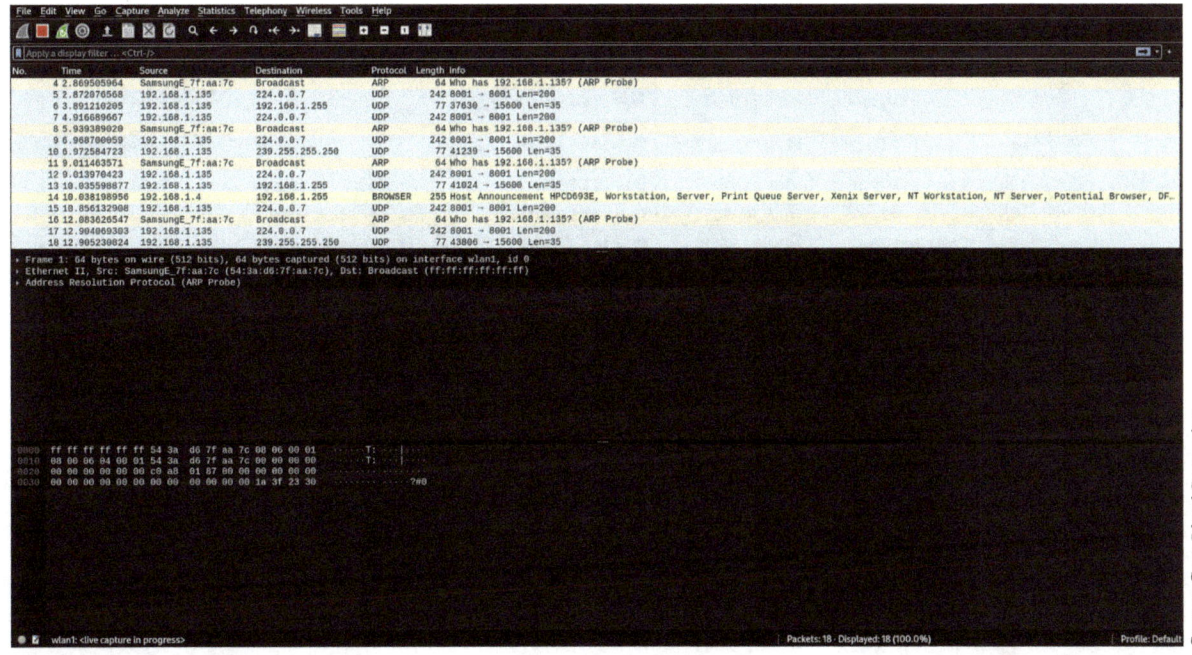

Wireshark

Snort – Snort is a highly customizable open-source IDS application which can be used as a real-time traffic analyzer. It comes with basic rule sets for some of the most common attacks and users can create their own custom rule sets to maximize Snort's capabilities. It is freely available software that includes the option of annual subscriptions for immediate access to the most recently updated rule sets which will alert on all the latest attack vectors. The only difference between the paid and free versions is when the user gains access to the new rule sets. On average, there is a 30-day delay before free users receive updates. This may be acceptable for small organizations unable to afford subscription costs, though the current price of $399 per year is reasonable for the level of protection received. Snort is natively a command-line tool which is perfectly fine for some users, but if you want a GUI front end, you can install Snorby. This will require some Linux knowledge of installing packages so be prepared to learn something new if you have not done this before.

https://www.snort.org
https://github.com/Snorby/snorby

	Aug 14 13:20:28	PRIVATE_WIFI5	10.0.5.4:45140	74.125.21.147:443 yv-in-f147.1e100.net	TCP:PA
	Aug 14 13:19:52	PRIVATE_WIFI5	10.0.5.4:46118	50.16.228.90:80	TCP:PA
	Aug 14 13:19:45	PRIVATE_WIFI5	10.0.5.4:45140	74.125.21.147:443 yv-in-f147.1e100.net	TCP:PA
	Aug 14 13:19:23	PRIVATE_WIFI5	10.0.5.4:45140	74.125.21.147:443 yv-in-f147.1e100.net	TCP:PA
	Aug 14 13:19:15	PRIVATE_WIFI5	10.0.5.4:46118	50.16.228.90:80	TCP:PA
	Aug 14 13:19:12	PRIVATE_WIFI5	10.0.5.4:45140	74.125.21.147:443 yv-in-f147.1e100.net	TCP:PA
	Aug 14 13:19:06	PRIVATE_WIFI5	10.0.5.4:45140	74.125.21.147:443 yv-in-f147.1e100.net	TCP:PA
	Aug 14 13:19:03	PRIVATE_WIFI5	10.0.5.4:45140	74.125.21.147:443 yv-in-f147.1e100.net	TCP:PA
	Aug 14 13:19:02	PRIVATE_WIFI5	10.0.5.4:45140	74.125.21.147:443 yv-in-f147.1e100.net	TCP:PA
	Aug 14 13:19:01	PRIVATE_WIFI5	10.0.5.4:45140	74.125.21.147:443 yv-in-f147.1e100.net	TCP:PA
	Aug 14 13:19:01	PRIVATE_WIFI5	10.0.5.4:45140	74.125.21.147:443 yv-in-f147.1e100.net	TCP:PA
	Aug 14 13:18:56	PRIVATE_WIFI5	10.0.5.4:46118	50.16.228.90:80	TCP:PA
	Aug 14 13:18:47	PRIVATE_WIFI5	10.0.5.4:46118	50.16.228.90:80	TCP:PA
	Aug 14 13:18:42	PRIVATE_WIFI5	10.0.5.4:46118	50.16.228.90:80	TCP:PA
	Aug 14 13:18:40	PRIVATE_WIFI5	10.0.5.4:46118	50.16.228.90:80	TCP:PA
	Aug 14 13:18:39	PRIVATE_WIFI5	10.0.5.4:46118	50.16.228.90:80	TCP:PA
	Aug 14 13:18:38	PRIVATE_WIFI5	10.0.5.4:46118	50.16.228.90:80	TCP:PA
	Aug 14 13:17:29	PRIVATE_WIFI5	10.0.5.4:45714	74.125.21.97:443 yv-in-f97.1e100.net	TCP:FPA
	Aug 14 13:17:29	PRIVATE_WIFI5	10.0.5.4:45714	74.125.21.97:443 yv-in-f97.1e100.net	TCP:FPA
	Aug 14 13:17:01	PRIVATE_WIFI5	10.0.5.4:50923	173.194.219.17:443 ya-in-f17.1e100.net	TCP:FPA
	Aug 14 13:16:59	PRIVATE_WIFI5	10.0.5.4:45714	74.125.21.97:443 yv-in-f97.1e100.net	TCP:PA
	Aug 14 13:16:44	PRIVATE_WIFI5	10.0.5.4:45714	74.125.21.97:443 yv-in-f97.1e100.net	TCP:PA
	Aug 14 13:16:35	PRIVATE_WIFI5	10.0.5.4:45714	74.125.21.97:443 yv-in-f97.1e100.net	TCP:PA
	Aug 14 13:16:31	PRIVATE_WIFI5	10.0.5.4:45714	74.125.21.97:443 yv-in-f97.1e100.net	TCP:PA

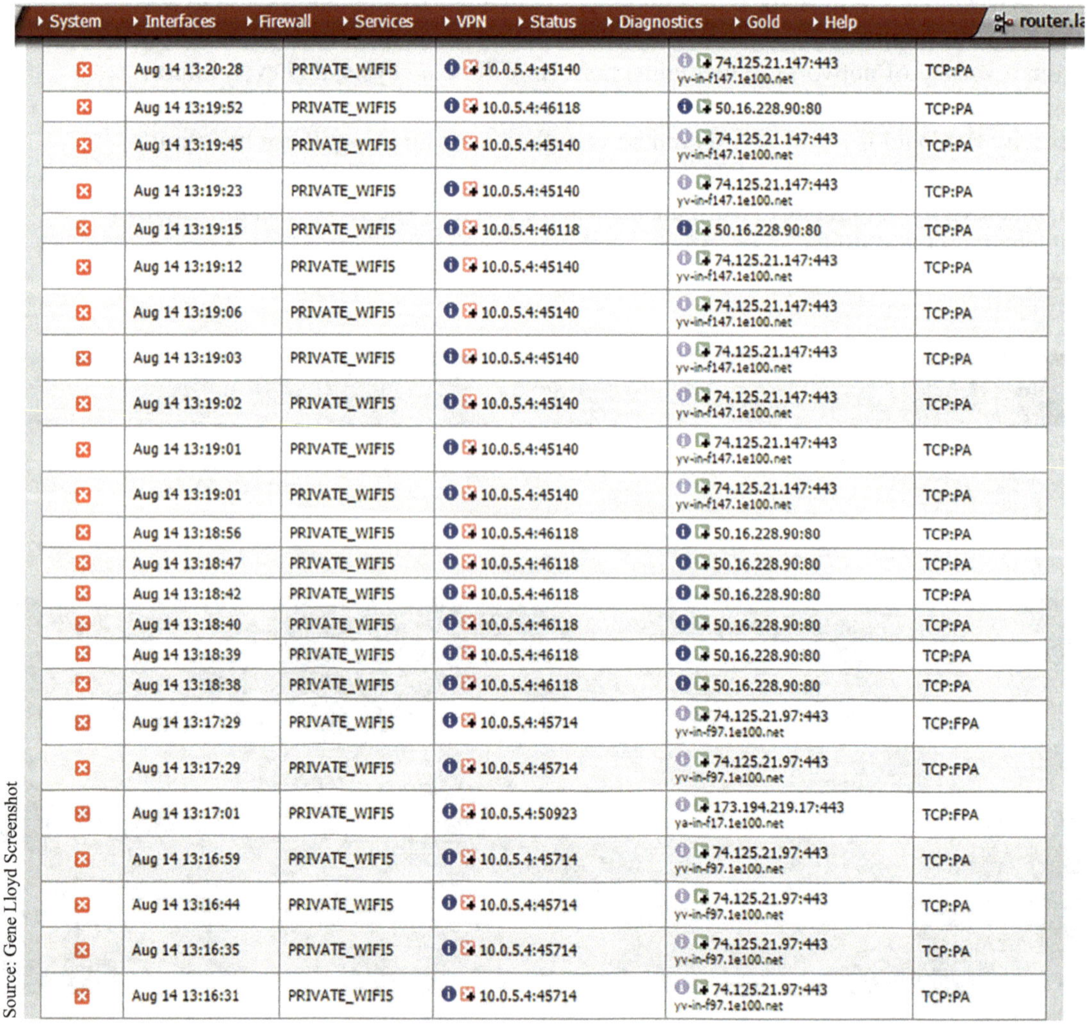

Source: Gene Lloyd Screenshot

Snort

NMAP – NMAP is a command-line network auditing tool used in vulnerability assessments and penetration testing to find ports or services that could potentially be exploited. It can also be used by network administrators as a troubleshooting tool. It works by scanning user-specified IP addresses and reports which ports are open, closed, and filtered. NMAP comes with a slew of options to broaden or narrow its focus, depending on the goal of the user. In real-world applications, it is best to keep it narrow in quiet. In training environments, NMAP can be let loose with its most intense options to discover more information about the network.

List all options	man nmap
Simple IP scan	nmap 192.168.1.1
Simple IP range scan	nmap 192.168.
Ping scan	nmap -sp 192.168.1.0/24
Singe port scan	nmap -p 80 192.168.1.1
Multiple port scan	nmap -p 1-1000 192.168.1.1
	nmap -p 22, 80, 53 192.168.1.1
Top ports scan	nmap –top-ports 20 192.168.1.1
	Note: this scans the top 20 used ports, change it for more or less
OS detection scan	nmap -A 192.168.1.1
Fast scan	nmap -T4 192.168.1.1

Many of these options can be combined, creating custom scans for any particular task. NMAP can also be used to look for vulnerabilities or systems infected with malware using its advanced NSE scripting options. Practice some of these scans on your home network to see how the results change and how long it takes for individual scans and ranges of scans. You can also run Wireshark on a separate computer to watch what the traffic looks like when someone is running a scan against your network. This gives you two forms of practice at the same time.

NMAP

NESSUS – NESSUS is a vulnerability scanner which includes a database of more than 60,000 known vulnerabilities. It scans the target network or IP address and reports back on any potential discovered vulnerabilities. This is not a tool you start with; it is one you use after you have looked for open ports with NMAP and know what you want to target. NMAP will show you what is open, NESSUS will show you if a vulnerability exists on that open port. NESSUS requires registration to receive a key to activate the downloaded software. The free version is limited to scanning no more than 16 IP addresses at a single time and is perfect for practicing. More capabilities are unlocked with purchase. NESSUS has a simple-to-use GUI interface that only requires inputting target addresses and ports to get it running.

https://www.tenable.com/products/nessus

Source: Gene Lloyd Screenshot

Nessus

PFSENSE – PFSENSE is a freely available firewall that can be deployed in many different environments. As with any other firewall, it blocks or allows traffic according to its configuration. The standard install blocks all incoming traffic by default and users need to actively open ports to allow traffic originating outside of the network to cross through the firewall. It is highly customizable; so much so it allows for the installation of additional packages within its framework. One of those packages is the snort IDS which makes it a great two-in-one device for smaller networks and saves you the extra work of installing Snorby.

https://www.pfsense.org/download/

Chapter 3: Traffic Analysis

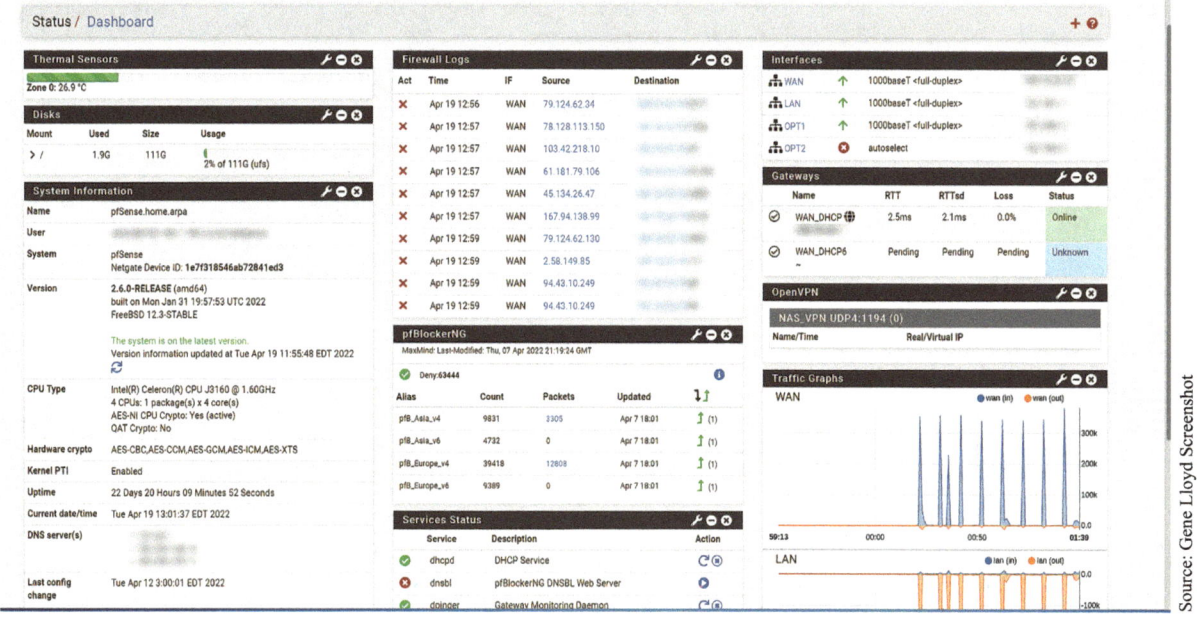

PFSense

Working in the cyber security arena requires constant research and learning to stay ahead of the latest hacker techniques and knowing which new vulnerabilities may affect your network or systems. Several easily searchable online databases exist allowing you to search for vulnerabilities based on operating systems and specific applications, letting you quickly look for anything concerning specific configurations in use on your network. It is a good idea to check these sites every week for newly identified vulnerabilities; whenever you are considering installing new applications to make sure they do not have inherent vulnerabilities which cannot be mitigated.

Chapter 3: Review Questions

1. _____ network traffic is a core function of cyber security.
   a. deleting
   b. monitoring
   c. addressing
   d. managing

2. Analysts work to _____ traffic that squeezed past defenses.
   a. detect
   b. modify
   c. eliminate
   d. ignore

3. A traffic analyst must _____ how traffic flows.
   a. ignore
   b. watch
   c. understand
   d. control

4. Patch _____ is the term for when Microsoft releases patches.
   a. Monday
   b. Tuesday
   c. Wednesday
   d. Thursday

5. Analyzing traffic requires _____.
   a. focus
   b. sleep
   c. desire
   d. intensity

6. It is not possible to analyze _____ traffic.
   a. bad
   b. all
   c. web
   d. email

7. _____ from network devices should be included in analysis.
   a. configuration
   b. listings
   c. commands
   d. logs

8. _____ are unsophisticated hackers.
   a. government employees
   b. teenagers
   c. script kiddies
   d. administrators

9. _____ incentive is a major motivator for hacking.
   a. financial
   b. personal
   c. corporate
   d. relationship

10. NIDS is a _____ device.
    a. difficult
    b. active
    c. passive
    d. hardened

11. Network _____ can affect NIDS sniffing ability.
    a. volume
    b. users
    c. administrators
    d. managers

12. NIPS is an _____ device.
    a. difficult
    b. active
    c. passive
    d. hardened

13. Analysts need to be aware of false _____ with NIPS.
    a. negatives
    b. alerts
    c. packets
    d. positives

14. An IDS/IPS can be placed on the _____ network.
    a. perimeter
    b. internal
    c. DMZ
    d. All of the above

15. Analysts need to know the _____ on the network.
    a. users
    b. open ports
    c. computers
    d. administrators

16. _____ is the most common action taken against malicious traffic.
    a. blocking
    b. ignoring
    c. testing
    d. securing
17. Patching is the _____ layer of defense.
    a. hardest
    b. fastest
    c. highest
    d. easiest
18. Buffer overflows take advantage of _____ buffers.
    a. network
    b. video
    c. memory
    d. game
19. It is always better to be _____ in cyber security.
    a. proactive
    b. reactive
    c. fast
    d. slow
20. _____ is a network protocol analyzer.
    a. Explorer
    b. Wireshark
    c. NMAP
    d. Telnet
21. _____ is a network auditing tool.
    a. Explorer
    b. Wireshark
    c. NMAP
    d. Telnet

Vulnerability Assessment

CHAPTER 4

The best way to locate vulnerabilities on a network is to conduct a thorough vulnerability assessment. Vulnerability assessments scan systems and devices looking for known vulnerable services and probe to determine if the currently used version can be exploited. These assessments do not attempt to exploit or break into any systems. They scan and record what is discovered so security professionals can make the appropriate changes. This is the number one method an organization can use to locate and eradicate known vulnerabilities on necessary services and applications. As you have already learned in an earlier chapter, there are many thousands of vulnerabilities in existence across the entire landscape of software and computing. It is highly likely some of those applications are used on your network. In many cases, they are necessary applications needed to conduct business and simply need to be patched with the latest update or replaced with the latest version. In other cases, the applications can be deleted altogether.

The purpose of these assessments is to find what is wrong and fix it before someone else tries to exploit the weakness. Unfortunately, one existing hurdle is the perspective that a network is not important to a hacker, or that security is so strong it could never be hacked. This is security arrogance, and it leads to… you guessed it, hacked systems. Never assume your network is off the radar. There have been many instances where newly announced vulnerabilities were exploited all over the internet with just a few days. The WordPress plugin, Easy WP SMTP, which had a discovered vulnerability in 2019, is a great example of this possibility. Hackers began scanning for vulnerable sites immediately after the vulnerability was announced, wreaking short-term havoc on many websites before administrators had a chance to install the patched version of the software. Never assume hackers do not care about your systems. There are many ways they can utilize your resources for their gain. Stay vigilant, and scan regularly for any possible security risks.

Pause for a moment and think about risk. What risk really exists against your network? Who would ever want to hack into the systems of a small company focused on serving the residents of a small town in the midwestern U.S.? Why do you need security, or vulnerability assessments, if you are so small and insignificant that no one will ever likely target you on purpose? That way of thinking has put many organizations in a bad situation when hackers took over their networks. It is dangerous to assume you are safe because you are unknown. Hackers scanning the internet for open ports do not see company names, they see IP addresses. The IP address they scan could be the home of a CEO, Senator, or average person. The scan does not differentiate between the who, it is only looking for the what. The open port. The vulnerability. Personal home networks get scanned constantly every day as do the IP address ranges of many internet service providers. The risk of being hacked exists equally for everyone.

A good risk management principle is to eliminate as many risks as possible. Vulnerability assessments pinpoint the risks that need to be eliminated and help leaders and technicians determine the best path forward in updating software applications, removing old systems, or redesigning infrastructure into a more security-conscious posture. If you have never conducted a vulnerability assessment, you may be surprised the first time to find some vulnerabilities on your network. You can run an assessment against your own home network and will likely discover open ports on Windows-based systems that could be vulnerable to specific types of attacks. This is very common. We scan systems to find and plug the security holes. It is not designed to be a witch hunt to fire employees who have failed to keep a particular system secure. The job of a system administrator can keep them stretched thin and cause some tasks to fall off their list. These scans help to prioritize the importance of security and find the vulnerabilities before a hacker has a chance to gain access. It keeps us one step ahead of the game. Working together as a team to identify and rectify every possible vulnerability generates the best outcome for everyone.

At a bare minimum, vulnerability assessments should be conducted every six months. Scanning on a more frequent basis is an even better idea but is not always practical or possible. Unless your organization installs new software applications on a frequent basis, twice a year scanning should be sufficient for this level of analysis. Scans should also be run against new software applications, preferably on a system not connected to the network, so potential vulnerabilities can be corrected prior to placing the software on the live network. You may think at first glance this plan is too aggressive. But consider how aggressive a hacker is when looking for a new target. These methods take time and resources and are needed to keep your network off the list of a hacker's next round of planned attacks. Prevention is a powerful weapon against an attack, and most attacks are completely preventable as long as security professionals stay vigilant. Hackers only need to be correct one time to gain access, security professionals need to be correct all the time to keep them out. A proactive process of scanning is an easy way to maintain the upper hand and not have to endure incident investigations at a later time.

Every organization should maintain a list of approved applications along with the version currently installed on their systems. The vulnerability analyst should compare this list with software manufacture patch announcements and inform system administrators when new patches are released. It takes very little time to check on the status of patches and updates, so there are no reasons for it not to be accomplished every week. If this process is strictly adhered to, the chance of a vulnerability being exploited is very low. The issue of patch management cannot be overstated. Most vulnerabilities occurring in the wild are a result of unpatched systems.

The simple process of checking for and installing updates can be the difference between exploited and ignored. It is a mundane process, but it is better to be mundane and protected than run over by digital warlords. This application list should also be used when running full vulnerability assessments to know the expected ports and protocols applications are using for communication.

These assessments are conducted with a full understanding of the network configuration and layout. Penetration tests attack the network blind, with as little knowledge as possible of infrastructure, available services, or security configurations. Vulnerability assessments want to locate every possible vulnerability and get it fixed. So, current network maps, listings of all network services, firewall configurations, and operating system policies should all be reviewed prior to scanning. You are looking for the weak link and reviewing the landscape prior to the assessment will help to focus attention on potentially weaker areas. These tests are not designed to defeat your coworkers in a digital attack. It is a team effort where everyone focuses on the same goal of securing every inch of the network. The classic "us versus them" mentality in the security world tends to get in the way. Throw that ideology away right now. It has no place in a healthy team environment.

Vulnerability assessments require a lot of coordination because they will stress the network and potentially slow communication capabilities needed for operations. It is best to deconflict schedules with system administrators, the perimeter security team, and management to conduct the assessment on a day no other major upgrades or operations are taking place. It is typically good practice to do this work on a weekend when the least number of employees are in the office. This allows plenty of time to run tests, review results, and potentially install easy patches—all on the same day. If consistent patching has been conducted throughout the year, the scans will reveal little to nothing, securing peace of mind and confirming that the security team is doing a great job. Follow-up scans should be conducted after all patching and remediations are conducted, which may require an additional day of scheduling. It can be a tedious process at times but is necessary and very worth the effort.

One area that needs more attention than others is rarely-used systems that tend to fall off the radar of regular maintenance and updates. It is a good idea to have a conversation with the system administrators about these types of systems. Sometimes they are legacy systems used for a singular purpose that may not be needed anymore. They could also have useful functions with software that has never been updated by the manufacturer. This does not mean they are automatically vulnerable to attack, but special attention should be given because of the nature of their use. Systems that are rarely used tend to be forgotten, making them a great potential hiding place for hackers to store their tools and set up long-term backdoors. A more intense scan of these individual systems is warranted, and it would also be wise to recommend alternative applications in your final report to eliminate any unnecessary additional risks.

When conducting a vulnerability assessment, be sure to scan everything. Every port should be scanned because there may be some applications you may not be aware of, and in some cases, user-installed software that was never approved. Scanning for what is known is good, scanning for what is not known is better. This allows you to conduct a systematic review of every possible vulnerability. Do not leave out any system, any segment of the network, or any device on the network. There are no silos in cyber security. Full coverage is important because even one, single vulnerability can provide a doorway for someone to gain unauthorized access. Larger networks will take more time to scan so plan accordingly and start at an appropriate time. Most scanning operations are automated once they get underway, freeing the assessor to prepare for other elements of the assessment while the scans are underway.

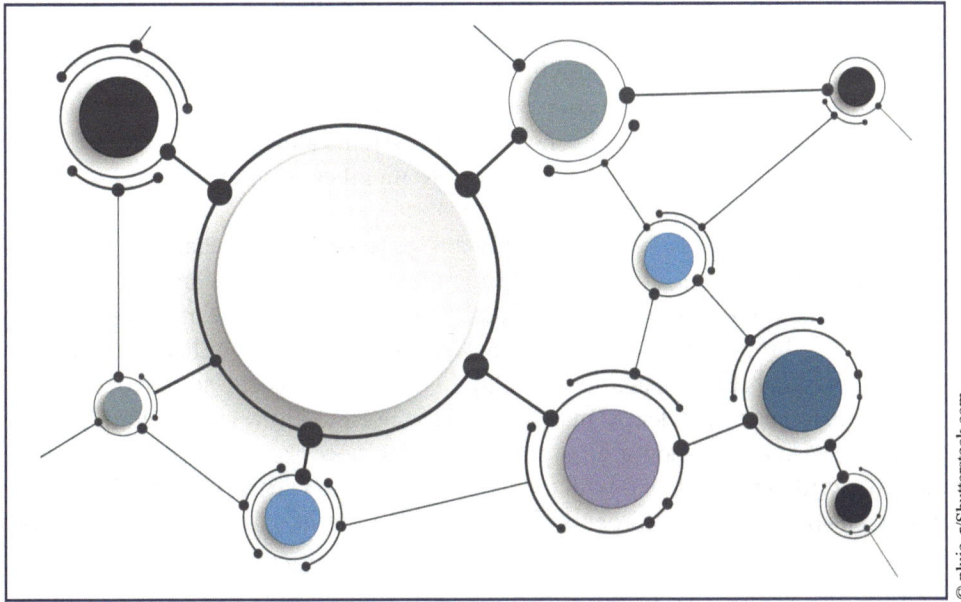

Conduct your initial scan with one tool, then broaden to include the use of other tools as you discover services specific applications may be used to exploit. Every scanner has slightly different capabilities and techniques, as do hackers, so looking from multiple angles will help flush out something you may have otherwise missed. Vulnerability assessments need to be taken seriously and not simply viewed as an item to be checked off the list a few times each year. The livelihood of the organization, employees and customers are all at stake. One successful attack could cause a small organization to go out of business and result in secondary and tertiary effects in individual lives. These tests can make those scenarios much less possible. Scan, scan some more, change your perspective, and scan again. Every corrected vulnerability is one less possibility of attack. It is also good to run scans from internal and external positions.

External scans will show you what is visible to any user outside of your network, while internal scans will show you everything a network user can see. Penetration tests are typically run from outside of the network because that is the focus from which most hackers will operate. A vulnerability assessment starting on the outside and then moving to the inside can provide multiple perspectives. You may think scanning from the outside is enough because the attacker can only exploit what the firewall makes available. This would be true if all attacks originated from outside of your network, but that is not always the case. Some attacks anticipate user behavior that creates an outbound stateful connection a hacker can ride back into the network. Insider activity where an employee intentionally creates vulnerabilities to steal data or disrupt capabilities would also not be discoverable from an external scan. One scan will confirm the firewall is configured properly and the other scan will conduct a deep dive into all capabilities. Both perspectives are important.

Alerts generated by internal and external IDS devices should be reviewed to make sure they respond properly to every scan. This is an element most people forget to think about during a vulnerability assessment. The IDS, as you have already learned, functions to alert on potentially nefarious activity. These scans will test its capabilities as well and reveal where any fine-tuning is required. An IDS is only as effective as its programming, so tweaking the rules that trigger alerts will help with day-to-day security activities. In fact, you may find new exploits that the IDS is not yet aware of and be able to close that loop as the result of the vulnerability assessment. The assessment is not for user systems alone, it is also to check the security devices and capabilities in place. Remember, testing every system and capability is the best methodology.

Vulnerability assessments should always generate a report that provides management with a listing of problems, recommended fix actions, and timelines for when the vulnerabilities will be eliminated. This is a critical piece of the pie because some vulnerabilities may require purchasing new applications or hardware to fully correct the problem. Scanning tools often generate reports automatically that include many technical details managers do not need to know and would likely not understand. Analysts should incorporate only the necessary details into a professionally written report along with advice for any needed decisions. This is the necessary business side of the process allowing for long-term tracking and comparison.

If the same vulnerability pops up every six months, it could be a sign of a larger problem or systemic issue needing to be corrected. Those issues almost always involve managerial decisions, and those decisions are easier to make with the readily available historical data these reports provide.

One thing you cannot scan for, but need to be aware of, is zero-day exploits. These are exploits to vulnerabilities that have not yet been discovered or publicly announced by manufacturers but have been discovered by someone else. With these types of exploits, the world is unaware they exist until an attacker strikes. It is very difficult to protect against an exploit you do not know about, which is why we have other security mechanisms in place. Paying attention to news alerts related to cyber security is a good way to monitor for zero-day exploit attacks. One of the more famous zero-day exploits in recent history was the attack against Sony Pictures Entertainment in 2014 where hackers gained access to a treasure trove of sensitive data. Some of this data, including unreleased copies of movies, was released on the internet potentially causing financial loss. No one knows for sure who the culprit was, or the totality of damage, but it highlighted then, and now, the importance of vigilance in all areas of cyber security.

There are also other types of targeted scans vulnerability analysts can conduct, more specific to user access and activity. Even if all vulnerabilities are patched, a weak password or untrained user can easily become a broken link in the security chain. Checking password strength alongside vulnerability assessments helps to fill in one potential gap that normal scans will not detect. This is accomplished by running a password hacking tool against the network accounts to determine if any user password is easily broken. Running this tool for 30 minutes is enough to find the weakest of passwords. The goal is to identify weak passwords and force those users to immediately make a change. The other area users tend to fall short on is dealing with emails that include malicious links. Savvy attackers can craft an email that looks legitimate to convince a user to click a link that downloads a malicious file or initiates a connection from inside the network. This is known as a phishing email, a term you are likely already familiar with. Crafting and sending the same type of email to all users as a test can identify training deficiencies and serve as a reminder for everyone not to click on links from unknown sources.

While you conduct assessments a few times or more each year, you should also scan new systems before they are put onto the network. It is always best to know new vulnerabilities are being placed on the network instead of waiting until the next round of scanning to discover a glaring problem. These are much easier to conduct because it typically involves a single IP address, or a single application, and can be completed very quickly. Any potential vulnerabilities should be addressed and fixed before the system is put online. Some organizations have administrative teams, sometimes called a configuration control board, that provides formal approval for new systems. This creates a more rigorous process for all network changes, ensuring interoperability and security concerns are addressed prior to any change taking place. It can be a burdensome process at times and should be streamlined as much as possible, but it is a valuable method that can stop security deficiencies before they happen.

Test Networks

One great method of early scanning is to create a small test network that mimics the real network configuration and using that enclave for the testing of all new systems and applications. This is one of the easiest ways to keep vulnerable systems and applications from creating a problem on the live network. It is always easier to keep something off the network than to clean it later when it becomes a problem. As a general rule, every organization should conduct some type of offline test prior to putting anything onto the live network. This is true of new applications, updated applications, system patches, and any other change. You never know when even the smallest change can create a big problem that sends everyone into a frenzy to figure out the culprit. Test networks eliminate a lot of needless headaches and extra work.

A test network can be made up of physical network devices and systems or be fully virtual. It can be expensive to purchase and maintain identical versions of routers, firewalls, servers, and user systems. This would be the most ideal setup but is not always practical. Virtual test environments are easier and cheaper to manage. They do not perfectly mimic the real network environment but are more than capable to fill this needed role. Most applications will run inside of a virtual environment without recognizing it is not on a physical system. It is also easier to reset a virtual system if a tested application turns out to include malware. Whichever option is available for your needs, the key is to keep it isolated from the rest of the network and consistently use it for all changes before implementing those changes on production systems.

This is also a good place to practice vulnerability assessments without affecting the rest of the network. If you conduct a real vulnerability assessment every six months, you can also run practice assessments on the test network more frequently to become familiar with the process and learn how to easily recognize the most common vulnerabilities. Practice makes perfect, as the saying goes, and training is often the key to making this process more effective. Vulnerable systems can be placed on the test network for trainees to discover, administrators to patch, and penetration testers to exploit. You can also practice this on your own computer at home, at least on a smaller scale.

Policies

Vulnerability assessments should always start with a review of policies. The creation and following of sound security policies is a major key to keeping a network safe. Policies should be updated or reviewed at least annually, practically implement requirements, and should exist for all the following areas:

Acceptable Use	Mobile Device and BYOD
Access and Data Control	Open Source and Free Software
Account Monitoring and Data Privacy	Passwords
Administrative Access Oversight	Patch Management
Antivirus and Malware	Penetration Testing
Backups	Perimeter Security
Change Management	Physical Security
Checklists	Remote Access
Cloud Storage	Security Awareness Training
Disaster Recovery and Continuity	Social Networking
Documentation Review	Storage Device Management and Disposal
Email	System, Server, and Network Device Security
Encryption	Technology Ethics
Equipment Inventory and Disposal	Visitor Management
Incident Response and Unauthorized Data Access	Vulnerability Assessment
Key Control	Wireless Network Access

Common policies that should be reviewed

A vulnerability in any of these areas can create an opportunity for someone to gain unauthorized access to systems or data. Policies are where security really starts. Organizations determine what will be allowed on the network and then implement those requirements through various physical and technical controls or measures. A vulnerability assessment that includes reviewing adherence to policy provides an additional layer of risk analysis. There are two things you need to determine when reviewing policies. First, does the policy provide the necessary requirements for a sound implementation of security? Maybe it did when it was first developed, but technological advances can force the need to update policies on a regular basis. Second, are the policies being followed? A policy does not have much value if employees ignore it, and management does not force compliance. Answer these questions for every policy you review and make it part of your final report.

Users love to bypass security measures and ignore policies they consider to be burdensome or irrelevant to their particular job. This will always be a challenge. There are many ways users can work around security features designed to keep them confined within a secure computing box. This is often in the realm of making connections outside of the network, prohibited by policies or technical controls. The common method to control web access is through the use of a proxy server configured to prohibit access to websites that contain content the organization chooses to prohibit, typically adult themed or malicious websites. Security organizations provide lists of known IP addresses in these categories making implementation very simple. But a savvy user can easily bypass these restrictions by setting up their own web proxy, which is unlikely to be blocked if it is unknown to the larger security world.

It is difficult to detect these types of vulnerabilities because the connections often originate from within the network and connect to IP addresses not known to be malicious or on any restricted lists. Users who take these actions are not necessarily trying to intentionally cause harm. They just want to have the ability to access other content and not be restricted by company policy. Monitoring for this type of activity can be difficult. It is not feasible to monitor all web-based outbound traffic because the volume of traffic is too large to effectively analyze every packet. Randomly filtering web activity based on internal IP address is one method to look for this type of activity but is hit or miss. The vulnerability assessment team can narrow the focus by looking at all outbound traffic connecting to commonly used web proxy port numbers. Ideally, this traffic will not exist. If it does, it will be a much smaller amount and likely come from a single user attempting to bypass the rules. Users create risks, sometimes on purpose and sometimes accidentally. Security professionals need to be on the lookout for both.

Some particular policies that can cause more problems than others are the use of company laptops, remote access, wireless network access. Laptops issued to employees should be brought into the office often enough to receive regular updates and patches. These systems are notorious for lagging behind the rest of the network when new security measures are rolled out. Employees who have extensive travel schedules may find it difficult to bring the laptop to the IT department usually leaving many vulnerabilities open the next time it is connected to the internet. The last thing you need is for a company laptop to be breached while connected to a public network and used as a type of trojan horse to bring malware back into the company network. This scenario could quickly ravage a network as malware replicates through systems. Your assessment should include every device allowed to make a connection to the network.

Remote access that allows connection to the internal portion of the network is much less common today than in previous times. We have become much wiser to the idea of keeping external connections isolated to network segments containing no sensitive data. This is not always possible if traveling employees need to connect to customer databases or similar content and that is when remote access connections can take a dangerous turn. Just as with the laptop scenario, malware can easily be copied across a remote connection as if the system was physically in the office. The remote connections also typically originate from the company laptops showing once again the importance of keeping those systems secure. Any of these systems discovered to be insecure by a vulnerability assessment should be barred from any connection until updated. That level of response will force the user to bring the laptop in for updates.

Insider Threats

The insider threat is one of the most difficult to detect. Insider threats are employees or other individuals who have authorized access to the network and a desire to steal data or cause some form of harm to the company. The challenge with these types of threats is you rarely know about them until action is already taken. It is difficult to guess who might steal data and sell it to a competitor until one day you discover one of the system administrators left with a treasure trove of information. These create a challenge for anyone in the security field because we cannot treat every employee as if they are a potential criminal and we also cannot allow every employee unfettered access to every portion of every system. This is where checks and balances need to be put in place to help eliminate insider threats and make it very difficult for their actions to go undetected.

Edward Snowden is a great recent example of an insider threat. He was upset because concerns he highlighted were ignored and he believed a great crime was being perpetrated against the American public. That is a synopsis of his version of the story. The other side is that he was disgruntled for some reason and decided to smear the intelligence community through the release of many of their clandestine operations. Regardless of individual opinion on his actions, Snowden firmly fits in the category of an insider threat. He had high-level privileges on the network and access to a treasure trove of data. His access enabled him to copy data without anyone noticing and remove that data from a secure facility, only to later provide it to his chosen media conduit. This is a classic example that can play out in any organization and it received international media attention because of the organization involved.

How much damage can an insider actually cause? It depends on their actions. A disgruntled system administrator can shut down services in the middle of critical operations, delete technical data needed to complete a project, or sell data to competitors. The actions they take are only limited by their access and creativity. What does this have to do with vulnerability assessments? An insider threat is a huge potential vulnerability. Vulnerability assessments have traditionally been conducted from behind a keyboard, but as this chapter has already highlighted, reviewing policies and procedures for other gaps in security can help identify those areas where the risk of insider action is higher. Every potential vulnerability should be analyzed as part of the overall process. Policies determine much of the activity within an organization. Those policies are what will make or break the mission of maintaining a solid security footprint.

Reporting Timelines

An in-depth vulnerability assessment as described in this chapter will generate a lot of information. All that information needs to be sorted, formatted, and presented to management for action. The time it takes to prepare these reports can easily be more than the assessment itself. It may take several weeks to properly assemble concerns, recommendations, and supporting data. This can pose a problem if vulnerabilities are discovered, as the systems will remain vulnerable until the responsible party is notified. A listing of vulnerabilities should be provided to the appropriate personnel prior to the completed report so they can start the work of mitigation immediately. There is no good reason to leave something vulnerable for several weeks while a formal report is being generated. Get the problem fixed as soon as possible and discuss the reasons for the vulnerability after the risk is eliminated.

Vulnerability assessments are not difficult to run but they can force employees to answer difficult questions if glaring security issues are discovered. All vulnerability assessments uncover something. Sometimes it is already known, benign, and no further action is required. Other times it is a new vulnerability not previously identified on the network—which requires some work to get it corrected. And very rarely it is a vulnerability previously discovered that was never fixed. That is the worst possible outcome. You never want to see the same vulnerability pop up on a new assessment. This is a clear sign someone did not take the process seriously and they will need to answer for their lack of action. The bottom-line goal here is to make sure nothing on the network is vulnerable to an internal or external attack, as well as to ensure policies and procedures are effective and being followed. The assessor is not the bad guy pointing out everyone's mistakes, they are a secondary layer of security confirming hackers will have a difficult time breaching the system.

Practical Application – Tools of the Trade

Many great commercial vulnerability scanners are available on the market, which are highly effective in running vulnerability assessments. Open-source tools, such as Nessus, which was mentioned in Chapter 3, can also be very effective in these scans. Some people assume that a product which costs money will be better than a free product. This is true in many areas, but in the open-source software world, many great tools exist that can accomplish the same tasks without spending a dollar. There are some pros and cons to both approaches, generally centering around cost, capability, and support. Commercial applications of this magnitude can be expensive, ranging from approximately $1,500/year to more than $30,000/year depending on how many devices you need to scan. Major corporations with millions of dollars in revenue can easily absorb these costs, but smaller organizations have a lot of trouble making this software fit into the budget.

Commercial scanners come with technical support and great user documentation, giving you a tool that can be learned and deployed without a lot of customization or experimentation. Technical support can help when you run into a problem and walk you through how to get everything working for your next scan. Both options are valuable, but they usually come with added costs. On the other side of the equation, open-source vulnerability scanning software comes without the price tag, and without any official support. This can be a challenge if the user is not

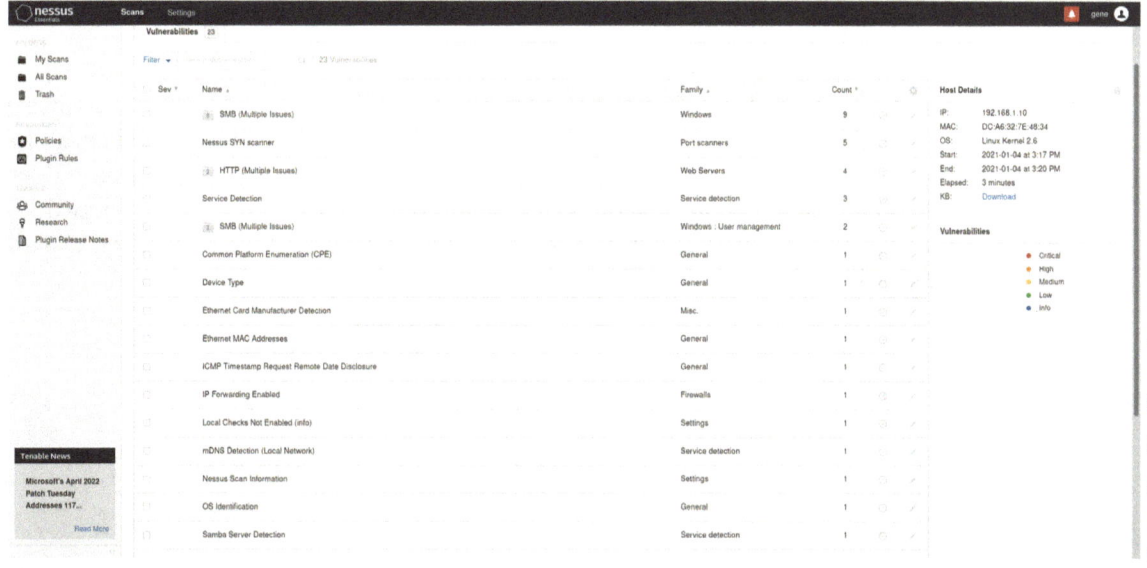

Nessus

familiar with the software and is not willing to learn the specifics on their own. Some organizations also assume open-source may be synonymous with poorly coded or potentially malicious. This is rarely the case with well-known tools but can be true of random applications from untrusted sources. Ultimately, what you choose to use will depend on budgets, management, and skill levels.

Nessus is a popular scanner because it fits in both categories. Home users and students who are learning about vulnerability scanners can download and use it for free with the only limitation of not being allowed to scan more than a small number of IP addresses at one time. These capabilities are perfect for a beginner, and if needed, expanded licenses can be purchased to provide more capabilities. Most scanning tools are GUI-based with very similar features, capabilities, and use cases. They are mostly straightforward and intuitive to use for scanning small or larger networks. The normal process follows a path similar to the following:

- Create a new scanning operation
  - Some applications include templates that can be used to speed up the process of getting started.
- Select IP addresses or IP address ranges
  - Only scan IP addresses where explicit permission has been granted
- Select port numbers or port number ranges
  - Some applications allow for ranges with deselection of specific ports
- Select additional settings
  - Use known vulnerability settings to run targeted scans with more specificity
  - Provide default usernames and passwords to test logins for certain devices
  - Use malware signatures to look for infected systems
  - Utilize policies to verify compliance
  - Customize scans as needed for specific requirements
- Run the scan
  - Depending on the network size, these scans can take a significant amount of time. Do not expect an instantaneous response.
- Review scan results
- Prepare scan report

Cyber security professionals utilize these types of tools to locate and eradicate vulnerabilities on the network. They are fairly simple to use, and in the hands of a knowledgeable person, can be a surgical tool to locate even the most well-hidden vulnerable application. Practice often with your tool of choice on test networks, home networks, and anywhere else you can legally do so, to gain as much experience with different types of systems as possible.

Chapter 4: Review Questions

1. The best way to locate vulnerabilities on a network is to _____.
   a. Run a vulnerability assessment
   b. Look through configurations
   c. Talk to administrators
   d. Review software installations

2. A common hurdle is the idea that _____.
   a. Systems are impenetrable
   b. The firewall is enough
   c. The network is not important to an attacker
   d. The data is worthless

3. The risk of being hacked exists _____.
   a. Only on sensitive systems
   b. Only on weak systems
   c. Only for important users
   d. Equally for everyone

4. Systems are scanned in order to _____.
   a. Plug security holes
   b. Fire employees
   c. Locate potential risks
   d. Both and c

5. Vulnerability assessments should be conducted at least _____.
   a. Every month
   b. Every 6 months
   c. Every year
   d. Every 2 years

6. _____ is a powerful weapon against an attack.
   a. Augmentation
   b. Deprecation
   c. Prevention
   d. Reporting

7. How much time does it take to check for patches?
   a. Very little
   b. A long time
   c. Unknown
   d. A few seconds

8. Penetration tests attack the network _____.
   a. Blind
   b. With all knowledge
   c. With partial knowledge
   d. As administrators

9. Vulnerability assessments should be _____ before running.
   a. Monitored
   b. Tested
   c. Deconflicted
   d. Mastered

10. Rarely used systems should receive _____ attention than others.
    a. Less
    b. More
    c. The same
    d. No

11. What ports should be scanned during an assessment?
    a. Every
    b. Minimal
    c. 1-100
    d. 500-1000

12. Looking from multiple _____ will help find more vulnerabilities.
    a. Fields
    b. Systems
    c. Networks
    d. Angles

13. Vulnerability scans should run from _____ the network.
    a. Outside and inside
    b. Only outside the network
    c. Only inside the network
    d. The external firewall

14. What is something you cannot scan for?
    a. Old exploits
    b. New exploits
    c. Zero-day exploits
    d. Foreign exploits

15. A _____ should always be generated after an assessment.
    a. Report
    b. Penetration test
    c. Installation plan
    d. Email
16. Password hacking tools locate _____ passwords.
    a. Strong
    b. All
    c. Some
    d. Weak
17. _____ systems should be scanned before going _____.
    a. New, Online
    b. New, Offline
    c. Old, Online
    d. Old, Offline
18. A _____ should be used for new patches before they go live.
    a. Live network
    b. Small network
    c. Mimic network
    d. Test network
19. Virtual test networks are _____ to manage.
    a. Expensive
    b. Difficult
    c. Cheaper
    d. Impossible
20. Users love to _____ policies and security measures.
    a. Follow
    b. Ignore
    c. Improve
    d. Plan

Penetration Testing

CHAPTER 5

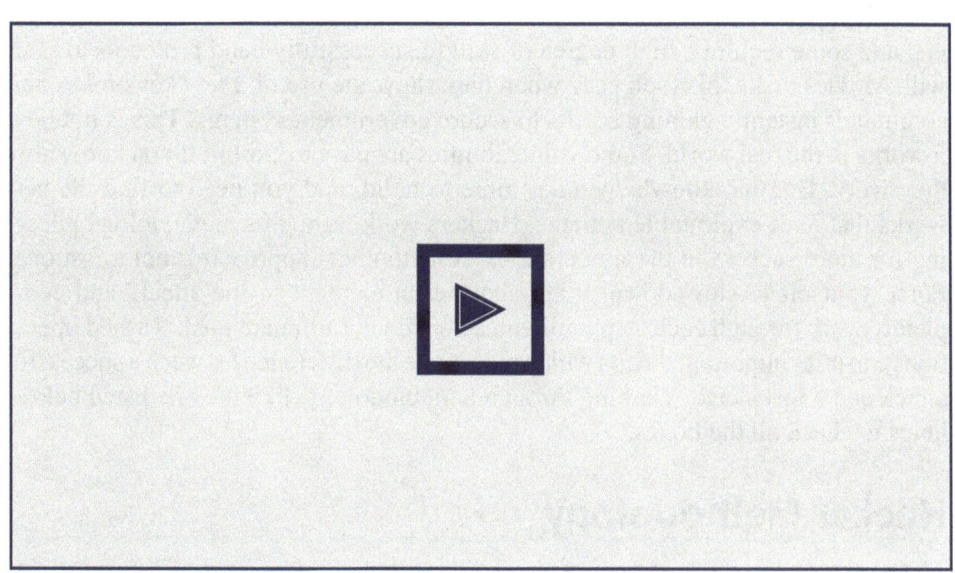

Penetration testing is a rigorous process of locating and exploiting vulnerabilities on a network. It is more rigorous than a vulnerability assessment because it takes the process one step further in an attempt to manipulate a discovered vulnerability. Vulnerability assessments report what could be vulnerable and the risk of leaving it unresolved. A penetration test proves the vulnerability is a risk and reveals how much damage could be caused if that vulnerability is successfully exploited. It is essentially two sides of the same coin, and can be conducted by the same people, depending on how deep of a test is required. The advantage to a penetration test is in its ability to reveal a more quantifiable level of risk. Vulnerability assessments make risk assumptions for 'what if' scenarios, while penetration tests reveal actual risks allowing management to estimate financial damages and costs to secure and recover victim systems.

These tests should be run annually and target the external portion of the network to mimic the actions of a real hacker. Hackers do not have the luxury of entering your office, plugging into the internal network, and then running a scan. They must attack from the outside, so a penetration test should work from the same perspective. The goal is to locate a vulnerability, maybe one discovered in the previous assessment, and then attack with the appropriate tool to gain access. Once on the internal network, testers dig deeper looking for passwords, other weak systems on the internal network, and try to spread throughout as much of the network as possible. Gaining administrative control and accessing sensitive files is always a major goal. Real hackers may take it to the next level by destroying data, wiping systems, or encrypting data and holding it for ransom. Penetration testers do not do anything destructive. They work to gain access and show what could be done in a real attack. Administrative access to data is an end game scenario.

This can be a tedious process requiring a lot of patience and tenacity to work through any potential exploits. Some vulnerabilities are easier to exploit than others, and some require a high degree of skill to successfully bend protocols to your will. Movies make this look easy when they show the use of a few keystrokes and commands instantly gaining access to secure government systems. This is not how it works in the real world. Some vulnerabilities are easy to exploit if you know how they work. But that knowledge takes time to build, and you need to find the networks that have exploitable systems. Hackers work through a methodology allowing for more success in these operations. A methodical approach is not a fast one. Force yourself to slow down, think about each element of the attack, and completely work through each step until you achieve your ultimate goal. Rushed operations can miss important details which may make the difference between a successful attack and a lost cause. Working through a methodology, like the one listed below, helps to check all the boxes.

Hacker Methodology

- Research – the best type of attack is one that includes a lot of research prior to initiating a scan. Once a scan is conducted, the victim network analysts will know you are interested in gaining access. So, it is best to conduct as much research on the target ahead of time. Where you find information will depend on your target. Large organizations tend to have a large online footprint with a lot of publicly available information. Smaller organizations will require a little more digging to find something you can use in your attack. The goal of this stage is to gather information which could be beneficial in later stages. For example, knowing the names and email addresses of senior executives could help you construct a potential list of usernames. If you discover the standard username and email address format, you will even be able to guess with a high probability the usernames for any employee publicly listed on websites or social media. Review websites for employee and management names. Look for any personal information that may help break a password or discover a username. Catalog IP addresses of any server offering a public service. This is much like an intelligence operation conducted by a nation prior to taking any action. The more you collect in this stage, the more you will be able to leverage later in the operation. It is easy to locate a target and launch an attack, but this stage requires patient and systematic research. Highly skilled attackers may spend a long time in this stage.

- Scan (Vulnerability Assessment) – scanning is the first active act against your target. This is where you start to probe the IP addresses you collected earlier to see which ports are open and what services are running on each port. It is easy to think scanning every port of every known target IP will speed up the operation, but that is actually a foolish method. An IDS will quickly alert when a large scan is conducted, so take it slow. Tools allow for scanning thousands of ports all at once and those are the types of easily identifiable scans that end an attack before it ever starts. Scan one port, wait a few minutes and then scan another. Rushing the process leads to mistakes and subsequent blocking action. Try to make your scans look like normal traffic. Slow scans can easily be hidden with the mix of all the other traffic hitting the network and will be difficult for an analyst to detect. If possible, change external IP addresses as you scan, to further hide your activity. Public Wi-Fi in coffee shops and hotels is often a good place to use, as you can easily change locations and get a new IP address. As you scan, record any information you discover and do a little more research to see if there are any potential vulnerabilities associated with the discovered ports and services. Take your list and search through online vulnerability databases to locate a potential avenue of attack.
- Penetrate – this is where the rubber meets the road, and your patient research approach potentially pays off. It is now time to attempt an exploit against your chosen target. This will set off some bells and whistles if security devices are in place, so you will need to be prepared to work quickly and efficiently before someone shuts off your access. Nighttime operations may yield better success while the majority of cyber security personnel are sitting at home. This is especially true for smaller organizations without a 24/7 defensive operation. It is important to note that every attack is not successful. If you are not able to gain access, and you have not yet been blocked, pick another potentially vulnerable port, and try again. Do your best to stay under the wire of detection for as long as possible, and you just may find yourself with a little success.
- Establish Foothold – at this point, the methodology can veer off in a few different directions depending on the goal of the attack. In most cases, hackers want to establish and secure access on their victim system so they can more easily connect again, at a later time. The exploited vulnerability may be patched at some point, so creating a new open door allows for potentially long-term access. This is known as backdoor access. There are many different tools allowing backdoors to be created and it is a good idea to be familiar with the ones you use so you can get it up and running quickly. This is also the point when any custom tools are copied over to the victim system to help

further penetrate the network. Gaining or creating user credentials, preferably with administrator access, is also attempted in this stage. Once access is gained, user privileges should be upgraded to an administrative level which gives unfettered access to all portions of the victim system. The tools listed in the practical application section will help escalate the privileges. Long-term actions will be greatly limited without escalation but that does not mean the operation is a bust. Actions can still be taken to expand access or manipulate data.

- Grab Passwords – how much additional access could you gain if you are able to acquire the administrator password for your victim system? Here is a secret you may not know. It is very common in system administration to use the same local administrator password on every system throughout a network. It is a horrible security practice, but it makes the administration job a lot easier. Administrators who need to remotely connect to a system to perform some function find it less burdensome to keep all the high-level passwords the same. This is to your advantage. Gaining this password allows you to leverage it to connect to many other systems on the network, potentially without the need for additional exploits.

- Scan Internal Network – this is the step where hacking starts to feel cyclical. Once you have secured your access on the network, it is time to look around and see what other internal systems are available to exploit. Another round of scanning is needed at this point to look for additional IP addresses and open ports. This could be a much larger list and you will need to select your next target carefully, so you do not waste time needlessly bouncing through insignificant systems. Look for servers, systems holding sensitive data, or anything else that does not look like an ordinary user workstation. The nice thing about this additional scanning is very few networks monitor internal network activity for security breaches. If you have made it this far, it is unlikely your internal network activity will be immediately detected. People often wonder how a hacker could dig so deep into a network or maintain long-term persistent access. The answer is no one is watching what is happening inside the house. This further highlights the need to keep the perimeter secure. Sometimes, the first victim is the primary target and additional scanning is not required or necessary, but in most cases, this is the stage where we spread further into the network.

- Penetrate New Victim – as with your first round of attacks, you once again need to exploit a vulnerability and gain access to an additional system. This process can go on for a long time if there are many vulnerable systems on the network. It is also not uncommon to find the same vulnerability on multiple systems throughout the network.

- Take Action – at some point, hackers will reach their ultimate target. This is when they take the intended action to complete their overall goal. It may be to steal secret plans for the new death star, copy fake information into a database, wipe out years of research to eliminate competition, or really anything at all relating to the use of the target system. The possibilities here are endless.

- Clean Up Tracks – once the goal is accomplished, it is time to clean up any evidence you were ever on the system. Hacking can leave a lot of evidence in the victim system and the network devices. This portion of the methodology falls more in line with a real hacking event and not what a penetration tester would typically do—unless they were hired to accomplish their mission with zero detection. Cleaning up requires removing programs and hooks that allow you to return. Delete user accounts and wipe permissions for any access created as part of the operation. Clear out any accessible logs that may leave breadcrumbs of what you accomplished. Leave the system as close as possible to the way it was when you found it. If done correctly, no one will ever know the level of access gained.

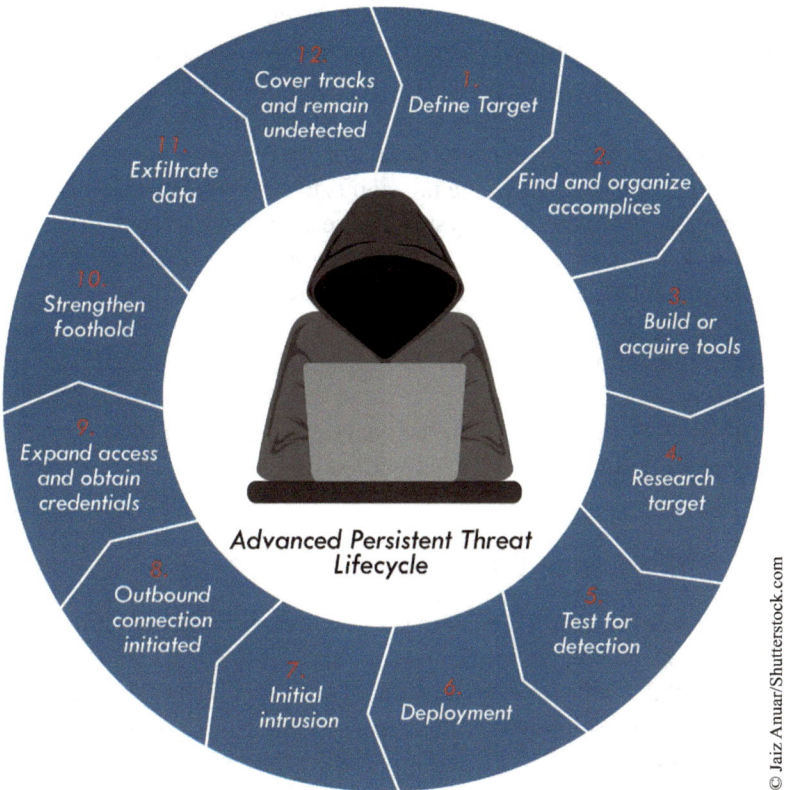

Professional Tips

Hacking can break systems, and often crashes services. You may not be able to regain access after a service crashes until someone reboots the system. This is one point of common frustration for anyone new to this field. Losing access in the middle of an event destroys momentum and forces a pause until the system is reset. This is why establishing a solid foothold after an exploit is such an important element. Sometimes a service will immediately crash as the result of the exploit, keeping you from ever gaining access. Manipulating software to do something it was not designed to accomplish can cause unintended cascading effects. This is a reality you will learn to deal with over time. Expect the unexpected and do not be surprised if you manage to lock yourself out in the process of a penetration test. These crashed services can also alert savvy system administrators to your attempts. One crash may result in a quick reboot. Multiple successive crashes will force an investigation that leads to discovering your activity.

If your methods are not working, pivot to a new idea, look for a new exploit, or stop and rethink the scenario. There are many different ways to access data once you are on the victim system, so do not assume one method will always work. Also, consider the possibility in place security is keeping you from continuing in your operations. A vulnerability may allow you to gain access, but the rest of the system or network could be locked down keeping you from expanding any further than the initial attack. Take time to work through every feasible variable and if they all fail, consider your work finished for this piece of the puzzle. Every system is not hackable and that is a good thing! We want systems to be so secure that penetration testers and hackers alike are unable to gain any level of access.

Enlisting the help of other security personnel can also be very beneficial in these engagements. Analysts, for example, are not typically involved in penetration testing activities because part of the mission is to see if the attackers can be stopped before gaining access. A good analyst can have a lot of great input in these activities because they know how to move around without being detected. When possible, moving personnel into different roles helps to stretch their knowledge as they view events from different perspectives. The perspective of an analyst who has viewed hundreds of hours of traffic can provide new attack strategies previously unconsidered. Similarly, a seasoned penetration tester can key in on more difficult-to-spot exploits when working in the role of an analyst. Researching new ways to conduct these tests on a regular basis will keep your skills sharp.

Best Skills for a Penetration Tester

Penetration testing requires a variety of skills to successfully work through a network full of different hardware, operating systems, applications, and security mechanisms. Some of these skills will come from reading books and many others will come from hands-on practice. The more you learn, the easier it will be to achieve your objectives. Some of these are technical skills and some are intangible emotional states, actions, or perspectives. The key here is to be well-rounded in as many areas as possible, providing you with a greater degree of flexibility during an operation.

- Patience – Hacking can be a frustrating practice when you find yourself up against a door that will not budge. Those who are new to this profession tend to give up early without considering other alternative approaches. Do not be afraid to experiment and keep hammering away until you find a way in or determine that a particular service is currently unbreakable. Here is a big tip for you: not every system is hackable. Some organizations have very strong security and are good at keeping attacks at bay. Patience is a virtue well employed by a penetration tester as is the recognition that it may be time to move on to a new target.

- Operating System Knowledge – Microsoft Windows remains the prevalent system in use on the planet today, but UNIX, Linux, and MacOS are well peppered throughout the internet landscape, so having an understanding of each provides a lot of flexibility. A singular understanding of Windows will not help when you run into a Linux web server. You will suddenly feel like you are in a foreign country attempting to use a language you do not understand. If you plan to work alone, take the time to learn the functionality and administration of each popular operating system. Otherwise, build a team of individuals who have expertise in different areas and be prepared to trade off who is sitting in the driver's seat when their particular expertise is required.

© Stanislaw Mikulski/Shutterstock.com

- Command Line Expertise – Graphical user interfaces (GUI) have spoiled users into making computers more intuitive and easier to use. This is great for the everyday user working on normal projects, but a security professional needs to take it to the next level. A few decades ago, the command line was more common than the GUI. That pendulum has swung to the opposite side of the spectrum today, so much so that many new computer scientists are very uncomfortable with even basic command-line operations. In the hacking world, you will almost always end up staring at a command prompt after exploiting a system, and the commands are different depending on the operating system. Many of the tools used in this field also depend on command-line options. Learn the command line. Become as knowledgeable as you can with this skill. It is incredibly important.
- Programming/Scripting – If you have worked your way through any type of computer science degree, you have likely encountered a few programming courses. Maybe it was Python, C++, or Java. Maybe it was more web-focused like PHP. Regardless of the language flavor, you would have learned many of the same common programming concepts such as loops, variables, arrays, input, output, and if statements. If all this is foreign to you, pick up a book on programming or read through a good website and learn the basics. You do not need a large amount of programming knowledge to work in cyber security, but you need to understand enough that you can recognize what a program is trying to accomplish. Scripting languages are equally important here. Familiarize yourself with both of these competencies.

- Internet Searches – The ability to craft an internet search that returns what you are looking for can save a lot of time in penetration testing. The early stage of collecting information can take a significant amount of time, especially for larger targets. That timeframe can be narrowed through an understanding of how search engines work and the types of keywords they expect. We sometimes call this Google fu, as an analogy to having greater martial arts skills. Most people do not know that Google, specifically, has advanced search operators allowing searches against specific domains, limiting results based on time, and excluding what is returned based on a variety of variables. Some exploits are easily discovered with a well-crafted Google search. Other search engines have similar capabilities as well.
- Metasploit – Metasploit is like a Swiss army knife of tools wrapped up in a well-structured, but sometimes complicated, package. It is a commonly used tool by hackers and security professionals alike and is covered in this chapter's practical application section. It is mostly command-line based, though there is a GUI front end available. Learn the ins and outs of this application. Many vulnerabilities can be exploited using Metasploit, including capabilities to more easily route your way through a complicated network. Programs with this level of capability come with a steep learning curve requiring a lot of practice. Once you get the basics, the rest will become fairly intuitive.

- System Administration – System administrators make some of the best penetration testers. The reason is because years of experience provide an in-depth understanding of how an operating system functions, where system files are located, how to modify passwords, create users, and disable security functions. Of course, there is so much more to system administration, but these specific areas are of great interest when testing the security of a network. Once you land on a system, you need to go to work establishing your long-term foothold and that is only possible if you are able to navigate your way around the victim's files and folders. This is closely linked with the command-line skills along with the added understanding of where to look, what to modify, and how to avoid security traps. Take time to learn at least the basics of system administration on Windows and Linux.
- Network Device Experience – Network devices are always part of the equation in hacking. Computers are connected to networks that may have a variety of routers, firewalls, or switches in place. Understanding how they work and how they respond to connections allows for more streamlined attacks. Firewalls and routers have their own command-line structures that can be used to reroute traffic on a network or allow a hacker to gain direct access to a segment normally unavailable. The only way a penetration tester can successfully pull this off, other than rare luck, is if they have experience configuring these types of devices. This is also an area where working as a team can pay off.
- Network Configuration – Similar to system administration, managing a network infrastructure also provides experience in the way data is commonly routed through a network. Most infrastructures have a router, as least one firewall and a switch at the demarcation point. But what about the rest of the network? Can you draw a diagram as you route your way through an internal network you have never seen before? Those who have configured network devices and designed network segments can quickly determine the critical pieces of infrastructure and know which devices lead to weaker or more sensitive systems. This ability will also help keep you from going in circles when systems have multiple IP addresses assigned. Study common network diagrams and maps to familiarize yourself with these capabilities.
- Password Cracking – If you are going to attempt breaking into systems, you will always end up in a place where you need a password to gain higher level privileges. The aforementioned Metasploit can help dump passwords in plaintext in some situations, so learn to use that function. In most cases you will only be able to grab the encrypted password hash. Cracking the hash will make the password available for other systems as you route your way through the network. Here's a secret: large networks commonly have the same administrator password on every system. It can be difficult to manage many different systems when all the passwords are different, so administrators make them the same to uncomplicate their jobs a little. This can be advantageous for a hacker who gains an administrator password. Practice with the tools in this practical application section to familiarize yourself with breaking passwords.

- Physical Security – We often say that once someone gains physical access to a computer, the battle is already over. Physical access affords the opportunity to quickly boot into an operating system on a USB drive, reset the administrator password, and reboot into unfettered access. If someone can walk into a building, talk their way past security, and make it to the server room, the game is over! In the early days of hacking, the ability to bypass physical security was one of the easiest ways to gain access. Physical security has become a lot stronger today in large organizations, but small ones still tend to have a variety of deficiencies that can be exploited. In these situations, a good penetration tester can gain total control over a network in a very short amount of time. You can practice this skill every day by casually looking for physical security shortfalls in every restaurant, office, or store you walk into. Thinking like the bad guy in these scenarios tends to make weaknesses stand out.

- Encryption – Encryption can save a system from some of the physical security shortfalls just mentioned. Third party software can encrypt all data on a computer's physical drive when it is not in use. This is known as encryption at rest, and it protects a system from being modified if a password is not entered to decrypt the drive when initially booted. Booting onto a USB drive in these situations will be pointless because you will not be able to access the main operating system. Encryption can also be used to protect sensitive data, and when good encryption is used in the best way, it is close to impossible to break. Learn to recognize when encryption is being used and work towards attacking weaker targets on the network.

- Tenacity – Do not give up so easily. A good network will have some defenses in place that will need to be overcome or defeated. Every computer and every network are not hackable, but do not give up if your first exploit fails. Look for other potential ways to gain access and keep trying until you are certain every door is securely locked. It is easy to try the one vulnerability you are familiar with and then move on to a new target if that fails. This is a bad practice. Be willing to put in some extra time until you find an opening or know for sure the system is locked down tight. This does not mean spending years looking for a potential vulnerability. Work hard and be willing to walk away when it is clear no vulnerabilities exist.
- Morality – Penetration testers will come across sensitive data during their operations. A high level of morals and ethics is necessary to ensure private data is not shared with anyone else. Criminal hackers do not tend to have high morals. Their goal is to steal and disrupt, so this is not a common area of development in their lives. Security professionals, however, need to operate with an understanding they are being trusted with incredibly sensitive information and should protect it in the same way they would protect their own private information. Never fall for the trap of sharing juicy information with your friends.
- Wireless Networks – Wireless networks, if poorly configured, can be an easy way into a network. The early days of wireless security were easily defeated as the wired equivalent privacy (WEP) protocol could be broken in a matter of minutes allowing access to any system connected to that network.

Wireless protected access (WPA) and the later WPA2 were created to make things more secure but it also had its own set of weaknesses allowing the password to be easily snatched out of the air and potentially cracked offline. Wi-Fi provides us with incredible capabilities and will not be going anywhere. In fact, it will likely expand into more capabilities in the future. Some of the newer security being implemented on Wi-Fi is more effective, but it will take time for everyone to upgrade to the devices and software capable of using newer technologies. Be aware of the vulnerabilities and include Wi-Fi in your penetration testing. Some networks have been hacked from the lobbies of large buildings because of open Wi-Fi access points.

Many of these listed skills are gained during traditional work in the broader field of information technology or computer science. Most people in this field start out in entry-level positions working with users at the help desk to resolve minor issues and eventually work their way into other positions of system administration. If you have worked in the computer science field for more than ten years, you have likely built up skills in a variety of areas that will be beneficial for you in cyber security. Someone can certainly jump straight into the security arena, but they will need to put in a lot of extra time learning what they would normally have learned in a natural career progression. There is a lot of value in learning the foundations of computer science, not just from books and classes, but from practical hands-on knowledge. Building on a solid foundation makes learning how to conduct penetration tests much easier.

Penetration tests can be performed by external organizations or employees who are part of the security team. Regardless of who is involved, a type of "get out of jail free" card is used in case someone is physically caught in the act. This is usually in the form of a formal letter signed by a C-level member of the organization specifically authorizing action. The letter should contain the dates for the operation, any systems that are off limits, explicit authority to hack into the network, and if attempts to gain physical access are authorized. You should never conduct a penetration test without this level of permission. Hacking without permission is illegal in most countries and verbal permission alone will not keep you out of jail. There are numerous stories in this field of hackers with and without authorization being questioned by law enforcement or corporate security. Keep a copy of this authorization close by in case it is needed.

Work as a team! As you think about all the skills required to pull off a successful penetration test, you may have come to the realization it can take many years to be an expert in every area. This is true. But you do not need to be an expert all by yourself. A team of professionals with different levels of skills can operate as a type of digital special forces unit, each with their own unique qualifications. Each member can step in when their specialty is needed for a particular portion of the operation. For example, the Windows expert can work on gaining initial access and then hand the keyboard to the Linux expert to pivot into an Ubuntu server. One person does not have to do all the work. One person does not have to be an expert in every system or application. Differing skills among a team make you more effective.

Practical Application – Tools of the Trade

Many of the hacking tools available in Kali Linux or downloadable across the internet are utilized by malicious actors, penetration testers, and even professional hackers working for their government. The existence of a hacking tool does not automatically make a program evil. Many objects can be used for good or evil purposes depending on who is using the object. Physical weapons, for example, in the hands of a trained military force are used to defend their nation. Those same weapons, in the hands of an evil person, can be used for violent actions against innocent people. The weapons themselves are inanimate objects. It is the people using the weapons that determine their use. The same is true in the digital world. You will come across applications that can be used for both good and evil purposes. The applications below fall into this category, so be sure you maintain a high degree of morals and ethics as you put them to use in securing systems.

Metasploit was mentioned earlier as a necessary skill to be effective in this area of cyber security. Some people used to think that Metasploit was only for script kiddies and less knowledgeable security professionals because it includes so many of the common exploits where less research is required. This is a bad perspective though because, although it does make a lot of functions easier, a significant amount of knowledge is still required to use it effectively. You cannot use an exploit against an invulnerable system. You can try, but you will fail. Some people have tried using Metasploit to throw exploits at systems in this way hoping something will eventually stick. It is very obvious to an analyst when this occurs and almost always results in an immediate block. But, in the hands of an expert, this tool can be used for the purpose it was created, to target systems already known to be vulnerable and further infiltrate victim networks.

Metasploit Exploits

Metasploit is used after scans have concluded that a system is vulnerable. A penetration tester can load the associated exploit from Metasploit's database, configure the necessary settings, and if the system is truly vulnerable, gain access in just a few minutes or less. Expertise with this program requires a significant amount of practice as it comes with a steep learning curve. The capabilities of each option can be overwhelming at first, but very rewarding once you understand how to employ them for the right purpose. Metasploit contains thousands of potential exploits, each one associated with a specific known vulnerability. Knowing which one to use with specific vulnerabilities is what sets experienced users apart from new ones. Metasploit also includes Meterpreter, which provides an interactive shell a hacker can use to navigate a system, execute code, and continue the process of gaining additional levels of access. Metasploit is most powerful as a command-line tool, though the Armitage GUI front end can be beneficial for new users who are learning how to use the application. Your goal should be to become familiar with the command-line version because you will need it as you work your way through different victim systems. Listed below are some of the basic commands for using Metasploit. A fuller listing of Meterpreter commands can be found in Appendix 2.

msfconsole	starts the Metasploit command line console
show	lists modules of a particular type
search	searches for modules and descriptions
use	selects the exploit to use
set	sets various options for the exploit
exploit	runs the exploit against the target

A simple exploit from Metasploit may look something like this:

```
use exploit/windows/dcerpc/ms06_040_netapi
set RHOST 192.168.22.5
set PAYLOAD windows/meterpreter/bind_tcp
exploit
```

```
File  Actions  Edit  View  Help

msf6 > use exploit/windows/smb/ms08_067_netapi
[*] No payload configured, defaulting to windows/meterpreter/reverse_tcp
msf6 exploit(windows/smb/ms08_067_netapi) > set RHOST 192.168.120.120
RHOST => 192.168.120.120
msf6 exploit(windows/smb/ms08_067_netapi) > set RPORT 445
RPORT => 445
msf6 exploit(windows/smb/ms08_067_netapi) > show options

Module options (exploit/windows/smb/ms08_067_netapi):

   Name     Current Setting   Required   Description
   ----     ---------------   --------   -----------
   RHOSTS   192.168.120.120   yes        The target host(s), see https://github.com/rapid7/metasploit-framework/wiki/Using-Metasploit
   RPORT    445               yes        The SMB service port (TCP)
   SMBPIPE  BROWSER           yes        The pipe name to use (BROWSER, SRVSVC)


Payload options (windows/meterpreter/reverse_tcp):

   Name      Current Setting   Required   Description
   ----      ---------------   --------   -----------
   EXITFUNC  thread            yes        Exit technique (Accepted: '', seh, thread, process, none)
   LHOST     192.168.1.186     yes        The listen address (an interface may be specified)
   LPORT     4444              yes        The listen port


Exploit target:

   Id  Name
   --  ----
   0   Automatic Targeting


msf6 exploit(windows/smb/ms08_067_netapi) >
```

Metasploit Attack

Remember one part of hacking methodology is acquiring usernames and passwords. Sometimes the best you can do is grab a hashed password file that requires breaking offline. This is where John the Ripper comes in handy. John the Ripper is a password cracking program which can be used to break weak passwords. Passwords are not stored as plaintext files on computers. Well, they should not be stored in this way. You will encounter passwords stored as a hash, which is an encrypted version of the password, and the password hacking process is an attempt to determine the plaintext that was turned into the hash. For example, a password of "H@ckisc00l" could be displayed in hash format as:

A437060EA66C78C46EEAECB7CD18BFBF29F8EA9EFF0B
552C8A056FEBC70619C

Password cracking tools attempt to break the password by hashing dictionary files full of common words and comparing each generated hash with the hashed password. If a match is found, the program will display the associated plaintext password. These tools are incredibly effective at finding weak passwords, especially those that are simple words. They have become more sophisticated over the years and will also replace i's with exclamation points, e's with 3's, s's with dollar signs, and others, following what has become the custom in password creation. So, using "Dr@g0n" as a password may fool a basic dictionary attack, but it will be easily cracked with a program that replaces letters with commonly used numbers and special characters.

John the Ripper

The next level after a dictionary attack is known as a brute force attack where every possible variation of letter, number, and special character is used in the hopes one of them will be the correct password. This is a long process and rarely yields great results unless the password is short, and the computational power of the system used to run the brute force is significant. The general rule of thumb is that a strong password is highly unlikely to be broken using brute force techniques. An advanced method that can speed up this process is using Rainbow Tables. These tables are pre-created lists of hashes generated using the different encryption methods utilized by common operating systems. They are similar to a dictionary file in that the list is run against the password hash to see if there is a match. The major difference is that a Rainbow Table's listing is generated in a similar fashion as brute forcing by hashing every letter, number, and special character combination ahead of time. This eliminates the need for massive amounts of computational power during the password-hacking process. The challenge with Rainbow Tables is that they can be incredibly large and need to be generated for different password lengths as well as different algorithms. It is likely the only people with full Rainbow Table listings are government agencies with access to supercomputers. Some are available for download online but are typically incomplete.

Take time to practice with these tools as they are two of the most common used in the industry. There are many other tools, of course, and each cannot be covered in one book or one chapter. As you come across vulnerabilities you have not previously encountered, look for tools created to specifically deal with that vulnerability and take some time to learn something new. Practice really does make perfect!

Chapter 5: Review Questions

1. Penetration testing is the _____ of locating and exploiting vulnerabilities.
   a. Simple
   b. Difficult
   c. Rigorous
   d. Normal
2. How often should a penetration test be run?
   a. Annually
   b. Monthly
   c. Weekly
   d. Whenever Requested
3. _____ make hacking look easy.
   a. Hackers
   b. Script Kiddies
   c. Con Artists
   d. Movies
4. What is the first step of a hacker methodology?
   a. Attack
   b. Research
   c. Crack Passwords
   d. Scan
5. In what stage of hacker methodology does exploitation take place?
   a. Attack
   b. Research
   c. Crack Passwords
   d. Penetrate
6. Which password can be leveraged to connect to other systems on a network?
   a. Administrator
   b. Firewall
   c. Router
   d. Email
7. Which of these is typically missing on internal networks?
   a. Users
   b. Security Devices
   c. Antivirus
   d. Servers
8. What is a common element of hacking?
   a. Falling Asleep
   b. Mountain Dew
   c. Going to Prison
   d. Crashing Services
9. What should you do if your methods fail?
   a. Look for a new target or exploit
   b. Give up
   c. Scan more aggressively
   d. Try physically breaking in
10. What skill keeps a penetration tester from becoming frustrated?
    a. Practice
    b. System Administration
    c. Patience
    d. Tenacity
11. Having skills in multiple _____ provides more flexibility in hacking.
    a. Operating Systems
    b. Tools
    c. Areas
    d. Programming Languages
12. In the hacking world, you will almost always end up where?
    a. Jail
    b. GUI
    c. Command Line
    d. Web Server
13. Crafting a quality _____ is a key skill to save time in penetration testing.
    a. Internet Search
    b. Script
    c. Exploit
    d. Keyboard
14. Who makes some of the best penetration testers?
    a. Firewall Technicians
    b. Email Administrators
    c. Linux Experts
    d. System Administrators

15. Many penetration testing skills are gained during _____ work in the broader field of computer science.
    a. Traditional
    b. Routine
    c. Monotonous
    d. Low Level
16. When someone gains _____ the battle is already over.
    a. Physical Access
    b. Server Access
    c. Internal Access
    d. External Access
17. This formal authorization keeps you out of trouble if you get caught during an authorized penetration test.
    a. Pardon Card
    b. Company ID
    c. Get out of jail free card
    d. Driver's License
18. Working as a _____ is the best way to conduct a penetration test.
    a. Sole Hacker
    b. Team
    c. Loner
    d. Operation
19. Which of these tools is commonly used to crack passwords?
    a. Metasploit
    b. Snort
    c. Wireshark
    d. John the Ripper
20. Which of these tools is known as a Swiss army knife of hacking?
    a. Metasploit
    b. Snort
    c. Wireshark
    d. John the Ripper

Incident Response Evidence Collection

CHAPTER 6

Cyber security always leads to one inevitable question: what do we do if we get hacked? This is an important question to think about before an incident occurs, so you are prepared to take the necessary actions limiting damage and disruption to the organization and securing the rest of the network from a similar attack. Putting all the correct defenses in the proper places helps to limit the possibility of an attack but operating on the internet carries an inherent risk. It has often been said that the only secure network is one disconnected from the internet. We can never say a network is 100% protected, even after all the assessments, patches, updates, and aggressive measures to keep hackers out of systems. There will always be some level of risk, even if it is a very small level. If you can get your

network to a 99% protected status, and keep it there, you are unlikely to deal with much more than scanners looking for potential targets. But, in the instance someone makes it past the defenses, it is best to already have a plan in place.

Incident response has been split into two chapters to divide both sides of the coin in the way this operation takes place. The first part is evidence collection, and the second part is evidence analysis. This first half will focus on collecting evidence after an attack has taken place and been discovered. As with any other good investigation, the amount of collected evidence will determine if criminal activity can be fully reconstructed and if the crime can be successfully prosecuted. This is arguably the most important phase of incident response. Every proverbial rock must be overturned if you want to determine every action. Apart from an investigation, the victim system can simply be wiped, reloaded with a fresh operating system and necessary software, and put back into use. That is good for short-term operational capabilities but horrible for long-term success. An ignored vulnerability will inevitably be hacked again at some point in the future. The only way to eliminate these issues is to determine what happened.

Investigating an incident on the network is incredibly important because we need to discover how someone gained access to make sure they do not gain access again. If you discover someone has a copy of a key to your front door, you know the action needed is to change the locks so that the key no longer works. If someone breaks the glass to get into your home, you know the action is to place alarm sensors near the glass to immediately sound the alarm and send the criminal running. You could also install bullet-proof glass so the criminal cannot break it, but that method may be too expensive and will also eliminate the capability of opening the window. We need to take a similar approach in the digital world. If someone successfully gains unauthorized access, practical defensive measures need to be put into place to make sure no one else can use that method again to gain access at any point in the future.

The other reason we investigate is to determine exactly what the attacker accomplished after gaining access, or as much as possible based on the available evidence. This is important because any action taken by a hacker needs to be reversed, so long-term issues do not plague the network. A simple blocking of an IP address without any investigation will not fix the problem. Hacking tools left on systems can create continuous problems if they are not discovered and removed. This is especially true for backdoor applications establishing outbound connections to an attacker's system. Blocking actions on incoming ports will not keep these connections from taking place. A complete investigative process is the only way to discover what took place, fully secure the network from future attacks, and clean all residue from the victim systems. Anything less is a poor response inviting more malicious activity to take place.

The goal of some investigations is to have some form of attribution that holds the attacker accountable. If China hacks into U.S. government computers, the U.S. government should have a way to hold China accountable. But the first step in that process is to fully identify the true source of the attack. Proper identification is needed in order to successfully prosecute a case in court or levy complaints to governments when high-level attacks take place. If a hacker located in Las Vegas breaks into your server and steals secret data, one element of your investigation should focus on positive identification. You cannot prosecute a cybercrime in court without proof of who conducted the attack. These types of prosecutions are rare because it can be difficult to definitively point the finger at a bad actor. The possibility of plausible deniability is always available. An individual could claim no knowledge of the attack and assert they were victims as well when a hacker breached their system and used it to attack someone else. The only way to refute this is for law enforcement to seize the attacker's computer and conduct forensics on it to determine what took place.

© AVN Photo Lab/Shutterstock.com

You may be thinking at this point that conducting a forensic examination of an attack for the purpose of attribution is too difficult. You are not wrong. It is a difficult and uphill battle most of the time, which is why we do not see regular announcements in the news of hackers being prosecuted. The digital landscape of the internet provides a degree of protection for those who want to conduct nefarious attacks. And in the case of nation-states, blame can always be shifted to a rogue citizen operating of their own volition. Major hacking incidents that cause widespread problems across the internet, usually in the form of a worm or other malware, tend to catch the eyes of the FBI within the U.S. and similar agencies in other countries because of the widespread nature of the attack. But even that level of interest rarely results in criminal prosecution.

What is the investigator to do? Why put effort into an investigation that will ultimately only protect the victim network? Well, that alone should be enough of a reason. The possibility for attribution should be considered a peripheral goal while the primary goal should be to eliminate the exploited vulnerability and restore the victim system to operational status as soon as possible. If in the course of the investigation, it becomes clear where the attack originated and who the attacker was, that is icing on the cake. In those rare instances, law enforcement will need to take over the investigation to ensure proper techniques are used to successfully prosecute the case in court. The role of the internal incident response team will mostly end at that point. These are all important elements to consider before an attack takes place, so the investigation can immediately commence without the need for discussing the necessary actions.

Successful attacks are typically noticed by an analyst reviewing logs or monitoring live activity coming across the wire. When analysts think they spot this type of activity, they immediately inform the incident response team which takes a deeper look to confirm the attack took place. This is when the investigative process starts. In smaller organizations, the analyst and incident response team may be comprised of the same people. In larger organizations, they tend to be split up with the more advanced analysts taking on the role of incident response. Regardless of the structure, once the attack is identified, the wheels of the investigation should immediately start spinning. You cannot afford to wait a few days until other projects are finished. The longer the hacker has access to the network, the more damage they can cause. Investigators need to dive in immediately and start taking action to plug the breach.

The first real step is to validate if an attack resulting in unauthorized access actually occurred. This is an important first step that verifies an analyst's work before resources are spent on a full-fledged investigative process. Some alerts may appear at first to be a successful penetration with deeper analysis determining it is benign. This is known as a false positive. It is always better to have a second set of eyes when a suspected incident occurred. Experienced analysts should review the alerts from the intrusion detection systems and any additional data, then determine if an incident occurred.

Consider this scenario: a hacker has successfully penetrated your defenses, gained access to a user system containing common everyday work documents, but nothing sensitive in nature. The hacker snuck past because of a misconfigured port on the firewall which is easily fixed and was not able to expand his foothold any further than this single system. The security mechanisms in place on the network kept the attack boxed in and limited the hacker from going any further. In essence, he did not do any real damage, and the hole that allowed him in can be fixed in under a minute. It is certainly a concern and should not be dismissed, but the level of effort put into fixing the problem could be wrapped up in short order. He got lucky this one time and was able to practice his skills in the real world. What action should you take at this point?

Here is another scenario: a hacker uses a zero-day exploit to access the contents of your corporate database which contains sensitive customer and employee data as well as product information. She changes the prices on a handful of items, reducing the cost by 90%, and makes subsequent purchases on the website, costing your organization several thousand dollars in lost revenue. You do not know how she gained access. You do not know if she was able to expand into any other systems. And you do not know if she acquired a copy of the personal information in the database. This is a significantly different situation because the hacker has shown a high level of sophistication in bypassing security mechanisms, utilizing a previously unknown exploit, changing systems for personal gain, and acquiring physical products at a highly reduced price. Her digital actions had actual real-world physical effects. What action should you take at this point?

What is the difference between these two scenarios? The glaring difference is the amount of immediate and potential damage caused. One was mostly benign while the other struck with some level of force. One was a known vulnerability with a misconfiguration while the other showed a high degree of sophistication using an exploit previously unseen in the wild. Should you treat them differently? Should you investigate them differently? Even if your goal is to simply secure the network

and get operations back to normal, you will still need to determine the necessary actions to secure what was manipulated. You will not know those actions without an investigation. You also will not fully know what occurred unless you take the time to methodically look at every action the hacker took, from the point of entry until they were removed. In fact, you will not even know if they still have a presence without the investigation. The bottom line is every incident, regardless of how benign it appears on the surface, needs to be fully investigated using a good digital forensics process.

If you have watched any television programs about law enforcement, you have heard the term forensics in some capacity. You may not fully understand what it means, but you probably know it involves digging deep into an activity to discover, analyze, and document as much detail as possible regarding a particular event. Forensics is primarily used in the investigation of a crime. Digital forensics is very similar to the process of collecting and analyzing evidence from physical crime scenes, except you do not need to worry about accidentally stepping in a gooey substance or protecting your nose from foul odors. The concepts of preserving evidence in the exact state it was found, not altering it in any way, and examining it for evidence are very much the same. In fact, many law enforcement agencies include digital forensics as part of their larger forensic operations.

You have probably seen a few criminal television programs which include some level of forensic evidence collection and analysis. Physical forensic science has grown over the years as investigators have developed new techniques and lab analysts have discovered better methodologies for processing evidence. The broad idea is to collect evidence without modifying or corrupting it so it can be used to determine exactly what occurred. If the evidence is damaged or modified in any way, it can lead to different results and alternate assumptions. Working to put a potential criminal behind bars is a serious job. We cannot afford to get it wrong. We do not want the wrong person to be punished for a crime they did not commit. Evidence definitively showing what occurred and who the perpetrator was is best for courtroom and television dramas. Many of the techniques in physical forensics have been transferred and translated into the digital world to create the same high degree of rigor and accuracy.

The physical evidence in the digital world consists primarily of storage devices. If you can gain access to the actual system used to commit the crime, physical forensic measures can be utilized to recover fingerprints, etc. This is not possible in most cases, so it will not be covered here. Your primary evidence is the data stored on victim systems and network devices showing the activity of the hacker. Collect enough of this data and you can piece together the method of the attack, timelines, actions taken, data stolen, and which systems were affected. It can be a painstakingly slow process requiring intentional focus to uncover every bit of affected data and every move the attacker made. Television shows solve crimes in under an hour. Real digital forensic investigative processes can take several days for simple cases and weeks or longer for complex hacking situations. Be prepared to roll up your sleeves, drink some coffee, and put in long hours.

Evidence Collection

What is the first step you would take when discovering a hacker successfully broke into your network? You could disconnect the victim system from the network, severing any active connection the hacker may have in place. You could even completely power down to kill connections and running processes. These are knee-jerk reactions that can destroy evidence, so it is better to snapshot what is happening on the system before taking these types of actions. Every incident response team should have a form of emergency plan they can use to quickly acquire several pieces of information from a potential victim system. This is critical evidence that is immediately lost when the system is turned off or disconnected from the network. It is also an evidence preservation step so the captured data can be thoroughly analyzed during the larger investigation. At a minimum, these items should be immediately captured:

- All active network connections – This will show any active connection from the attacker with IP addresses, ports, and protocols currently in use. This information can be later correlated with device logs to follow the trail of activity. This is a key piece of the puzzle that cannot afford to be lost. A large gap in time between these connections and device logs will point to the possibility of other systems being hacked at an earlier time. Specifically, look for external connections as well as connections to other internal systems.
- All running processes – This will show everything running on the system which could disclose a particular application the hacker is actively using to maintain their connection or further manipulate the system. This can also show applications the hacker copied onto the victim system and is actively using. It is not uncommon for great hackers to modify malicious programs just enough to avoid detection by antivirus systems. Those can be uncovered during this step.
- All memory contents – Memory contents can be used to acquire some peripheral information during the analysis stage. Sometimes plaintext passwords used for outbound connections are still floating around in memory. It is not always the most valuable data but can be used to fill in some gaps if needed.
- Antivirus status and signature date – This will show if the antivirus application is functioning properly and the last time it was updated. Grab this to compare with the latest signatures and to see if the running version should have caught the attack in progress.
- Patch levels for every installed application – Outdated patches can create vulnerable systems. Knowing the patch levels of each application could narrow down the avenue of attack. Similar to antivirus signatures, patch levels will tell us what may have been vulnerable on the system.
- Copies of all system logs – Logs provide so much detail and can fill in a lot of gaps. We are often left guessing about what actions the hacker took without the level of detail provided by logs. Logs are often overwritten after a period of time, so make sure these are copied soon.

You need to move through this quickly. Creating a small program to grab all of this data is the fastest method, streamlines the process, and ensures nothing is forgotten. A program of this nature could collect this data in a few minutes or less. Manually working through this process to issue each command, find each file, and copy it to another location will take significantly more time. This content will not take up a lot of space. The logs and memory dumps will be the largest portion and could fluctuate in size depending on the amount of memory installed in the victim system. A high-speed USB drive with a decent amount of storage, 16GB or higher, should be more than enough for storing this content and moving it to a forensic system. Storage devices are much cheaper today than in the early days of digital forensics, so it is fairly inexpensive to have a few of these USB drives ready for use if an incident occurs.

It is important to always start with the identified victim system. Consider this the initial point of attack until your investigation leads you in another direction. After noting active network connections, it is a good idea to check network devices for any other open connections to the same external IP address. This will identify additional victim systems where you can then take the same evidence-collection actions. Also, take note of active connections between the victim system and other systems on the network. This can provide another layer of detail in the hacker's access footprint. It is difficult to know how far the attacker has penetrated the network until your initial look at the collected data. The quicker you move through this process, the quicker you can implement blocks shutting off all access. Grab the needed data, make a quick search for other potential victim systems, then move on to securing the network.

At this point, you can block all activity from the offending IP to cut off the hacker's access. Occasionally, in law enforcement investigations, it can be a good idea to not put a block in place so the hacker's activity can be monitored further. This could lead to new evidence and details about the methodology being used, enabling easier prosecution. Other organizations can do this as well if they are looking to learn more from ongoing attacker activity. This can be a dangerous practice without making configuration changes that box-in the attacker, so they only have continued access to the victim system. Leaving the network-wide open for this type of operation is asking for trouble. A basic laptop with multiple network ports could be placed in between the victim and the attacker to fully monitor all activity. Network routing could then be configured to route all hacker IP activity to the laptop, acting as an intermediary passing traffic through to the victim. This is not a common methodology and can be complicated to configure perfectly, but it can yield interesting information.

You can disconnect the victim system from the network after the block is in place and the critical data is collected, then the larger forensic process of imaging the system drive begins. Never conduct a forensic examination of the original victim system drive. Always make a copy and store the original in a safe place. An accident during forensics can damage data and you do not want to damage the original copy. This is especially true if you plan to present evidence in a court case, but even apart from that scenario, it is a good practice to have a known, good copy you can return to if something goes awry. To get an exact copy, you will want to duplicate the drive bit by bit. This will give you an exact replica. One of the best tools for this is the dd command which is included in all versions of Linux. Work through the examples in the practical application at the end of this chapter for practice with this command.

In addition to the imaged drive, you need to capture data from every network device the hacker's activity passed through during their operation. This is important to grab as soon as possible because many network devices are set to automatically overwrite the logs after they are full, or after a specified period of time. Logs can be overwritten in less than a day, so it is a good idea to obtain a copy before imaging the victim system or have another member of the team working on it concurrently. Every router, firewall, and switch can contain time-stamped connections and attempted connections from the attacking IP address. Intrusion detection and prevention systems will have additional data on the attacker's activity. All this data will need to be correlated to paint a larger picture of everything that occurred. You want to recreate as much of the timeline as possible during your investigation. If you think something could be valuable, collect it for further analysis.

Check all company accounts accessible by the user whose system was hacked. If the attacker was able to access usernames and passwords, they may have used those credentials to also access external accounts. If the affected user was responsible for purchasing equipment, the attacker could leverage acquired information into making illegal purchases using company credit cards or customer accounts. Conducting investigations requires the investigator to think like, to some degree, the attacker. What would they do if they gained access to a credit card number? What would they do if they had access to an account database? How could they leverage this for more gain? And possible secondary connections should be considered as potential avenues of attack and reviewed to ensure no other malicious activity took place. We live in an interconnected world that uses many online resources every day. Each computer on a network is likely connecting to network shares, cloud drives, and other everyday resources. Think about where the hacker may have gone and follow that trail until you are sure you have found every bit of unauthorized activity.

An additional option to consider is the possibility of hiring 3rd party experts to assist in both portions of incident response. This can be valuable if the team is struggling to solve every aspect of the case. In these situations, it is important to have all 3rd parties sign non-disclosure agreements for anything they view while working on the investigation. Non-disclosure agreements are common practice today anytime someone may have access to private information. They provide a high degree of legal protection that can be enforced by courts. There is typically some form of punitive clause—usually in a monetary amount—levying a penalty on individuals who break the agreement and disclose information. These penalties are stiff enough to create a high certainty no one will release information. If a 3rd party is contracted to work on the investigation, the non-disclosure agreements should be signed before they are given any level of access or information.

Legal counsel is also advisable to protect the image and reputation of an organization. Public disclosure of a successful attack can create a lot of headaches and require a lot of communication even before the investigation is underway. Some laws require releasing information regarding the theft of individual personal data according to a particular timeline. This leaves no option except full disclosure to those affected and is a fair process to make individuals aware of the possibility of identity theft. Requirements for releasing information regarding the theft or manipulation of private company data are less common and companies may want to keep that information in-house to protect and maintain customer confidence. The laws are different nation to nation and even within different states within the U.S. Legal counsel can provide needed advice and expertise in this arena to help protect interests without breaking any applicable laws or acting in an immoral way.

There are many rules regarding how evidence should be handled if criminal prosecution is desired. Those rules cannot be covered in-depth here and legal counsel should be consulted if prosecution is the desired outcome. The process of collecting the data will need to be fully documented at every step of the way to maintain a proper chain of custody. Chain of custody ensures evidence is properly collected, transported, and stored throughout the entire process to eliminate any possibility of tampering. If criminals can gain access to the evidence, it can easily be destroyed or modified causing the legal case to crumble. Law enforcement officers are well trained in these processes and should be involved if a legal case is pursued. This is rarely the case with incidents involving private organizations but more common when government organizations fall prey to a cyber-attack, though it never hurts to operate with this level of rigor in all investigative situations.

Problems that can occur in evidence collection:

- Too much time spent searching for evidence and devices. Equipment should be labeled for easy identification.
- Logs have been overwritten. A log set to overwrite every hour is not very effective. Many incidents are discovered after the fact and a small logging window can eliminate a large chunk of evidence. Set the logging timeline much higher or implement a logging server where all network logs can be stored for long periods of time.
- System administrators try to hide evidence. Employees may think their job is on the line if they forgot to put a patch in place or inadvertently left an opening in a firewall. They may quickly try to cover up their mistake to stay out of trouble.
- Employees just want to get back to work. Losing a computer for any reason results in reduced production, loss of profits, and frustrated employees who cannot do their jobs without a dedicated system to work on.
- Investigations take time and can easily lead to temporary increases in employee salaries due to overtime.

Many of these potential problems can be dealt with before an incident ever occurs. Checklists and procedures should be developed long before incident response is needed. It is relatively easy to think through hacking scenarios and develop standard responses for different scenarios. An incident responder should be able to work through the steps of a checklist instead of flying by the seat of their pants, hoping they do not forget any vital steps. These checklists can also be updated after an incident occurs to include any new ideas or make the process easier the next

time it is needed. Look for potential pitfalls in this process and find ways to constantly improve each step. A strong security posture will lessen the need for an incident response plan, but it can never be fully eliminated. There is always the possibility, even if very small, an attack can occur. Stay vigilant in maintaining a solid process should the need arise.

There are differences of opinion on how each of the steps in evidence collection should be processed. No one does it quite the same way. Some prefer to block access and disconnect victim systems before collecting any evidence. Others like to box in their opponent to learn as much as possible about their technique. Some even deploy honeypot systems, designed to attract hacker activity for the purpose of studying methodology or wasting the hacker's time so they do not go after real targets. There is much variation in this arena, some based on expertise, some based on personal preferences, and some based on organizational requirements. Most of them are great ideas you can incorporate yourself. There are also many lists available online of "best practices" providing ideas for how an investigative process should be structured. Except for legal requirements, these ideas are born from the experience of investigating many incidents. Experience is a great teacher in this field and can help to fine-tune how we conduct many different operations.

The forensic collection of digital evidence continues to improve as new software applications are developed, new technologies give easier access to data, and security devices make it easier to track network activity. What you are learning now will inevitably change as technology continues to advance. Technology advances very quickly and often outpace even the publishing of new books. A great incident investigator will blend the totality of what they learn in the field, into their own customized methodology. Apply what you are learning, tweak it over time to create a methodology of your own, and pay attention to new capabilities you can add to your toolbox to become an even better incident response investigator.

Practical Application - Tools of the Trade

dd – This is one of the most versatile copy commands available on Linux systems. It can be used for a variety of operations such as creating images for bootable USB drives (or CD/DVD if you are old school), copying specific sectors of drives, converting data formats, and creating exact duplicates of drives. It is this last option we are mostly interested in when conducting digital forensics, as it gives us the capability of examining a drive without damaging or modifying the original contents.

Example: dd if=<source file name> of=<target file name> [Options]

Windows and Linux both have default locations where logs are stored. This makes it easy for a forensics examiner to copy those logs off of a victim without hunting all over the hard drive. The majority of logs in Linux are stored by default in the /var/log tree. The majority of Windows logs are viewable using the built-in event viewer application. Some applications may store logs in different locations, so be prepared to dig deeper if unique software is in use on the victim system.

Autopsy is a digital forensics tool available as an open-source download and is also bundled with Kali Linux which can be used to analyze mobile devices and digital media. It includes the ability to analyze timelines, search for indexed keywords, extract content from web browsers, find and recover deleted files, and hash and filter along the way to eliminate duplication of effort. Autopsy is free, which is always a bonus, and has a low learning curve for anyone already versed with basic computer and networking terminology.

Write blocker – write blockers are hardware devices that allow us to connect and copy in one direction eliminating the possibility of accidentally writing to a victim drive. They should always be used when conducting imaging operations. We never want to modify anything on the original drive and keep the evidence is completely preserved. A write blocker makes this possible.

Many other forensics tools and applications exist, too many to mention here. Look for applications to assist you in conducting specific forensic actions and building out your own forensic kit. Kali Linux has many forensic tools as well as the SANS SIFT distribution. Ultimately, the specific tool used is not as important as the skills of the investigator. Know what you are looking for, where to acquire it, and how to analyze it for anything suspicious. Over time, you will develop a keener sense of recognizing common hacker activity and will be able to more quickly locate needed evidence.

Chapter 6: Review Questions

1. Cyber security always leads to what question?
   a. Is this a virus?
   b. What happened to my email?
   c. What do we do if we get hacked?
   d. Why do we need a firewall?
2. We can never say a network is _____ protected.
   a. 100%
   b. Completely
   c. Totally
   d. All of the above
3. Incident response determines _____ someone gained access.
   a. How
   b. Why
   c. Protections since
   d. None of the above
4. Any action taken by a hacker needs to be _____.
   a. Managed
   b. Encrypted
   c. Ignored
   d. Reversed
5. Some investigations have the goal of _____.
   a. Deniability
   b. Attribution
   c. Covering up
   d. Managing expectations
6. It is difficult to _____ a hacking incident.
   a. Investigate
   b. Analyze
   c. Report
   d. Legally prosecute
7. Successful attacks are typically first noticed by _____.
   a. Penetration testers
   b. Analysts
   c. Incident responders
   d. Managers
8. Forensics is the process of _____ and _____ evidence.
   a. Collecting, Destroying
   b. Analyzing, Collecting
   c. Collecting, Analyzing
   d. Analyzing, Managing
9. Incident response teams should have _____ for how to handle an incident.
   a. Plans
   b. Procedures
   c. Diagrams
   d. Protocols
10. The first action after identifying an incident is to _____.
    a. Hide evidence
    b. Block attacker
    c. Disconnect victim from network
    d. Grab data from victim
11. Active network connections will show _____.
    a. IP address of connections
    b. Port of connections
    c. Source of connections
    d. All of the above
12. _____ can provide greater detail into hacker activity.
    a. Logs
    b. Antivirus
    c. Processes
    d. Memory
13. Initial victim evidence collection needs to move _____.
    a. Methodically
    b. Quickly
    c. Slowly
    d. None of the above
14. Block the attacker and disconnect the victim from the network _____ the initial data collection.
    a. Without
    b. During
    c. Before
    d. After

15. _____ conduct a forensic examination on the original victim system drive.
    a. Carefully
    b. Always
    c. Never
    d. None of the above

16. Acquire _____ from all network devices.
    a. Logs
    b. Antivirus
    c. Processes
    d. Memory

17. Some problems in the incident investigation include:
    a. Overwritten logs
    b. Administrators hiding evidence
    c. Frustrated employees
    d. All of the above

18. Incident investigations take _____ to do the job correctly.
    a. Money
    b. Time
    c. Internet connections
    d. Legal action

19. _____ is advisable to protect other elements of the organization.
    a. Legal counsel
    b. A professional hacker
    c. Legal action
    d. Manipulation

20. _____ is a difficult outcome in hacking investigations.
    a. Establishing defenses
    b. Identifying victims
    c. Criminal prosecution
    d. Full understanding

Incident Response Evidence Analysis

CHAPTER 7

Continuing the process of incident response takes us from collection to analysis. The collection piece is relatively easy as it mostly requires copying content from each affected or involved device or system. These actions require quick engagement as many logs are set to overwrite themselves after they reach a pre-determined size and the contents on the victim system have a certain level of volatility. After everything has been collected, the systematic process of analyzing each piece begins. Collecting data is what allows you to do the rest of your work. You should sort this data well, in order to stay organized and make immediate backups to be stored on an external drive and collocated with the original imaged hard drive from the victim system. The order you work through your analysis can vary based on personal preference, but a methodical process of stepping through the timeline is typically the best way to conduct a completely thorough investigation.

Put yourself into the mindset of a detective. Think back to all the police dramas and crime shows you have watched where investigators step through a process of analyzing evidence to find the criminal. Those shows provide investigative solutions in under an hour, which is a great thing of fantasy in the real world. Your analysis process can take several weeks or longer as you dig through each piece of evidence. The greater the effort and success of the hacker, the greater level of time and energy will need to be spent on the analysis. Work like a detective looking for each new clue. Some may seem insignificant at first but could prove to be the key element that solves the case later in the process. Log everything. Dig several levels deep into each piece. Be as methodical as possible as you work through your process. If a hacker made it into your network, you know the connections came through the firewall, so that is a good place to start.

Firewall logs provide basic incoming and outgoing network connections. Search this log for the attacker's IP address to locate when the initial connections took place. If the firewall logs happen to be backed up regularly, you should also search through the archives to find any earlier attempts to connect, from that same IP address. You may remember scanning precedes attacks and your investigation could reveal scans that took place earlier in the day or even several days earlier as the hacker looked for a target. Pay close attention to timestamps of when connections were allowed into the network and the port numbers in use. An open port on a firewall allows data to pass through to the internal network. For example, if port 443 is open on the firewall, it will be configured to forward those requests to a web server. If this particular attack came through port 443, it would lead your investigation to the web server, as that would be the next system where the hacker established a connection.

© Mega Pixel/Shutterstock.com

Router logs will provide similar information and sometimes show more or fewer connections depending on the amount of traffic coming into the network, and specific configurations. Keep the configurations for these devices close by and reference as needed to follow the trail. Each entry in these logs will show the source and destination ports as well as the IP addresses. The source ports are rarely of any use in the investigative process because systems generally grab any available high-level port for transmission. The destination port is the key piece to zero in on. Earlier scans may show the attacker looking at many different ports before settling on the one ultimately exploited. This is a common practice when scanning for vulnerabilities and can give you some clue in their level of sophistication. Scans that hit thousands of ports may be a sign of a less sophisticated hacker looking anywhere for a potential target. Contrast this with a scan of only a few ports, showing a level of sophistication looking for very specific vulnerabilities.

[router logs]

Zero-day exploits are a great example of narrowly targeted scans. When a hacker discovers a vulnerability yet unannounced to the public, it creates an opportunity to hit vulnerable targets with a high probability of success. For example, if a new vulnerability is discovered in an audio program that listens for a connection on port 77, attackers can scan that single port on many systems to locate that singular vulnerability. The Easy WP SMTP vulnerability discovered in 2019 allowed hackers to scan WordPress sites across the globe for any site using this vulnerable plugin, and by some estimates, affected more than 500,000 websites. This is a significant amount of success from a single vulnerability. This was not the work of script kiddies who launched broad scans with the hopes something would stick. It showed a greater degree of sophistication by attackers who knew what and where to look for a vulnerable target. Most of the exploited systems were set to redirect their visitors to advertising or malicious websites in Russia (NY). This highlights the need to pay attention not only to the connections themselves but the way in which the connections were attempted or established.

Pay attention to timestamps as they can help you narrow down where to look for activity on the victim system. Every entry in a log should have a timestamp showing when the connection was made. You can use this information to help focus your initial investigation on the most likely areas the victim system was manipulated. It does not make sense to search for changes to data that occurred a day before the event. Focus your attention first on the timeframe you know the attacker was on the network and expand from that point. It is easy to go in many different directions at once during this process; the investigative process requires determined focus if you want to discover every bit of activity. If the hacker gained access at 11:25 P.M., start looking for activity at that time on the victim system. Start small and expand outward as the evidence leads you in new directions.

Most IDSs have the ability to conduct historical searches for other activity from the attacking IP address to see if any past scanning or penetration attempts were recorded. Your attacker may have been "casing the joint" for weeks before their attack, but stayed under the wire keeping the IDS from generating an alert. An IDS should be configured to collect as much data off the inline as possible, even if it does not generate an alert for every packet. This gives you the ability to grab historical data. For example, you may capture all the web traffic coming across port 80, but only generate alerts for specific types of malicious activity. The rest of the packets can be stored in the IDS logs or database for a period of time to provide this historical capability. Earlier activity is another potential sign the hacker may have a higher degree of sophistication.

It is typically easy to tell the difference between a sophisticated or experienced hacker and someone new to the game. A professional will have the patience to step through a methodical process until they achieve their goal while a less experienced person is more likely to rush the process and trip every alert imaginable along the way. When conducting an investigation, you should pay more attention to the incidents showing a greater degree of experience. This is especially true if an incident is discovered without any corresponding IDS alerts. Someone who makes it into your network undetected, and gains any level of access to a system, is a greater threat than the script kiddie running every automated tool with the hopes of getting lucky. The experienced ones are more likely to have expanded their foothold internally gaining a greater degree of access to data and control over network capabilities. This does not mean less sophisticated attacks should be ignored. But they are likely to be solved much sooner with less effort.

If a hacker has gained a significant foothold on the network, their back doors could have set up listeners on ports on multiple systems creating unusual inbound and outbound traffic. This can be a huge clue to the true source of the attack and to what the attacker is trying to accomplish. Analysts should pay very close attention to all traffic associated with the victim system as well as any odd traffic leaving the network. Establishing an outbound connection from an internal system is easily accomplished because firewalls are rarely configured to block outbound traffic. This type of connection is often referred to as a reverse shell because it can spawn a command-line shell connection on the attacker's system. This also establishes a stateful connection through the firewall keeping the outbound port open for as long as communication continues to flow. This makes long-term connections more viable because it is unlikely an organization is going to detect every command issued by the hacker and every bit of exfiltrated data.

Pay attention to outbound traffic coming from the victim system. It is highly probable the destination for those connections is the true source of the attack, or at least one of the systems the hacker controls.

Digital Scavenger Hunt

This can start to feel like a scavenger hunt as each reviewed log may send you off to another system to look for additional activity. Any system touched by the attacker should also be forensically examined using the process in the evidence collection section above. Initial recognition of an incident may not reveal all the systems the hacker gained access to after pushing into the internal network. The IDS sitting at the perimeter is limited in its ability to see what happens on the internal network. It is only one piece of the puzzle and only has partial information. Incident investigations need to go deep, looking under every proverbial rock, to discover every action an attacker took. No investigation will be perfect, and you will not always find every trace of activity, but you want to find enough evidence to piece together what happened, so it does not happen again. This is a fundamental goal of incident investigations.

There are other goals of course, and they are driven by organizational policies or the desires of leadership. Some organizations want to see hackers criminally prosecuted for their actions. This is not always possible because it can be difficult to definitively point the finger at a specific individual. Even the most thorough investigation can determine the vulnerability that led to the attack, the exploit used to gain access, and what the attacker accomplished after establishing control, but cannot determine with 100% accuracy the original source of the attack. The internet is vast. Billions of people around the world are connected to the digital landscape and anyone could perceivably conduct an attack against any system located anywhere on the planet. Hackers can also weave their way through multiple systems before launching their final attack on their ultimate target. This creates a challenge for investigators, and it is where the digital forensic process greatly differs from the physical world.

A hacker sitting in Lithuania can break into the system of an elderly woman in Florida, and subsequently, use that system as a launching point for many other attacks. To the victim, it will appear as if an IP address in Florida is attempting to steal data from their database. But in reality, the attack is occurring from a much further distance. The victim of the attack could not drive to Florida and conduct a forensic examination of the attacking IP address. This is the job of law enforcement. So, what can an organization do at this point? How much time and energy do they want to spend cleaning up a single hacking incident that had little impact on their day-to-day operations? The elderly woman is just as much a victim in this process and certainly cannot be prosecuted for a crime. Even if law enforcement conducted their own investigation and discovered connections coming from Lithuania, what then could they do?

Incident investigators need to consider the challenges of the process and accept the possibility that many incidents will result in zero action being taken against the perpetrator. We get lucky on occasion and can prove in a court that actions were taken by a specific individual and hold them accountable. But this is rare because of the obfuscation injected into the hacking process. This is to the advantage of the hacker. In the physical world, an identifiable piece of evidence left at a crime scene, such as a hair or fingerprint, can be used to help prosecute a criminal. This is a much more difficult feat to pull off in the digital world because an IP address is not always enough to tie an actor to a crime. If legal jurisdiction exists, systems are seized, and analysis reveals the attack definitely originated from those systems, a case for prosecution could be successful. Most investigations, however, end in assumptions that cannot be proven without a doubt. Sometimes we even know who the bad guy is, and they are still out of reach.

Hackers working to achieve national interests as employees of their nation—known as state-sponsored hacking—could conduct attacks against enemies of competing nations for the purpose of intelligence collection, theft of secret data, or a myriad of other reasons to gain some type of advantage. We may know that an attack came from North Korea. We may know that the hacker is part of a team that works for the government. Our investigation may reveal this level of detail, and yet we still cannot take any legal action. No court in any other country has jurisdiction over North Korea, so a lawsuit would be a fruitless response. Governments can simply deny awareness of the attack and claim they were not involved. Will a nation go to war over a cyber-attack? How great of an attack would need to occur to warrant launching missiles, shooting guns, and taking lives? North Korea is an easy example here, but the truth is many nations are involved in cyber warfare-type activities on a daily basis.

These are challenges that you must be aware of when investigating events. Some cannot be overcome, but that should not keep an investigation from occurring. An uninvestigated incident will certainly lead to another incident further down the road. It is imperative to discover how the attacker gained access and plug that hole before anyone else can do the same. Any forensic investigation that leads to securing the system and network from further attack is a successful one. Knowing the identity of the attacker is icing on the cake that could spawn law enforcement actions, but the ultimate goal is to make certain the attack cannot occur again.

Another thing to consider is, if law enforcement becomes involved, you will likely lose all control over the investigative process. They may take the victim system into evidence until their investigation is complete. This could take many months or longer leaving your organization one system short. Some activity will need to be reported to law enforcement because of the nature of the crime, but every successful hack does not need to have a full-fledged police investigation. Not to mention the reality that police departments do not have the resources to investigate every crime ever committed in the physical world, let alone the ones conducted in the digital world. Keep all of this in mind as you consider the direction an investigation needs to go and advise organizational leaders on specific actions that should be taken.

Some organizations take the opposite approach of skipping the investigation and heading right into cleaning and securing the system. The mindset here is that it is better to get a system operational again than to spend time and money determining all the details of what happened. For them, the only concern is to eliminate the vulnerability and move forward. This is not necessarily a bad perspective. It will not yield the same fruit of the process of a full investigation and may not show all the hacker did after gaining access, but if you can be reasonably sure the attack was benign, a quick cleanup could be the best route to take. Even in these instances, it would be good to image the victim system and grab copies of all logs for training purposes and offline analysis when time permits.

Drive Analysis

After a thorough review of device logs, you can turn your attention specifically to the data collected from the victim system. This is where you will spend most of your time during an investigation. If you are lucky, the incident was caught early, and you will have very little to do. However, this is rarely the case, so get ready to do a deep dive into the hard drive to find the evidence of what the attacker accomplished. You do not need to review every file on the drive. Pay specific attention to what occurred during and immediately after the timeframe of the initial attack and let the evidence carry you on to other areas of the drive. Forensic applications can help you find new or modified files based on timestamps very easily. Focus on those files first.

It is important to note that having multiple members of the team working on different aspects of the investigation can speed up the process. You may be in an organization that cannot afford a full-fledged incident response team, requiring you to work solo. If it is possible to divide the work, victim system analysis can begin while the log analysis is also underway. This requires intentional coordination but can speed the process along and get the victim system restored to an operational status much sooner. You want to conduct a thorough investigation, but you also want to do it in a reasonable amount of time with the knowledge that someone is without a computer as long as you are still digging through evidence. In the business world, a non-functioning or unavailable system can result in financial losses, so keep this in mind as you work through your process.

The running processes will show you everything actively running at the point the list was generated. You can eliminate common processes used by the operating system and known user programs as long as their versions match what is expected. There should be very little left to analyze at this point and anything malicious could stand out. Look for the executable files that spawned the process and any additional files the suspicious process is using. You will want to look through the directory where these files are located as this can provide additional clues to other malicious activities. After collecting the files, run each one through a debugger or disassembler program to systematically step through each element of the code and determine what action the program is taking. You can also search for the filename online to determine if anyone else previously examined it and provided the results of their analysis; this can save you a lot of time.

A great practice that makes the investigative process even easier is to generate a hash of every file on a system before putting it into operational status. A free open-source tool, such as MD5, can be used for this purpose and making it part of the process for system deployment can make investigating future incidents a little easier. Hashing algorithms create a fixed-length string for a file, allowing a user to validate if the file has been modified. This is becoming a more common practice with file downloads from security-conscious websites. They will provide the hash

for the file so you can confirm you have the original content and not something which was modified. Using this hashing method for all system files can help you to locate any files a hacker replaced with their malicious version. Rerunning the hash tool on the victim system to compare the difference will show you all the changed files. Of course, files get changed and updated regularly, so the hashes will need to be recreated from a known good system after each round of updates.

Active connections at the time an attack is discovered will reveal any active backdoors, direct connections from the initial attack, and additional connections established by the attacker for the purpose of exfiltrating data or copying tools. Also, pay close attention to established connections between the victim system and other systems on the internal network. This could lead to discovering if the attacker was able to expand an internal foothold and which systems were involved. Look for connections that utilize commonly used administrative ports such as 3389 for remote connections to Windows systems. Each discovered internal connection will require stepping through the evidence collection phase for each associated system. An investigation is only complete after every known victim system is analyzed. Missing even one victimized system can allow the attacker to maintain a foothold long after the investigation has been completed. Being thorough is an incredibly important element in this process.

Hacking involves copying files to victim systems and any file left behind can continue to cause problems until it is removed. This can be in the form of malware disabling functionality, backdoor programs, or tools the attacker plans to use to continue their infiltration. They are usually hidden in places the average user does not actively access daily. Hidden files in the "Documents" directory on Windows are easily noticed, so do not expect hidden content to show up there or on the Desktop. Files could also be renamed to appear as normal system files when they are in fact malicious. Storing a ".zip" file full of tools on a computer and renaming it to have a ".ini" extension can allow it to hide in plain sight! Look for any newly created files from the point of attack, and especially look within folders where system files are stored.

Reconstruct Attack

The fun side of incident response is the investigative process of reconstructing what happened. Each piece of your analysis will provide another piece of the puzzle and allow you to chart the path of the attacker from start to finish. Some investigators use large whiteboards to create a visual timeline of everything that took place. This method allows for adding more information as the investigation continues and makes the later reporting process much easier.

Occasionally, the sophistication of the attacker is so great it is virtually impossible to reconstruct each malicious action. In these situations, reconstruct as much as possible and try working backward to determine specific ports used by the attacker to create new alerts on the IDS devices. The "how" gives us the information needed to keep the attack from occurring again. Even when that information is limited, it can still yield enough to adjust an IDS' signature to look for the same type of activity in the future.

Form Conclusions

All of your analysis should lead you to understand what occurred, why it occurred, and how to keep it from occurring again. This is the heart of most digital forensics processes within an organization. Law enforcement will have the added desire of prosecuting a case within a courtroom, but most internal investigations within a company will never be elevated to that level. Forming conclusions after all the investigative work should be easy if every rock was uncovered. You may end up with a simple statement at the end of an investigation which looks like this:

> The investigation has concluded that the attacker scanned for vulnerabilities on March 23, 2021, successfully exploited the SMB vulnerability at 12:22 A.M. on March 25, 2021, gained administrative access to one system on the internal network, and modified the contents of two low priority files.

Reporting

Every forensic investigation should end with a report of everything discovered, required clean-up actions, and recommendations. Keep detailed notes throughout your process in a format that can be easily copied into the final report. Many forensic applications also include a report function providing a lot of quality content. This is automatically generated as you work, is highly accurate, and contains technical data specific to the incident being investigated. These are rarely formatted professionally enough to be presented in a courtroom or even used as an official report within an organization, so do not expect to simply print out the application's report and provide it to your boss. You can add the provided data to your report along with all the other necessary details to provide the most complete picture possible.

Organizations providing forensic investigations as a service employ technical writers who take the data generated by these programs, along with everything provided by the investigator, and format it into a professional report. Large organizations conducting many internal investigations every year also have professional writers as part of the team. This is the best way to create this product but is not always feasible in smaller organizations without room in the budget for an additional employee. Regardless of how the report is created, make sure it is done professionally with detailed explanations anyone can understand. Avoid technical jargon in the main portion of the report. Save the highly technical elements for appendices where other technicians can look to determine required actions to rectify any vulnerabilities. Senior leaders do not need the details for every element of every broken widget. The report should state the facts, provide the bottom line, and give the leaders what they need to make decisions.

The investigation will reveal in detail what is already known. Someone hacked into a system and did some form of damage, stole data, or made changes to the victim system. Your revelations will give greater detail to what, when, and where questions regarding the incident. The most valuable thing included in the report, and what will be seen as the bottom line by leadership, are the recommended actions. Patching or eliminating the vulnerability will always be the first thing on the list. This could involve downloading an update, replacing an application, or eliminating a process altogether. Other common recommendations include additional training, more frequent patch and update schedules, process improvement, and policy adjustments. It is important to provide every detail of the investigation within the report so decision-makers will have all available data to take appropriate action. At no point should information be left out to protect mistakes made by other employees or to cover up negligence.

Secure and Recover

The final phase of any investigation is to restore the system to operational status by wiping all hacker activity, recovering deleted data, and securing the system from future attacks. This is often easiest accomplished through recoveries from backup servers to bring the system to a known good state and follow up with extensive patching. The victim system is unusable within the organization during the investigation which can hamper operational capabilities leading to lost revenue and lower production. A better practice during the investigative process is to allow the secure and recover phase to take place concurrently with the investigation. After the victim's hard drive is fully imaged and all the required data is collected, there is no real need to leave it sitting disconnected in the corner of a room. If no new evidence is needed, and a law enforcement investigation is not necessary, there is no logical reason to keep it out of operational use for several weeks. Incident responders should return the victim system to the system administrators as soon as they are finished with evidence collection.

Criminal investigations will require the victim system, or at least the original hard drive, to be secured as evidence until the long process of court trials is completed. The chain of evidence is an important process to prove guilt or innocence and many cases have been lost or dismissed as a result of evidence being improperly handled. Incident responders within an organization are rarely trained to handle investigations of this magnitude which is why law enforcement runs the process for specific criminal investigations. Typically, hacking activity that involves other criminal elements such as child pornography, theft, or other actions affecting individual lives needs to include notifications to local police departments to facilitate the proper investigations. The involvement of law enforcement is the only scenario where victim systems cannot be restored much earlier than is typically seen in most internal investigative processes.

In-depth investigations take time. A lot of time. Each new investigation makes the incident responder more proficient at the process which can speed things up a little, but the systematic approach will always require a significant amount of time to conduct a thorough and complete investigation. Each piece of the process is important, and nothing should be skipped. Some cases are more "open and shut" where the activity is known, the way in is known, and the actions are known. Even in these cases, more data can be collected to show every step of the attack. Do not allow preconceived notions or commonly seen attacks to sway you from taking every necessary investigative step. The outcome of these investigations should result in a more secure network less vulnerable to attack than prior to the occurrence of the incident. It has been said that "leaving something better than you found it" is a good practice throughout life. This is also true in incident response investigations. The victim system and network should be better as a result of the investigation greatly lessening the possibility of future attacks.

Practical Application – Digging for Evidence

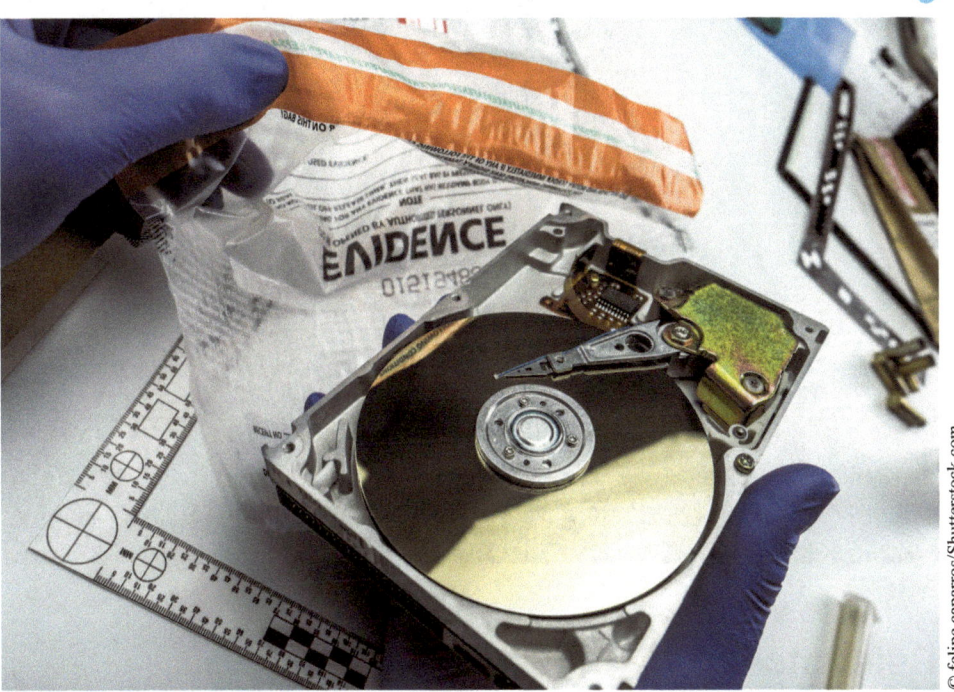

© felipe caparros/Shutterstock.com

Evidence collection may be the easier part of the investigative process. The sorting, digging, and the searching process is where the real work starts. This can be a mundane process or an exciting one. It all depends on perspective. The only way to fully determine what occurred is to conduct a thorough examination of every victim system. This is not a cursory look, but a detailed examination of everything the attacker accessed. Consider these tips as you work through your process:

1. Be methodical – do not rush through any piece of evidence. Methodically look at every line, every file, and every potential clue to see if it yields any new information. Even the smallest clue can help solve the case.

2. Follow the breadcrumbs – reconstruct the attack from the point of entry and into the first victim. Analyze every action and additional connection. Follow the trail wherever it leads.
3. Record everything – be meticulous in recording all discoveries and conclusions for your final report.
4. Reverse engineer applications – analyze hacker tools to determine how they work and what they accomplish. Consider sending key elements to antivirus vendors for inclusion in future signature files.
5. Consider how an IDS could have caught this attack more quickly and provide details for IDS rule construction.
6. Work as a team – when possible, have other experts review your findings and identify any missing elements or incorrect conclusions.

© Dusit/Shutterstock.com

References

NY: https://its.ny.gov/security-advisory/vulnerability-wordpress-easy-wp

Chapter 7: Review Questions

1. The analysis process can take _____.
   a. Several months
   b. Several years
   c. Several weeks
   d. All of the above

2. Firewall logs show _____.
   a. Incoming connections
   b. Incoming and outgoing connections
   c. Outgoing connections
   d. External connections

3. Router logs show _____ content as firewall logs.
   a. Similar
   b. Different
   c. Malicious
   d. None of the above

4. The _____ port is an important element to key in on.
   a. Origin
   b. Source
   c. Destination
   d. Ephemeral

5. _____ scans of single ports are targeted for specific vulnerabilities or services.
   a. Wide
   b. Broad
   c. Narrow
   d. Single

6. _____ help to correlate activity between systems.
   a. Methods
   b. Files
   c. Users
   d. Timestamps

7. _____ searches can provide earlier information about initial scanning activity.
   a. Annual
   b. Historical
   c. Timeline
   d. Daily

8. Professional hackers tend to use a _____ process.
   a. Methodical
   b. Simple
   c. Rushed
   d. Paranoid

9. Inexperienced hackers tend to use a _____ process.
   a. Methodical
   b. Simple
   c. Rushed
   d. Paranoid

10. _____ can provide a huge clue to the true source of an attack.
    a. System processes
    b. Screen doors
    c. Front doors
    d. Back doors

11. Backdoors allow the hacker to maintain _____ access.
    a. Long-term
    b. Short-term
    c. Temporary
    d. None of the above

12. Logs can reveal additional _____ impacted by the attacker.
    a. Systems
    b. Networks
    c. Applications
    d. All of the above

13. Great hackers _____ systems to hide their true source.
    a. Bounce through
    b. Encrypt
    c. Manipulate
    d. Destroy

14. Investigators need to accept the possibility that _____ action will be taken against an attacker.
    a. Legal
    b. Zero
    c. Vigilante
    d. Immediate

15. _____ attacks are used by nations collecting intelligence operations or worse.
    a. Script kiddie
    b. Automated
    c. Worm-producing
    d. State-sponsored
16. When law enforcement is involved, the organization _____ control over the investigation.
    a. Maintains
    b. Loses
    c. Manages
    d. Oversees
17. Some organizations _____ the investigation and go straight to securing the system.
    a. Rush
    b. Outsource
    c. Skip
    d. None of the above
18. _____ teams can speed up the process.
    a. Small
    b. Large
    c. Minimal
    d. Communicative
19. _____ files of systems make it easy to locate modifications.
    a. Managing
    b. Copying
    c. Recording
    d. Hashing
20. _____ is the final phase of an investigation.
    a. Secure and recover
    b. Wipe and reload
    c. Wipe and destroy
    d. Default restoration

Hardening Windows

CHAPTER 8

Any good investigation into a hacking incident will generate a series of recommended actions to correct the problem(s) which opened the door to attack. Never assume the hacker just got lucky. Systems were successfully exploited and the vulnerabilities which allowed the exploits to take place, need to be removed before another attacker shows up looking to cause more trouble. The recommended fixes can include a variety of things including software changes, modification of hardware configurations, updates to company policies, and patching of vulnerabilities. Most of this work will take place on the local victim system. This is referred to as hardening because the implementation of better security practices puts the system in a more robust posture with a thicker version of virtual armor. Knowing how an attacker gained access, or how one may attempt to gain access provides all the information we need to create a strong defensive posture that deflects their attacks.

You do not need to wait to be attacked before you harden your operating system. These steps can and should be taken as proactive measures that eliminate or greatly lessen the potential for exploitation. A common challenge in the security world is the responsive nature often taken regarding hacking activity. Responding to an incident, repairing any damage, and securing the system is a good thing. But being proactive at developing a strong security bastion is a much better route to take. Who would not want to eliminate a hack before it happens? The cleanup process requires a significant amount of time and resources that could be spent on more important operational needs. In a sense, it is a waste of time on a situation that could have been completely avoided if the right measures were put into place from the beginning. Be proactive, not reactive. There are many actions that can harden Windows operating systems. Some of the most common will be covered here.

© Wright Studio/Shutterstock.com

The lack of available patches installed on systems is one of the most common vulnerabilities exploited by attackers. This is especially true for older vulnerabilities because they are easily recognizable during a scan. These types of vulnerabilities stand out like a sore thumb and instantly become a target. A patch is a modification to the code of an application or operating system that eliminates a discovered flaw. Not all patches are related to exploitable vulnerabilities, some are more cosmetic in nature or fix glitches with functionality. Regardless of their purpose, all patches should be installed with priority given to those that impact the security of a system. This is an area that has fallen through the cracks for many years, partially due to the mundaneness of the process, and partially as the result of not giving patching the importance it deserves. With the ease and automation of patching today, there is no good reason to ever fall behind on keeping software up to date.

The Windows operating system has maintained solid domination in the computing market for several decades and continues to be the most widely used operating system on the planet. It is no wonder attackers target Windows systems. They are everywhere! Microsoft has made it easy to patch systems with standard, monthly rollouts of patches for all their software, along with other releases as needed throughout the month. The automated process in Windows makes this easy for individual systems to stay up-to-date for any update, not just security patches. Many network administrators disable the Windows update feature on user workstations and push updates manually to all systems at the same time after testing to make sure there are no adverse effects with other applications in use. Regardless of how the patches are installed, the key piece is to install them as soon as possible after release. Widely used applications have been hacked in the few days after patches were released. Hackers do not wait a few months to get around to breaking into systems. They jump at the chance to exploit something new, so do not delay this process. More on this process later.

Any application installed on Windows is also subject to the same possibility of being exploited. It is important to have a list of all installed software and check websites for those applications regularly to see if any patches have been released or vulnerabilities announced. Windows makes this easy for Microsoft software by utilizing Windows Update to push updates to all installed Microsoft software. Other applications sometimes have an update process built-in, but they are not always automated. Add third-party software to your regular process of checking for new patches. Staying ahead of the curve and installing these as soon as they are released will go a long way in keeping one step ahead of hackers. Hackers watch for vulnerability announcements as well. It makes their job of finding targets much easier because they know only the most vigilant defenders consistently patch systems regularly. Do not allow them to gain a foothold, especially when patching is a relatively simple process. Password construction is another easy method to strengthen defenses.

Passwords are often the easiest user element to attack because a weak password can provide quick access to a treasure trove of data. Every network should force a strong password policy on every account. But what is a strong password really? In the early days, we pushed the idea of an 8-character password that included a number, capital letter, and special character. As time went this advice morphed into longer variations where multiple special characters, numbers, and capital letters were required along with a forced change multiple times a year. In some cases, users are forced to change passwords every 60 days. Is this overkill? How long is long enough and what is too long? How long of a password can a user effectively remember? A longer and more complex password certainly becomes more difficult to break, but is there a point where it becomes unnecessarily long? William Cheswick (2012) in his article, *Rethinking Passwords*, provided the mathematical possibilities of passwords of different strengths being broken within different periods of time. His conclusions are too long to mention here in detail, but he proved that, at least in 2012, a password of 12 characters made from letters, numbers, and special characters, will take almost 2 million years to crack. Why would we need to change this password every 60 days? Changing it once every year would be more than efficient. This is an area where mathematical probabilities and common sense need to be used together to form the most effective policies.

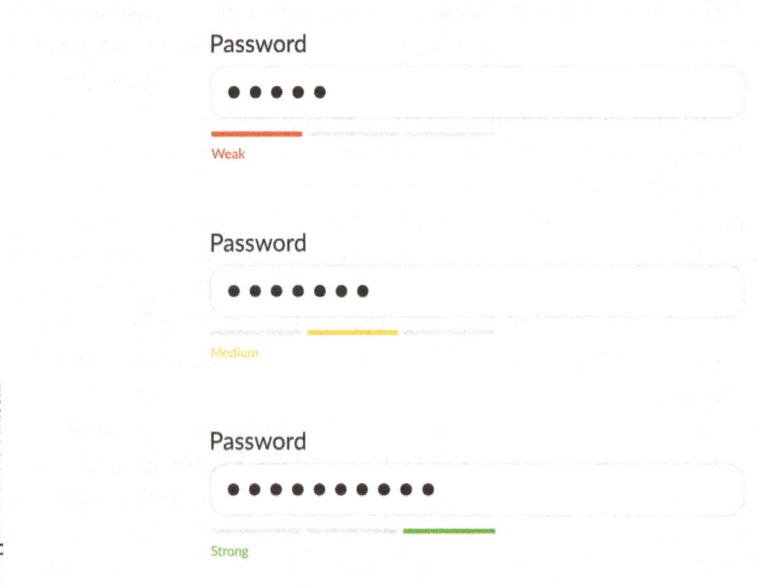

Rules for strong passwords should be enforced for every user account, but those rules should not be so burdensome users have difficulty remembering the passwords or coming up with new ones every other month. The difficulty in this process has created the insecure method of writing passwords down, which is a horrible idea, but the only one some users can utilize to log in each day. Technology has increased since Cheswick conducted his research, giving multi-core processors and high-end GPUs a lot more power to attempt breaking a password. But a magic bullet does not exist. It is still incredibly difficult to crack a strong password. Consider this—a hacker will not use the resources of his system 24/7 for two years to break your password. Practically speaking, they will move on to another task within a few hours or days at the most. Why waste time on a strong target when you can look for a weaker one? Governments with powerful supercomputers are the only ones with the resources to conduct long-term attempts at breaking passwords. And even in those scenarios, changing a password a few times each year is more than enough.

Organizational Policies

There is no reason not to have some form of antivirus application running on every system. A few decades ago, antivirus applications tended to slow down systems because they hogged a lot of resources, but in today's computing environment that is no longer the case. These applications can be fine-tuned to take very specific actions, lessening their burden on system resources and mostly running silently in the background. The technological advancements in this arena have created a lot of difficulty for malware creators longing to put their dangerous software on unsuspecting systems. Antivirus has advanced to the point that it can quickly detect most known malicious files and even some new variations, keeping systems secure from what can easily cause a lot of destruction and headaches. Free versions of this software also exist, so even users on a budget can be well protected. Get it installed and eliminate this particular risk.

One area of malware that has been prevalent in the past few years is ransomware. Malware was formerly designed to break systems, destroy data, or cause a nuisance to users. It was a hassle to remove it from a system, but one could easily accomplish it in a few hours or less. Ransomware changed the landscape by encrypting data and requiring users to pay a fee in order to receive the keys required to decrypt and once again access their data. Companies and individual users alike have been targeted with these types of attacks. The best method to defend against ransomware is a twofold approach of running good antivirus software and having an excellent backup process. Antivirus should stop any known ransomware attacks, but newer ones may get through before updates become available. If it makes it onto your system, you end up in a difficult situation. This is the worst for businesses because every hour of downtime equates to lost revenue.

Some organizations think paying a small fee is worth the hassle of getting their data back quickly. This may be true if the ransom fee is less than the cost of paying employee-overtime to restore from backups. The problem with paying the fee is that it encourages criminals to keep up their tactics because they know it is a profitable process. The U.S. government policy of not dealing with terrorists is a great one to apply in these situations. A system infected with ransomware can simply be removed from the network, restored from a known good backup, and put back online with minimal impact. Backups are not usually mentioned as part of security training or system hardening techniques, but they can save a lot of time and money when these types of attacks strike. Ask anyone who has lost data because of malware or even a crashed system and they will passionately advocate for good backups.

Windows operating systems have long included a remote-access capability, allowing users, typically administrators, to remotely connect to another workstation and use it as if they were physically sitting at the keyboard. It is a very useful capability for administrative tasks, especially when operating a large network, but can also be dangerous if a hacker makes their way into the network. Remote access of this type is most commonly used in troubleshooting problems users are experiencing, or to install new software applications. It eliminates the need to physically go to the user's location, which can save a significant amount of time if the user is located in a separate location. Convenience can be a big wrench in the work of security. Users and administrators alike tend to ignore some security rules for the sake of convenience. It is human nature to look for the easiest path forward and eliminating the need to leave the office to fix a problem is a good motivator.

Leaders need to weigh the capability this service provides with the associated risks to determine if it should be left in place. In most cases, it is not needed and should be disabled. This is a capability where a standard rule should be in place and exceptions should be approved on a case-by-case basis. Having the remote desktop protocol (RDP), as it is known in Windows, enabled on every workstation provides a sea of targets for an attacker. One administrative password could allow access to every system without any additional need for exploits. This is not a good situation for a network and is not the definition of a secure network. Newer versions of Windows come with the service automatically disabled, so unless your network has a mix of different Windows versions or someone enabled this service across the network, this hardening method may already be in place. If not, disable RDP right away.

Closely related to this is the use and management of the local administrator account. One of the first tasks a hacker takes—after gaining access to a system—is to increase privileges through the use of an additional exploit or by grabbing the credentials of the administrator account. It is fairly easy to locate the account with administrative privileges when it is named "administrator." This is the default name Microsoft has used for many years on Windows systems and there are a few different practices that help to obscure this account from a hacker's vision. The first is to rename the account to something benign so it appears to be a regular user account. Renaming it to superuser, privileged, or something similar will be just as obvious as administrator. Try something simple like johnsonb, hartfordm, or something similar that looks like a normal username and matches the naming convention used on the network. This small change can be enough to throw a hacker off the scent. This may not be enough for a more seasoned hacker who knows how to dig deeper into Windows account information.

Every account on a Windows system includes a security identifier (SID) which Windows uses for controlling access to files, processes, and other security-related matters. The username can be changed, but the SID will remain the same for as long as the account exists. Changing the name of the administrator account will not change the SID. A good hacker knows that every administrator account SID ends with the number 500. Several programs exist that allow for a listing of usernames matched with their corresponding SID. Even Windows itself has a built-in command to display this data, so a decent hacker can easily run a single command and discover that johnsonb's SID matches the standard SID of the administrator account. That small bit of obscurity goes away, and the hacker has an account to target. What good is it to rename the account if the hacker can easily locate it with one command? It does not make the system feel any more secure, but there is another method available to make this more difficult.

The second security practice you can use, and this one is much better than the previous, is to create a completely new account on the system with assigned administrator privileges. This will do two things. First, it will generate a SID that looks like any other normal user account. An attacker's ability to gain a list of SIDs will no longer be effective. Second, the username will also appear as a normal user account. It will not stand out when the attacker takes a quick look. When using this method, it is important to disable the built-in administrator account so it can never be used. It does not do any good to create a new account and keep the original one active on the system. The new administrator account should also not be made a member of the local or domain level administrator groups. That would be another clear giveaway to an attacker. This method is very sound and can make a hacker's attempts at upgrading access more difficult. It may buy the defender enough time to recognize the activity and block the attacker before any damage can be caused.

There is one problem with this method. On a domain with many systems and users, user accounts are controlled at the domain level, not the system level. It is unlikely a long list of local user accounts will exist on a user's system. A user will log in with a domain account and that account has the same privileges throughout the entire network. This can make the johnsonb account stand out because it would not seem logical to have a random normal local user account sitting on an individual system. This is especially true if no other local accounts exist on that system. Once again, the hacker may be able to easily recognize the administrator account. If your network is not controlled by a Windows server, creating a new administrator account is the right thing to do. On a domain, the better option is to disable all local administrator accounts and make the domain administrator account a member of the local administrator group. This will allow domain administrators the ability to locally log on to any system with administrative privileges and eliminate this particular privilege escalation threat at the same time.

Windows has also come with automatic update services enabled for several iterations, allowing systems to stay up to date with little interaction, other than a prompted reboot, from users. This has become a very beneficial feature because it almost completely eliminates many new vulnerabilities by automatically installing patches as they become available. It also provides updates to core operating functions, new drivers for hardware, and new versions of other Microsoft software if installed. For the average user, especially on home-based networks, this service should never be disabled. It provides a service formerly requiring regular interaction, which often led to insecure systems. Eliminating the need for interaction has certainly made many systems more secure. Some versions or configurations of Windows do not even allow the update process to be disabled or modified. This can be seen as a bit of overreach by a software provider but paying for the right version restores more user control over the system. So, why would anyone ever want to disable this capability?

Some networks and some custom configurations are very sensitive to change and need to have patches tested to make sure they do not accidentally eliminate a capability of a third-party application or completely remove needed services. Users with older applications or in-house custom-designed software can fall into the trap of their applications breaking after an update because patch designers generally consider broad integration and cannot account for every possible application in existence. The best long-term approach to these situations is to upgrade applications to a newer version, but until that becomes possible, these instances require a more nuanced approach to the update process. Every network is a little different and there are no cookie-cutter solutions that can simply be deployed across the world to solve potential security risks. There is always a balancing act required to make some security and operational capabilities work together.

Microsoft has provided the Windows Server Update Service (WSUS) to allow administrators to download updates to a centralized server and approve each one individually for deployment to workstations. This is an excellent workaround for networks needing a greater degree of control. Systems can be also placed in different categories allowing updates to be pushed to some systems while leaving others unpatched. And it provides the added benefit of only downloading updates from the internet one time instead of every system on the network pulling down the required files. This can save a lot of bandwidth, especially if every computer tries to grab updates at the same time. It also allows administrators greater control over the time-of-day updates are installed, limiting middle-of-the-day updates that slow user systems and hamper operations. Larger networks can take advantage of this capability and smaller networks of just a few systems can likely keep the auto-update feature enabled across the board.

One additional policy to consider is full disk encryption. Encrypting the entire hard drive renders a hard drive unusable if it is lost or stolen, as everything it contains has been scrambled. There are many different tools available on the market today that provide this capability. And do not worry if you are not familiar with cryptography or encryption, it will be covered more in-depth in Chapter 12. Essentially, the way it works is all data on a computer is stored in an encrypted state. The most secure implementations require a password to unlock the encryption when the system is powered on. It is mostly seamless for the user. They access and use files in the same way. The major difference takes place when the system is powered down. If someone was to remove the hard drive for analysis, they would not be able to access any of the information. Implementing full disk encryption on every system is rarely necessary for anything other than the most sensitive physical systems. Laptops used by traveling employees should also have this additional layer of security just in case the laptop falls into the hands of an unauthorized user.

Security Software

The firewall located at the perimeter of your network will do a great job at blocking access from external users for every closed port. Access will be granted for open ports and that data will be allowed to traverse the network as it is forwarded to the system—behind the firewall listening for connections on that port. This is a solid method, but it does not stop an internal system from scanning or connecting to other internal systems. It has often been said that networks have a hardened exterior and a soft interior. Network security includes more than perimeter security. Local system security controls provide a slew of additional options through various applications. One application is a software firewall running on each workstation. Average system hardware resources have improved enough to be able to run these types of applications without affecting system performance. A well-configured software firewall can stop insider activity and keep hackers from expanding their footprints if they gain access to the network.

A software version of an IDS can also be installed to provide detection capabilities throughout the network. Imagine a user decides to scan the internal network using their personal laptop connected to the company's W-Fi network. The first problem is that they were able to connect with a personal system; this will be discussed in Chapter 10. The second problem—if a firewall and IDS are not used on workstations, it is likely the user will go unnoticed because no one is monitoring the internal network. In this same scenario, the employee would be immediately noticed if these software applications are in place. Is this overkill? Some think so. Is it worth it to protect the internal portion of the network? Absolutely! Is it more expensive? Not really. All the top-tier antivirus applications available on the market today include some form of firewall and intrusion detection capabilities. One package can do all the work at the same time.

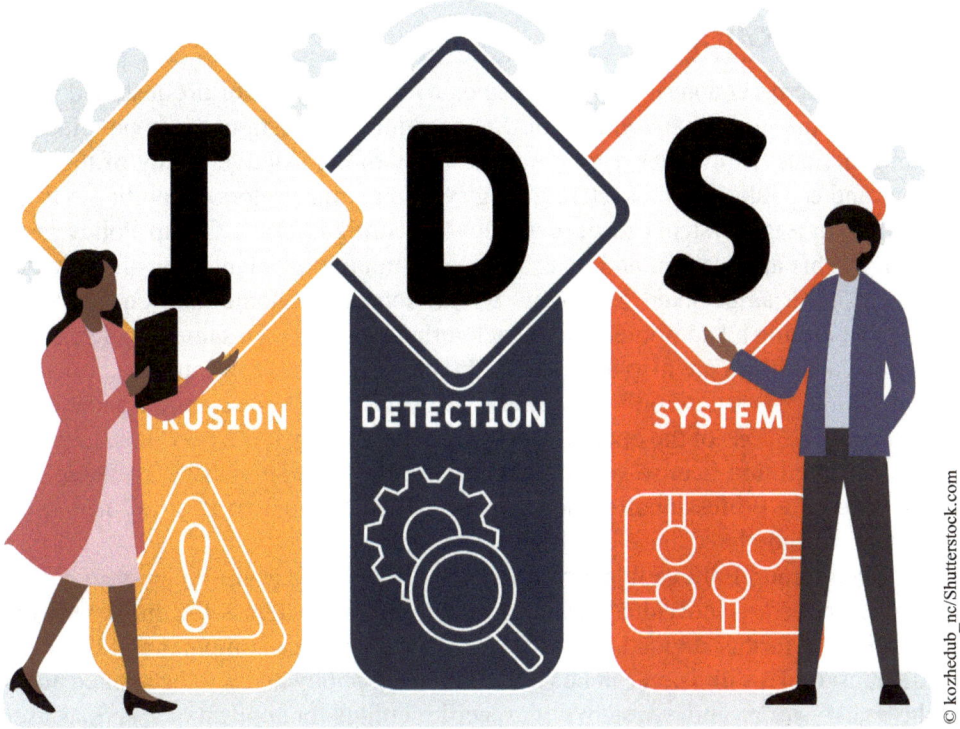

This type of third-party software is very effective at catching threats before they cause damage. Antivirus solutions have come a long way in the past 20 years. Some of the earliest versions crippled system performance by using up most of the available memory and processing power. The application was working overtime to stop threats at any cost, even if the system slowed so much it became unusable. This was not a good situation. Security should never hamper an employee's ability to do their job. Fortunately, antivirus and other security applications have been updated and fine-tuned to work well within the operating system and stay mostly hidden in the background—unless the user needs to be alerted to a situation. Hardware capabilities have also come a long way, allowing these applications the resources needed to effectively monitor the system and giving the user enough power to run many other applications at the same time.

Choosing to deploy host-based security measures, especially in a large network environment, should also include a centralized server to push updates to clients and receive alerts from each individual system. The last thing a security professional needs to add to their task list is individually checking the security logs of every system regularly. The smart method is to have all logs and alerts transmit back to a centralized location where they can be combined and analyzed more efficiently. Another method is to eliminate the server model and respond only when users provide a notification of an alert. This is not the best model but can work in smaller environments where budgets do not allow for servers or additional manpower for deeper analysis. Scaling up or down as needed to fit security within necessary budgets and manpower capabilities is an art form in the field of computer science.

Group Policies

Every modern version of Windows comes with a policy editor pre-installed which provides fine-tuning capabilities for user accounts, applications, and operating system functions. It provides a greater granularity of control over many of the functions and capabilities of a system giving system administrators the ability to tweak settings to align systems to needed network configurations. Group Policy is the name of this application, and its capabilities can be implemented on an individual system, such as personal computers within someone's home, and on networked systems forcing all computers on the network to maintain the same policies. Group Policy capabilities are also affected by the version of Windows installed on a system. Some options are only available when using the Professional, Education, or Enterprise editions of the operating system, which is why it is a good idea to pay for the higher edition license so more fine-tuning capabilities will be available. You also need the Professional edition to join a Windows network, so all networked systems already have these capabilities available.

Each Group Policy Object contains a collection of Group Policy settings that can be applied to individual users, groups of users, or across the entire network. Policies are further divided into those affecting the entire computer and those that affect users. This division can be valuable when a policy needs to be applied across the board—for an entire system with specific settings for applications, actions users are allowed to take, and system-wide security settings. This effectively boxes all users into the same configuration and can be a powerful way to secure capabilities on a system unable to be modified using other software. The user-based policies can be used in conjunction with the system variation to further restrict specific users or give some users more control and authority over a system. For example, a system administrator needs to operate with more control to fix problems, run updates, and conduct other routine business. A separate Group Policy should be applied to those accounts.

The real power behind Group Policies is the ability to set network-wide policies which can be created and updated in one centralized location and forced onto all systems connected to the network. When a Windows system participating in a network first starts up, it looks for new Group Policies on the network and accepts required updates. This keeps all systems synchronized to the same policies and makes it very easy to maintain the same security across a slew of systems. Policies are created using the Group Policy editor through a GUI containing many different drop-down options. Making changes is as simple as enabling or disabling one of the available options. At first glance, the number of available configurations can be overwhelming. There are many options available that affect not just security, but many other common actions an administrator may want to restrict or disable. Group Policies can also be backed up to be easily applied to non-networked systems after a new purchase or fresh install. The following list contains some of the most common and useful policies to lock down the security of Windows:

- Disabling or limiting access to the Control Panel.
- Modifying minimum password length.
- Modifying maximum password age.
- Completely disabling the Guest account.
- Blocking use of USB drives, optical drives, or any other removable media devices.
- Disallowing ordinary users from installing software.
- Disable or limit access to the command prompt.
- Disable forced restarts after Windows updates.
- Disable Windows Defender after installing third-party antivirus software.

There are many more policies an administrator can put in place. No two networks are configured exactly the same and different areas may require more or less flexibility. An organization that allows users to bring work from home will need to keep USB ports enabled to allow data transfers, creating a potential security risk. This can be mitigated by forcing an antivirus scan of every device connected to the network. The types of files allowed to be copied can also be closely controlled to eliminate the transfer of seemingly benign executables which are actually dangerous. No security solution is completely foolproof. There is always someone savvy enough to find a sneaky way past a technical control. Putting in common-sense controls will keep the majority of users boxed in and the remaining sneaky ones can be caught using other methods discussed in this chapter. The Group Policy Editor is an excellent tool for anyone wanting to lock down Windows a little more tightly.

These are just some of the methods you can use to harden Windows. Many books have been written on this subject containing hundreds of suggestions for many different industries. The key thing to remember in this process is to stay vigilant. Think about the actions a hacker may take and put a brick wall in their path. Just a few policies and technical measures will keep all but the most persistent and experienced hacker from going further than a cursory scan. This is not about passing a vulnerability assessment or keeping a penetration testing team from making you look bad. It is about creating a secure operating environment where employees can conduct business without the concern of someone stealing or disrupting their work. These methods allow a business to operate and make a profit, which is good for everyone involved. Hardening the system's employees use is an important piece of the puzzle, especially when the often-attacked Windows operating system is being used.

Practical Application – Simple Lockdown Steps

Locking down a Windows system is not difficult; it only takes intentional time to establish a secure configuration. It is wise, especially in larger network environments, to have baseline images that can be installed on new systems. These baselines make standardization much easier and reduce the amount of work required when systems need to be installed or refreshed. The baselines will need to be updated often enough to keep up with the most recent patches and updates but installations in-between these updates can simply be configured manually. These steps are enough to harden everyday Windows-based systems:

1. Remove all unauthorized software.
2. Remove all unneeded software pre-installed by manufacturers.
3. Update applications to the latest version after configuring on a test network.
4. Remove the built-in administrator account.
5. Create an inconspicuous administrator account.
6. Install all operating system and application patches after configuring on a test network.
7. Install antivirus or enable Microsoft Defender.
8. Install firewall or enable Microsoft Defender.
9. Install software-based HIDS.
10. Configure Group Policies.
11. Run internal vulnerability scan against the system and adjust setting based on results.

References

Cheswick, W. (2012). Rethinking passwords. *ACMQueue*. 31 Dec 2012. Vol. 10, Issue 12. Accessed at https://queue.acm.org/detail.cfm?id=2422416

Chapter 8: Review Questions

1. Operating systems should be hardened _____ an attack.
   a. During
   b. Before
   c. After
   d. Both B and C

2. Cleaning up from an attack requires _____ and _____.
   a. Time and resources
   b. Software and hardware
   c. Outsourcing and Employees
   d. All of the above

3. The lack of _____ is the most common reason for successful hacks.
   a. Routers
   b. Patches
   c. Firewalls
   d. Intrusion detection systems

4. _____ is the most common targeted operating system.
   a. Windows
   b. Linux
   c. MacOS
   d. Redhat

5. _____ can be exploited as easily as operating systems.
   a. Hard drives
   b. USB drives
   c. Memory
   d. Applications

6. A _____ can provide easy access.
   a. Strong
   b. Weak
   c. Complex
   d. Both A and C

7. Password construction needs to _____.
   a. Stay the same
   b. Be stronger
   c. Rethought
   d. Eliminated

8. Every system should have _____ installed.
   a. Antivirus
   b. Software firewalls
   c. Software IDS
   d. VPNs

9. _____ holds data captive.
   a. Managers
   b. Administrators
   c. Ransomware
   d. Antivirus

10. Ransomware can be defeated with good _____.
    a. Patching
    b. User training
    c. Backups
    d. All of the above

11. Paying ransom fees _____ hackers to attack again.
    a. Fund
    b. Discourage
    c. Encourage
    d. None of the above

12. _____ make the recovery process from an attack much easier.
    a. Backups
    b. Policies
    c. Procedures
    d. Administrators

13. Remote access needs to be carefully _____ and _____ in use.
    a. Considered, limited
    b. Disabled, limited
    c. Disabled, unlimited
    d. Considered, unlimited

14. _____ administrator accounts should be disabled.
    a. All
    b. Domain
    c. User
    d. Local

15. New administrator accounts should be created with a _____ name.
    a. Managerial
    b. Common
    c. Unusual
    d. Administrative

16. The Windows _____ can identify built-in administrator accounts.
    a. SID
    b. NFS
    c. DNS
    d. RDP
17. _____ Windows updates makes patching _____.
    a. Automated, confusing
    b. Automated, difficult
    c. Automated, easy
    d. Mandatory, difficult
18. A policy of _____ takes security to another level.
    a. Full disk encryption
    b. Partial disk encryption
    c. Mobile disk encryption
    d. Full disk decontamination
19. Software versions of firewalls and IDSs help against _____ threats.
    a. Insider threats
    b. External threats
    c. Both A and B
    d. None of the above
20. _____ provide greater granularity of control over user capabilities.
    a. Internet policies
    b. Network policies
    c. System policies
    d. Group policies

Hardening Linux

CHAPTER 9

Linux is not an operating system known for having thousands of vulnerabilities. For many years, Microsoft Windows was the most common target for hackers looking to exploit a system. This is still true today. And this is because Microsoft maintained dominance in the worldwide computing arena for decades. Naturally, the most commonly used operating system is going to be the most common target. Microsoft is sometimes viewed negatively for the number of vulnerabilities connected with their operating systems, but this is an unfair perspective because the amount of programming required to develop feature-rich operating systems cannot be expected to be flawless all the time. We need to accept the possibility some software will have glitches needing to be fixed when discovered. This reality is one reason we have layered security methods to block access at the perimeter before a criminal can exploit anything on the inside of the network. It is also a reason that other operating systems, such as Linux, continue to be part of a network environment.

Linux is also not commonly used as a workstation. It is more commonly used as a server or by more advanced users working in the computer science arena. Security professionals often use Kali Linux, as mentioned in earlier chapters, to conduct vulnerability assessments, penetration tests, or forensic analysis. Other versions of Linux can be used for these operations and only need to be properly configured with the needed software, though Kali is often the quickest and easiest to get up and running. At the server level, it is more common to see the Ubuntu, Red Hat, and Debian distributions. There are many other available distributions available, and each has its pros and cons. Hardening any Linux system is relatively the same process across the board. Understanding the common areas needing to be secured will be beneficial for any of the common distributions.

Many of the concepts for hardening Windows apply to Linux, though the implementation will be different. Implementing some form of encryption, forcing the use of strong passwords, disabling USB ports, and regular patch updates all apply in this operating system. When used as a server, or as a penetration testing system, USB ports should be enabled for administrative users to conduct necessary actions. The other commonality with Windows is the need to secure services and applications needed for the proper functionality of the system. There are plenty of potential vulnerabilities lurking on a fresh installation of Linux to keep a hacker satisfied and it is dangerous to assume that, just because it is not Windows, it is automatically secure. Many web-based services, such as websites and databases, run on Linux-based systems. One fatal flaw can temporarily remove an online presence from the internet or corrupt data and force an organization into recovery mode. Do not make the mistake of leaving a vulnerable Linux system plugged into a network.

File Permissions

Users should only have access to files and directories needed to perform their duties. This is known in the security world as 'least privilege.' A secretary does not need administrative access to the email server. The manager of the sales department does not need access to the human resources systems containing private employee information. Each user should only have access to the data required to perform their duties and nothing more. This can be controlled through the assignment of file permissions to users and groups allowing or disallowing access to different portions of the network file system. This is accomplished in Linux using the chmod and chown commands. The chown command assigns ownership of a file or directory to a user or group. Owners typically have full control over those files, but those permissions can be narrowed down if needed. The chmod command assigns the level of access a user has, to read, modify, or execute any particular file. Use these commands to designate specific permissions for each user and watch out for the dreaded permission creep.

Permission creep can occur over time when users move to different positions which require different levels of access. An employee in the finance department would have access to files containing budget information, employee salaries, and other financial documents. If that employee transferred to the sales department, they would need access to a different set of files and information. What often happens is administrators assign new privileges without removing the old ones. This transfer would negate the need for accessing financial data and that access should be removed when the transfer takes place. It usually stays in place giving a user an even broader level of access on the network. This permission creep can turn into a serious problem if not controlled. It is good to audit permissions regularly, remove what is no longer needed, and keep the permissions set well controlled.

Lock Down Services

The boot directory contains high-level system files which can crash a system if modified. The files in this directory are those needed when the system is initially booted, and in most distributions includes, master boot records, kernel files, and other configurations automatically generated by the system during installation. These are not files users, even administrators, need to manually modify and, as such, the directory should be modified to have read-only permissions. This eliminates accidental and malicious changes from taking place and the only way the modification can be reversed is by a root-level user. A quick change can be made to the file system table, more commonly known as FSTAB, that forces this directory into read-only mode for all users. This is a text-based configuration file located here: /etc/fstab. Adding this single line at the end of the file puts this security measure in place.

```
LABEL=/boot    /boot    ext2    defaults, ro    1 2
```

Secure shell (SSH) is one of the most commonly seen services running on a Linux system and provides administrators with remote shell access. Any scan revealing something listening on port 22 will almost always be SSH on a Linux or Unix system. It is that common! SSH is a very secure service but should be limited to specific users and modified to use SSH keys instead of passwords. It can be disabled if absolutely unneeded, but limiting access is a better way to handle this service. The sshd_config file, usually located in /etc/ssh, should be modified to eliminate the allowance of logging in as the root user and should specify which users are authorized. Logging in as root is frowned upon in security circles. A user rarely needs root-level privileges and can temporarily upgrade their access when it is absolutely necessary. Allowing root-level login through any remote service is asking for trouble. Limiting which users can utilize this service further narrows the opportunities for exploitation.

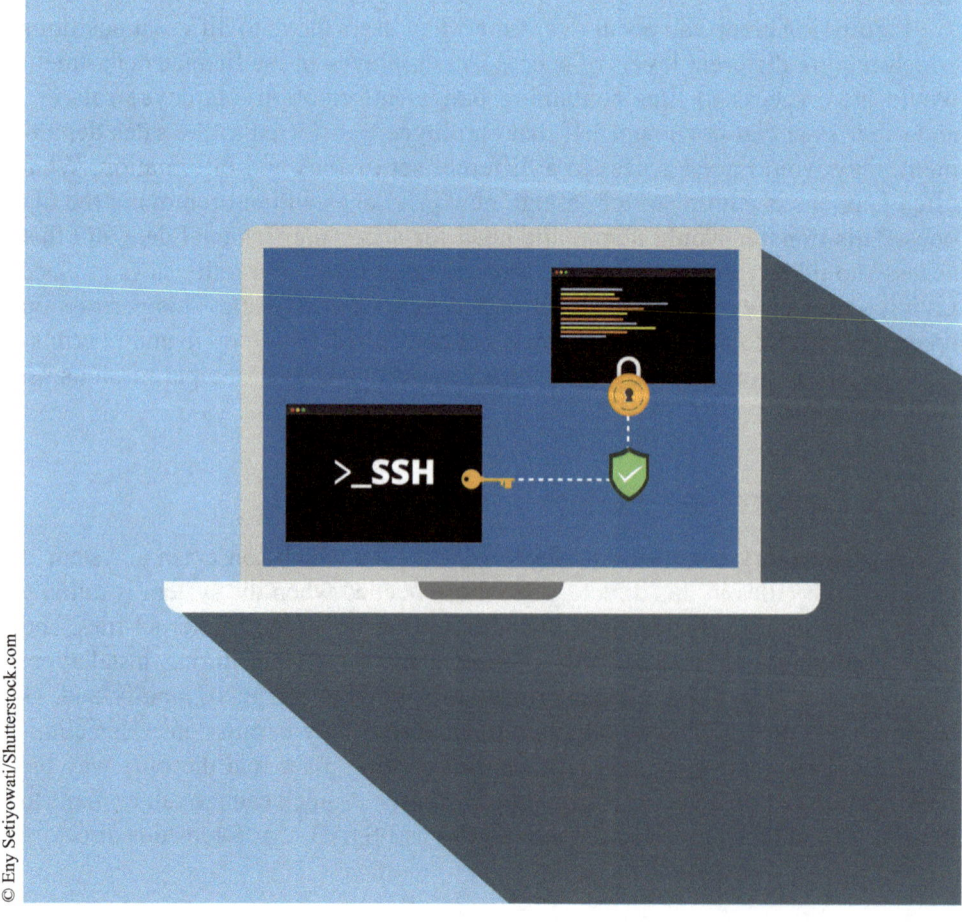

SSH can be accessed with usernames and passwords and can also be configured to use system-generated SSH keys. These keys boost security and make administration much easier. Everyone knows a password can be a weak link on a system. One weak password can bring down the entire kingdom. Adding SSH keys eliminate this risk, at least with this particular service, by using the public and private key system to establish secure connections. You will learn more about public and private keys in Chapter 12. The private key is stored on the user system and the public key is transferred to the server. The keys are used to authenticate the user anytime a session is initiated. The key itself has a passphrase that protects the system from being used by any random person, and the correct passphrase allows the connection to be established to the remote system. This is valuable because a hacker who obtains a password will not be able to log in to SSH without also having an SSH key. And she would not be able to copy the key to the server without already gaining access. Simple user authentication does not provide this level of security. Enabling SSH keys is a security practice every Linux system should have in place.

Another common communication protocol in use—on Linux-based systems—is the remote procedure call (RPC). This protocol establishes communication for client-server applications where the two systems need to communicate various functions with each other. The implementation is not as important here as the security vulnerability it presents. Several important and highly used applications, such as the network information service (NIS) and the network file system (NFS) are built on top of RPC. NIS is used to determine and distribute system configuration data, such as usernames and hostnames, between computers. NFS is a file system used on UNIX and Linux-based computers for sharing data across a network. It is easy to see from these two definitions that exploiting RPC could create a lot of havoc on a network. One common RPC exploit creates a denial-of-service situation where applications relying on RPC would not be accessible by anyone on the network. Much of the core communication between systems and servers would be disrupted effectively shutting down the network until the exploit event has been dealt with. Any Linux network utilizing RPC, which is pretty much all of them, should be running the latest patched version available.

As with Windows, Linux applications provide remote connection capabilities for convenient access. Virtual Network Computing (VNC) is a remote access service used for monitoring systems, technical support, and remote administration. As with many remote administration tools, VNC is very effective at making administrators' jobs a little easier by eliminating the need to physically move to another system. As you have probably guessed, there are some vulnerabilities associated with different implementations of VNC. VNC operates on a server-client model and most of the known vulnerabilities are on the side of the client connection. A successful exploit can cause a denial of service, disrupt the ability of remote connections, or gain unauthorized access in more extreme circumstances. If VNC is needed, use a strong password unique from other system administration passwords, limit connections from trusted IP addresses, upgrade to the latest versions, and never connect to a random VNC server. Having a list of all devices where VNC is installed will also help to keep track of what needs to be monitored for upgrades.

In some cases, the default capabilities of a system are not enough to provide security in very sensitive networks. SELinux is an add-on available for most Linux distributions that enhances security, similar to the Group Policies available in Windows. It gives greater granularity of control over files and system resources beyond what native controls are available from the command line. Typically, administrators lock down directories and files based on user account access using the chown and chmod commands to limit access or limit how a user can interact with a file. SELinux adds significantly more capabilities through a list of custom policies that can enforce actions beyond general permissions and file access. A user may need some level of administrative access to work with protected files, but not need the ability to configure network ports. SELinux allows the implementation of limited scope of access, giving the users what they need and nothing more. If available on your system, the configuration file used to enable SELinux is located at /etc/selinux/config. Changing the role to "enforcing" activates these increased security rules.

Many Linux servers are configured to run as web servers, offering up web pages to visitors from all over the world. Apache is the webserver software of choice for these systems. It is a robust and stable software platform that, like many other software applications, comes with some capabilities that could be manipulated and exploited by hackers. Any new installation of web server software running on any operating system should never be placed online until it has been locked down. Many administrators have made the mistake of placing a web server online too soon while they were still in the middle of configuration, only to find themselves hacked in short order. There is no reason to rush the process. Take the time to do it correctly and you will lessen the chance of needing to explain a security incident to management.

The first thing to do after an Apache install is to remove or disable all unnecessary modules. Apache comes with some installed modules an organization will not utilize, so it is wise to strip them out. You can see which modules are installed using the httpd -l command and can remove modules by editing the httpd.conf file. The next hardening method is to deny access to the root directory. This can also be accomplished in the httpd.conf file and ensures no web user will ever be able to view the contents of the root directory. After this, create non-privileged user and group accounts and update the same configuration file with this new information. Many services on servers run as a type of user account and they should be configured to run with the least number of necessary privileges. A webserver running as a root-level account that gets hacked will automatically give the hacker root-level access. If you get hacked, make the attacker work a little harder to gain this level of access.

Other areas of Apache to shore up are hiding the version and operating system information—keeping web users from knowing if the server is running a vulnerable version of the software. This is valuable when new vulnerabilities are discovered and gives you a little more time to get it fixed without worrying about a web crawler detecting the vulnerable version. Disabling directory listings are also important. You do not want visitors to the website looking through listings of every file in every directory. These additional options can be set in the configuration file mentioned above bringing the Apache webserver to a more secure operational status.

Other security risks may pop up with newer versions of software, so look for best security practices for your particular version. This is a good practice for all software applications, not just web servers. Keep in mind the webserver is the public-facing image of the organization designed to be accessed by anyone in the world. If anything needs to be locked down tight, it is this system.

Network Controls

Never rely on a single device to provide all the security for a network. A strong firewall and great ACLs on a router will provide a significant amount of security, but they are not flawless. One minor misconfiguration could allow packets into the network, that should never have made it past the first round of checks. A secure network is defined by having a secure posture with external security devices, updated and patched software, and properly configured hardware on every device. Many devices come with default configurations that need to be changed before being put in operation. Devices with default configurations are some of the easiest to gain access to because the settings are readily available in user manuals and on product websites. Wireless access points are a great example. Lists are available online of default usernames and passwords allowing anyone to log directly into the device with administrative control. Never put a network in that position! Configure new systems to the most secure state necessary. A good place to start on the networking capabilities is with network processes.

IP forwarding is a process that allows traffic coming in on one network interface to be transmitted back out on a different interface—when that traffic is meant for a different network. If a system has multiple network interfaces and each one is connected to a different network, such as 192.168.1.0 and 10.2.12.0, IP forwarding allows packets to be moved between the two. This is normally the function of a router, but a Linux system can perform this operation if IP forwarding is enabled. This is not inherently dangerous if the service is properly configured on each side of the connection and the destination has some form of software firewall in place. In practicality, it is rarely needed and can be disabled to eliminate the potential for future manipulation. The configuration file can be found at /etc/sysctl.con where the net.ipv4.ip forward parameter should be set to the disabled state of 0.

Some processes need network access, and some only need local access. It is important to understand the level of access every process actually needs and limit the ones which do not need to communicate beyond the local system. For example, running a SQL server on a local system purely for the purpose of internally tracking trouble tickets would not need to transmit or receive anything across the internet or communicate with other systems on the network. A software firewall could block communications, which is a good idea, but the process itself should also be configured to only bind to the localhost. This is accomplished within the configuration file of the specific application, so implementation will be different for every configuration. Check the documentation of the specific application to determine which configuration files need to be modified. Taking this action eliminates any communication from taking place with the process and effectively eliminates unauthorized users from establishing a connection.

You may have noticed a trend throughout this chapter of referencing the need to patch applications. It is just as important in Linux as it is in Windows. Patching an application, operating system, or installing the latest version is often the easiest way to eliminate vulnerabilities. Hackers love unpatched systems. They are easy targets that stand out like a bright red LED flashing in the night. Many well-crafted internet searches can locate vulnerabilities on systems offering public services saving attackers a lot of work simply because the vulnerable system is advertising itself to the internet. This is especially true when running web applications with multiple plugins. One vulnerable plugin can make the entire system insecure, and a well-crafted internet search can locate systems using that plugin in a short amount of time. The Easy WP SMTP vulnerability mentioned in Chapter 4 is a great example. Hackers were able to locate thousands of WordPress sites using this plugin and quickly take control of those servers causing traffic to be redirected to advertising servers in Russia.

Keeping a Linux system up to date is similar to any other operating system. Check for new updates regularly and install them as they become available. Use a test system before installing on an operational network to make sure the updates do not break anything. It is rare, but some updates will cause other third-party software to go haywire. It is always best to test first. Most Linux distributions use a package management system that can be updated from the command line. The syntax is a little different from distribution to distribution, but the process is basically the same. Look up the specific commands for the version of Linux in use on your network. These commands will do the job on Debian versions of Linux, such as Kali:

- apt update – updates the local cache from the distribution repository, so the local system knows what applications have newer versions available.
- apt upgrade – downloads and installs new application versions for everything on the system, with some operating system version exceptions.
- apt full-upgrade – upgrades the operating system to the latest available version.
- apt autoremove – removes applications that are no longer required, usually old packages no longer needed by larger applications.

Combine the patching process with a good firewall and a lot of threats can be eliminated. Iptables is the free software firewall available to Linux systems. It operates like many other firewalls by inspecting packets and comparing them to a set of rules. The general response in any firewall results in a packet being accepted or dropped. Packets that match a rule to deny entry will be dropped and unallowed to continue any further. The final line of firewall rule sets is configured to allow all traffic from all locations. This is known as an "implicit allow statement" allowing anything that was not already implicitly denied. Every implementation is slightly different, but the current, popular concept is to deny what you know is bad and allow everything else. Chapter 10 provides some alternative approaches to this strategy that can be implemented with any firewall. Iptables operates in the same fashion as other firewalls using a series of command-based rules to configure categories of accepted and denied traffic. As the name implies, multiple tables are used to determine how traffic is handled:

- Filter table – this is the standard table and the only one most users will ever utilize. Rules are applied based according to data coming into the system, data leaving the system, and data being routed through the system.
- NAT table – this table handles data that cannot be directly routed to destination networks using Network Address Translation.
- Mangle – the mangle table makes adjustments to the properties of the IP header.
- Raw – this table is used to exempt certain types of specified traffic from connection tracking.

Creating rules for Iptables is as simple as typing in a command with the necessary variables:

- List Current Rules: iptables -L
- Block IP Address – iptables -A INPUT -s 10.20.20.40 -j DROP
- Block Port Number – iptables -A INPUT -p tcp --dport 25 -j DROP
- Open Port Number – iptables -A INPUT -p tcp –dport 22 -j ACCEPT

Many of these options can be combined to block ports for specific IP addresses, block all access from a single or entire range of IP addresses, or even allow a specific list of addresses and block everything else. A great security posture, for a network that does not provide services to external users, is to block all inbound traffic originating outside of the network. Every packet will hit a brick wall and never make it into the network. Make exceptions for connections originating inside the network, as a communication stream will need to exist between the user and the external device. Some configurations use this method at the beginning of the ruleset and add allowed connections further down the list to ensure all vases are covered. There are a few different ways this can be implemented. The strategy below is one method; think about your own needs and customize the rules to implement the required security.

- Block all incoming traffic originating outside of the network
  - iptables -t filter -P INPUT DROP
  - iptables -t filter -P FORWARD DROP
  - iptables -t filter -P OUTPUT DROP
- Allow responses from external devices when connections originate within the network
  - iptables -A INPUT -m state --state RELATED,ESTABLISHED -j ACCEPT
  - iptables -A OUTPUT -m state --state RELATED,ESTABLISHED -j ACCEPT

Command Line Necessities

You may have noticed all the Linux hardening methods mentioned so far require the use of the command line. Anyone working in the computer security field should at least have a familiarity with how to navigate using commands. The original days of computing were all command-based and then Graphical User Interfaces (GUI)

came along to make things much easier and more intuitive for users. Much of the power in computing still resides in the command line, and Linux-based systems are typically managed using commands. GUIs also exist in those environments, but it is rare to not drop to a command line for a series of actions. When conducting penetration tests, testers will invariably end up at a command prompt after gaining access and will need to know how to navigate through both Windows and Linux systems, as well as other operating systems depending on the target. Take time to learn the basics of how Linux is structured, where system files are stored, and how to make changes to the many different available capabilities. A basic Linux command line cheat sheet is included in Appendix 1 to help you get started.

Unique Situations

Kali Linux is not designed to be a server-based system providing services to the world. It is designed as a penetration testing system. Some people attempt to harden Kali as soon as they finish the installation, then use it as their everyday Linux system. This can certainly be done but it is not the purpose for this distribution. In fact, hardening Kali is rarely needed if it is used for the intended purpose. A Kali system should not be connected to a network listening for connections and offering services to users. Do not use Kali as a web server, to host a publicly accessible database, or to serve as a storefront. If any of these is the purpose of the system, install a different version of Linux. The best practice for Kali is to install it on a laptop, or run it from a bootable USB drive, and connect it to a network as needed to conduct operations or run updates.

Other secure bootable versions of Linux exist which can be utilized for a variety of functions. If Linux is only used on rare occasions, booting it from a USB is more practical as it will not tie up a system that can be used for other purposes. Just make sure it is updated before using it for any operational purposes. Some people like to use secure bootable operating systems when traveling to avoid the possibility of picking up a virus or having their system penetrated while on a public network. These types of devices are configured to not save any data and revert to a default state after each use. This can be very beneficial in foreign nations—known to actively and aggressively attempt monitoring of all internet activity—including breaking into user systems when possible. A bootable distribution makes it impossible for anyone to gain a long-term foothold on your system. Any concern of malware or penetration can be solved with a quick reboot.

Tails is one such secure bootable system running on Debian Linux. It has been designed to eliminate as much tracking as possible. It does this through a variety of methods. First, Tails does not save any data to the USB drive or the drives within the system. Everything is conducted within memory space and lost when the computer is shut down or rebooted. Second, Tails routes all traffic through The Onion Router (Tor) network making it difficult for anyone to track a user's digital footprint as they traverse the web. Tor routes all traffic through a series of hopping points, 3 is the default configuration but that can be changed, bouncing every packet from one system to another before ultimately connecting to the site you intend to visit. All data flows through this multi-hop connection, supposedly making tracing efforts impossible unless an investigator or hacker has access to the systems used for the hops. This could allow close to perfect anonymity in online activity, but rumors in recent years have raised suspicion that Tor's algorithms have been compromised; though no one really knows for sure.

The third method of Tails to protect privacy is the prevention of tracking cookies used by many organizations for the purpose of advertising or data collection. Routing traffic through Tor obscures your true identity and location from these organizations. Tails does allow the ability to have some persistent storage where internet bookmarks and other regularly used documents can be stored. It would be wise to use this capability sparingly as it will reveal some minor information about internet activity if regularly used. It is best to use it for the intended purpose of secure, anonymous use of the internet. Some may think it could be used for criminal activity, and that is true, but it can also be used by journalists operating in communist countries, intelligence operators desiring to stay under the wire, and even crime victims attempting to escape dangerous situations. It never hurts to have a tool like Tails available just in case it is needed. And it is free, which is always an added bonus.

Intentionally vulnerable versions of Linux also exist as practice systems for penetration testing. Installing these in a virtual environment, or on an old system, can be beneficial for training, and also for practicing how to remove vulnerabilities or harden services. These distributions are purposefully riddled with vulnerabilities to show users how easy it can be to penetrate a weakened system. Damn Vulnerable Linux (DVL) is an older distribution that has been used for this purpose for many years. It is no longer maintained or updated but is still a good practicing target. One way to practice hardening Linux is to scan something like DVL and then systematically attempt to remove each vulnerability by installing patches, updating software versions, fixing configurations, or disabling unneeded services. Any type of regular practice will make the job of hardening a system in the real world much easier. Learn the common vulnerabilities for the systems you use and eliminate each one every time there is a new install or upgrade.

Hardening an operating system is not a difficult process. It can be mundane stepping through a variety of options and configurations with the hopes that each new modification makes the system slightly more secure from an attack. Just as a chain is only as strong as its weakest link, a network is only as strong as its most vulnerable system. A hacker scanning a firewall will see listening services from any operating system on the opposite end of the firewall. A smart hacker will recognize the differences and know if the responses are coming from one system or multiple. They will also know, with relative certainty, what operating system is being used. Attackers are just as keen to break into a Linux system as any other system. Maybe more so because it is more likely to be a server and provide a greater degree of access. Linux systems do not need as much patching and configuring as Windows, but some tweaks definitely need to be made to shore up weaker areas. Do not overlook any system in the hardening process.

Practical Application – Simple Lockdown Steps

Locking down a Linux system is slightly more difficult than Windows, but still relatively easy to accomplish. As with Windows, if multiple Linux systems are deployed, it is wise to have baseline images that can be installed on new systems. These baselines make standardization much easier and reduce the amount of work required when systems need to be installed or refreshed. The baselines will need to be updated often enough to keep up with the most recent patches and updates but installations between these updates can simply be configured manually. It is more likely Linux will be used as a server, except in odd cases such as pen testing, so a baseline may not be necessary. These steps are enough to harden Linux-based systems; you will see some similarities here with the Windows hardening chapter because the concepts are the same:

1. Remove all unauthorized software.
2. Remove all unneeded software pre-installed by manufacturers.
3. Update applications to the latest version after configuring on a test network.
4. Disable remote root logins.
5. Limit root-level access to specific needs through groups and the sudo command.
6. Install all operating system and application patches after configuring on a test network.
7. Install antivirus software.
8. Install iptables or another Linux-compatible firewall.
9. Install software-based HIDS.
10. Establish strong access controls to files and services.
11. Run internal vulnerability scans against the system and adjust settings based on results.

Chapter 9: Review Questions

1. Linux is _____ for being highly vulnerable to attack.
   a. Known
   b. Not known
   c. Renowned
   d. Famous
2. It is _____ to view operating system manufacturers negatively due to the amount of code involved in their programming.
   a. Unfair
   b. Fair
   c. Stupid
   d. Ridiculous
3. Linux is most often used as a _____, not a _____.
   a. Workstation. server
   b. Video editor, email server
   c. Server, workstation
   d. Domain controller, web server
4. Many concepts for hardening Windows are _____ for Linux.
   a. Different
   b. Identical
   c. Damaging
   d. The same
5. File _____ should be locked down.
   a. Names
   b. Permissions
   c. Locations
   d. Arrangement
6. The chown command _____.
   a. Assigns access level
   b. Assigns ownership
   c. Assigns encryption algorithm
   d. Disables external access
7. The chmod command _____.
   a. Assigns access level
   b. Assigns ownership
   c. Assigns encryption algorithm
   d. Disables external access
8. Permission _____ is the result of added access over time.
   a. Increase
   b. Allowance
   c. Jerk
   d. Creep
9. Regular permission _____ can curb unintentional higher access.
   a. Creep
   b. Review
   c. Increase
   d. Decrease
10. A system can _____ if boot-level system files are modified.
    a. Excel
    b. Run smoothly
    c. Crash
    d. Ignite on fire
11. _____ is one of the most common services seen on Linux systems.
    a. FTP
    b. SSH
    c. RDP
    d. NTP
12. _____ is the common web server software used on Linux systems.
    a. Edge
    b. Firefox
    c. Explorer
    d. Apache
13. Hiding the _____ and _____ makes it harder to attack Apache.
    a. Location, version
    b. Version, location
    c. Version, operating system
    d. Location, operating system
14. IP forwarding should be _____ in most configurations.
    a. Enabled
    b. Disabled
    c. Deleted
    d. Installed

15. _____ is the easiest way to eliminate vulnerabilities.
    a. Switching
    b. Routing
    c. Firewalling
    d. Patching
16. _____ is the common firewall application on Linux.
    a. IP Blocks
    b. IP Sheets
    c. IP Tables
    d. IP Routes
17. _____ versions of Linux on USB drives can be great temporary security solutions.
    a. Fast
    b. Efficient
    c. Safe
    d. Secure
18. Knowledge of the _____ is _____ for securing Linux systems.
    a. CLI, essential
    b. CLI, not essential
    c. GUI, essential
    d. GUI, not essential
19. _____ should not be used as an everyday system or server.
    a. Redhat
    b. Ubuntu
    c. Debian
    d. Kali
20. _____ vulnerable Linux distributions can be used for practice.
    a. Unintentional
    b. Intentional
    c. Dangerous
    d. Safe

Hardening Network

CHAPTER 10

Hardening a network starts with physical security. There is a simple reality in the cyber security world: once physical access is gained, the game is over. There are many ways to reset system administration passwords with bootable CDs or USB drives. Network devices can also be similarly reset. Easy access to a switch could allow someone to plug in their laptop configured with Kali Linux and immediately start scanning their way through the internal network. If you can gain physical access to a system or device on the network, you stand a great chance of acquiring administrator-level rights within minutes and establishing a strong foothold regardless of how many external security devices are on the network. Almost every physical device from servers to firewalls and even security systems have internal methods to reset lost or forgotten passwords. This is easy to take advantage of when that device is sitting in front of you. Physical security must be the first place we look when thinking about network hardening. Failing here makes much of the remaining work an easily defeated waste of time.

In the early days of cyber security, this was one of the easier things to pull off. Recall from your earlier reading on social engineering how a good social engineer could talk their way past security, secretaries, and other staff members with well-designed stories. This tends to be much more difficult today as years of training have heightened the awareness of even everyday users to notice and question those who do not belong. The physical security problem has mostly changed from poor awareness of visitors to authorized users having too much access and availability. Edward Snowden was able to siphon secrets and walk them right out of a highly secure facility simply because he had access. The proper motivation can provide an authorized user all they need to manipulate data, install malicious software, or set up connections accessible from external locations. Putting simple measures in place can limit users and system administrators from engaging in these types of activities.

As already mentioned, USB ports can be an easy point of entry into a network. An easy way to stop this is to disable all USB ports on all user systems attached to the network. This may be difficult if users routinely transfer files between systems or move content between home and work systems, but that is likely only a small number of people, so leaving these ports enabled on only necessary systems all but eliminates this risk. This also has the secondary effect of lessening the possibility of viruses inadvertently being copied onto systems. Any necessary files required to be copied onto a system can be moved by system administrators to ensure users are not knowingly or unknowingly inserting malicious content onto the network. Those systems with USB ports enabled should be configured with measures limiting the copying of executable files and only allowing traditional office-related documents. Most computers today do not include external media devices such as readers for CD, DVD, or Blu-ray discs, but disabling these on older systems, in the same way, is also imperative.

Firewalls are the primary gatekeepers on the network—controlling access through open and closed ports ideally denying any traffic not explicitly allowed. The only open inbound ports on the firewall should be those corresponding with internal services being offered to external users. The most common open ports are those for web servers, email servers, and VPN devices. Some organizations may also have software running on customized port numbers for clients to make connections, though, in today's computing environment, many of those applications are web-based and will route through the same web server ports. For example, the two common ports used for web servers are 80 and 443. Those ports should be open if you offer that service to the world. Port 22 is typically used for secure shell, which is a secure remote connection application. There is no reason to have port 22 open if there are no computers configured to receive secure shell connections. The fewer open ports, the fewer possibilities for hackers.

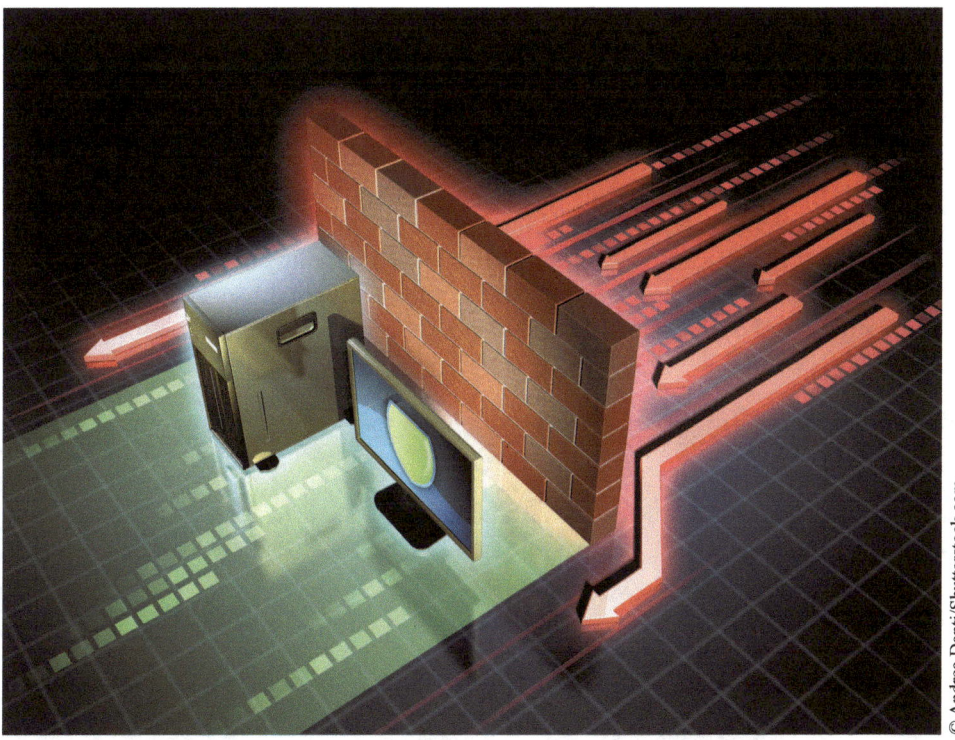

Think of the firewall as entry points to your house. Every unlocked window and door in your house is a potential entry point for a criminal. If you leave all the windows and doors unlocked 24 hours a day, you are providing many opportunities for someone to enter your house. Of course, the average person does not climb through a window to gain access, so those points can be cut off by locking the windows. Residents also do not generally walk through the back yard and enter through the back door, so that one can be locked as well. All that is left is the front door. Authorized visitors are either given a key to come and go as they please, or they are required to knock and request entry. Unauthorized users who knock can be turned away or simply ignored. We do not let everyone in our house, and we should not let everyone in our networks either.

When hackers first scan a network, the responses they receive are based on the open firewall ports. Imagine for a moment that you have four systems behind a firewall providing services to external customers. You have a web server running on TCP port 443, an email server running on TCP port 993, a VPN device utilizing TCP port 1194, and a Linux server offering secure shell connections on TCP port 22. A proper scan of the firewall will inform the hacker that these four ports are open and provide connections for these four services. If they attempt a connection to port 25, it will fail because port 25 is closed. The hacker in this scenario has four specific ports to check for vulnerable services that can be directly attacked. Any methodology they use will have to go through one of these ports or creatively work around them by manipulating user weaknesses.

VPN devices provide a secure, encrypted external connection for authorized users to remotely connect to the network, potentially from anywhere in the world. This capability essentially extends the network over the internet allowing the user to access resources on the internal network in the same way as if they were physically sitting in the office. VPNs are also used to provide users a greater degree of privacy when using the internet by routing all their traffic through a VPN service provider's system, effectively masking their activity from internet service providers. The first use case is most often used within corporate environments while the second use case is becoming more popular for individual users concerned about being monitored online. Both are valid uses, but the focus here is on the corporate use of VPN devices.

© Funtap/Shutterstock.com

VPN access can be controlled by limiting who can connect and what locations are authorized to establish connections. The typical application in a corporate environment is allowing certain users to establish connections from their homes. In these instances, VPN access can be restricted to a list of home IP addresses of authorized users. Usernames and passwords are also used to add a secondary layer of security. Other use cases are for corporate travelers who need to connect while on business trips. In these cases, restricting access to an IP address will be difficult because the address will always be different. Usernames and passwords should be used in these instances and those accounts should be disabled when employees return to the office.

The average network consists of a few network devices and a lot of systems connected to a single network segment. This is perfectly acceptable for a small organization with a handful of users and very little sensitive data to protect. For larger organizations, dividing the network up into multiple segments creates an additional layer of security where more sensitive data can be isolated away from unauthorized users. This lessens the possibility of insider activity—or authorized users choosing to use their access for malicious purposes—making it more difficult for hackers to expand a foothold if they are lucky enough to get past the perimeter. A secure segment on the network is a great way to harden sections where more sensitive data is stored, or sensitive operations are conducted. Secret plans for a flying car should not be on the main network. Those should be tucked away where very few people have access.

Network segments are configured by placing a router and firewall on the internal portion of the network to isolate it into its own proverbial island. These segments will have separate IP address ranges and the firewalls will be configured to disallow any communication between the main network and the isolated one. Any user on the main network attempting to access resources in the isolated segment will be denied by the firewall. Users on the secure segment may still have access to some internet capabilities or may be completely isolated, depending on the configuration. In even more sensitive arenas, separate networks that have no connection to the outside world or any other network segment can also be set up. If you do not want a hacker to gain access, this is a sure-fire way to do it. It is impossible to hack into a network that is not connected to the internet unless, of course, you have physical access.

Of course, every network has system and network administrators who have been trusted with a higher degree of access to systems, data, and devices. Restricting special access to a small number of individuals is a normal security process simply due to the nature of someone's job. But even system administrators can make mistakes that create vulnerabilities or succumb to the idea of using their access for other purposes. An easy way to combat these problems is through a rotation of duties. A sole employee managing all user accounts may be very effective at his job but have zero oversight on how those accounts are being managed. Old accounts from previous employees could still exist on the network. User accounts with too many privileges could accidentally be created, allowing access to sensitive data. Similarly, a sole administrator responsible for managing all firewalls could easily open unnecessary ports allowing potentially malicious traffic to flow through the network. Rotating these duties puts another set of eyes on the work to catch mistakes and verify high-level insider activity is not taking place. A good methodology is to rotate positions every few days, which also comes with several secondary effects.

Requiring administrators to rotate to different positions creates a more well-rounded team capable of working many, if not all, positions within their area of responsibility. It is rare for a Windows administrator to manage routers and firewalls and vice versa. Training users to do each other's job in a type of cross-pollination provides a secondary layer of security, lessens the chance for mistakes, and creates continuity during contingencies. Job rotation also keeps one individual from ever becoming indispensable because they are the only one who knows how to do a particular task. This happens quite often in unhealthy organizations allowing a single administrator to amass too much power. The story of Terry Childs, who formerly worked for the city of San Francisco, is a great example of this scenario. After being removed from his job, he refused to provide the passwords he alone knew, effectively holding the affected network hostage. He was eventually convicted of a crime but had he worked for a smaller company, the courts would have likely never been involved. Rotating duties eliminates this potential problem before it can ever be created.

A peripheral topic to rotating administrative duties is the separation of duties, which divides sensitive actions among several users, so no single user has unfettered control. This is more nuanced and may not be possible in all environments, but in situations where systems or data are extremely sensitive to the operation of a company, requiring this level of split access ensures no single individual ever has sole access. This is commonly seen in nuclear missile silos where two operators are always required to be present and the launching of any missile requires actions from both operators. This could also be implemented in a network environment through access controls that require multiple users to login in order to conduct any actions. This level of security eliminates the possibility of a single user stealing data, modifying systems, or creating potential vulnerabilities without anyone else's knowledge.

Normal users can also become unsuspecting security risks when permission creep affects their accounts. Permission creep occurs when an ordinary user has been assigned to many different duties during the course of a long career with the same company. Over time they begin to collect new levels of access as they take on a new position. It is common for a system administrator to simply add new permissions onto an account without auditing the account to see if previous permissions are no longer required. In the right scenario, a regular user could conceivably amass access to almost as much company data as executives and administrators. This is an oversight that can be easily corrected whenever users request new levels of access. System administrators should have a chart showing access levels required by each company position and, ideally, assign positions based on groups instead of individually granting specific levels of access. Permissions no longer required should be removed ensuring permission creep does not become a problem.

One of the major hurdles of advancement in cyber security was the inclusion of basic security training for all users. Normal users are a common target for attackers because they do not always understand how important their role is in the security process. It is the unsuspecting user who clicks a malicious link in an email, visits a website they thought was legitimate, or downloads a file that turns out to be a virus. It is common knowledge that if you send a well-crafted email with a malicious link to a larger organization, there is a high chance at least one person will click on the link. This is so well known that penetration testers tend to include this practice in their own process to test how many users fall for the bait. This does not mean users are stupid. It simply means they have not yet been fully trained on how to spot a nefarious actor trying to gain unauthorized access.

Another common test is to place a USB drive on a bathroom counter with an enticing label such as "pay raises," "layoffs," or "investigation" affixed to the side. It is very difficult for a curious employee to see this type of device and not want to plug it into their computer. The earlier mentioned security method of disabling USB ports keeps this from being a problem but imagine what would happen if the drive had malware on it. A user could introduce a slew of problems simply due to their curiosity and the savvy technique of a hacker. And this does not have to take

place in a company bathroom. This same type of drive could be left in a local restaurant or even on the ground in a parking lot. Untrained users tend to take the bait, and when they do, they can easily be snared into a serious trap.

How do we keep a user from clicking a link or inserting a USB drive? Quality training teaches not just what the problem is, but why the problem exists, and what can happen if the problem is exploited. Users need to know they are very much on the front line of defensive security. Training users on the basics of how these types of attacks work, the common wording seen in emails, the malicious activity that can take place if successful, and the potential aftermath will make them more aware of the reason certain measures are in place. Users can easily get frustrated when they are told USB drives are banned from all systems and links are disabled in external emails. They may see it as another attempt by security to control their activity. But explaining the reason why the policies are in place helps to educate users on the dangers, so they understand how to keep their systems safe, both at work and at home. Email security is a big piece of the puzzle.

Email is a great avenue for attack because it does not require working around a firewall or sneaking an exploit through an IDS. Email ports are already open, and users are ready to receive whatever is sent their way. Hackers can "go fishing" with a phishing email without the need for a lot of public reconnaissance. All they need is a list of email addresses and they are off to the races. Phishing is the attempt by hackers to convince a user to click on a link, follow some type of malicious resource, or provide personal information. Some phishing attempts are broad with the same link sent to thousands of users hoping at least one will be unable to resist clicking away. Other attempts, such as spear phishing, are more targeted towards a smaller subset of people such as all employees in the same department. Some spear phishing attempts can even be narrowed down to specific people if enough information is publicly available on the internet.

The reason this can be so effective? Because links clicked on the internal side of the network establish an outbound connection, bypassing the firewall's inbound rule sets. New connections established from outside of the network require the use of an open port to gain access. Outbound connections typically grab a high numbered port and establish a stateful connection with the external resource. In the case of a phishing email link, the user's computer would establish a connection to the hacker's server, typically triggering the download of malicious software. That software could be a backdoor providing the attacker with long-term access, a virus designed to wipe out the victim's hard drive, or any number of other malicious actions. It makes the hacker's job very easy when a user falls for this type of trick. Obviously, the hacker's goal is to get some type of content onto the victim system, and since email is always an open door, it can be targeted from anywhere in the world. Random USB drives left in bathrooms function similarly.

Users should be trained, at a minimum, on the following:

- Common attacks
- Potential impacts
- Security methods
- Personal methods

IDS and IPS devices typically do not need to be hardened after an attack. They may, however, need to have their signatures and alerts updated to catch similar attacks more easily in the future. If the IDS/IPS did not successfully catch the attack, it will need to be configured based on what was learned from the forensic investigation. If it did catch the attack, look for ways to optimize its capabilities to collect more data on this particular attack vector. The more we know about how an attack took place, the easier we can catch the attacker in the future.

A configuration control board (CCB) is a team of employees, usually made up of senior members of the IT department and other management, that approves changes to the network or individual systems. These teams are responsible for making sure company policy is upheld in all matters related to hardware and software. It can be annoying to request approval for simple changes, but as the gatekeepers, they ensure applications are not installed that may conflict with other services on the network, confirm new hardware is fully compatible, and attempt to keep anything dangerous from ever being used. For example, if a new server needs to be installed to replace something outdated, the CCB controls the timeline, testing, and contingency process that makes the installation as seamless as possible. A CCB typically meets on a regular schedule. It could be as often as every week in large organizations with a lot of moving parts, or as seldom as quarterly if changes are rarely made. Use these teams as a way to provide oversight on all updates.

Non-traditional ideas

Everything covered so far is standard for hardening a network and has been implemented in a variety of ways over the past two decades. Other more effective and drastic approaches exist that can eliminate more than 99% of the attack possibilities on the internet, but they come with a cost. Whitelisting can be the answer if an organization is willing to make a drastic change. Whitelisting is a method of limiting connections to a network based on a pre-approved list of known safe IP addresses or websites. If a company does not do business with China, there is no reason to allow connections from China onto the network. This is also true for any other country on the planet. Blocking an entire nation is not a difficult task, but we can narrow it down even further by outsourcing the webserver to a 3rd party and applying a whitelist that extremely restricts connectivity.

The first thing to determine is what access should be allowed. Employees tend to enjoy a liberal amount of web access from work. Outside of using a proxy server blocking adult content, known hacking sites, and similar content, workers are generally free to surf to their heart's content so long as it does not affect their work performance. Companies tend to put this in the morale category. Allowing an employee to check sports scores, read the news, and even do a bit of shopping makes the work environment less monotonous by giving employees something to do in between tasks. None of this is strictly necessary to the mission of the job, and some of it actually creates an opportunity for hackers to gain access. Not through a website per se, but because such broad access allows other connections to probe the network's defenses.

There are over one billion websites on the internet. There are more than four billion IP version 4 addresses. There are even more IP version 6 addresses. An organization never has a need for all those addresses to connect to their network. Even when involved in international business, the website is usually the primary connection point. A list of a few hundred websites could be added to a whitelist, allowing employees with some morale boosters, and the rest of the internet can be effectively turned off. What is the risk of being hacked when only 200 IP addresses can make a connection? What is the risk of being hacked from a well-known news website or store? The odds are incredibly low. A solid whitelist is a simpler method eliminating the need for many other layers of security. Even phishing becomes benign since the malicious links are not included on the approved list of IP addresses.

Why do more organizations not implement whitelisting? That is a good question. Some simply have not considered it. Others think it is too much work to manage. There are very few instances where whitelisting is not a great solution. It is one of the easiest and cheapest methodologies you can put in place to secure your network. Worried about ransomware? Set up a whitelist. Concerned about phishing attempts? Set up a whitelist. Worried about backdoors installed on a user system and establishing connections to an unknown location? Set up a whitelist. You get the idea. Whitelisting is not the most traditional idea, but it is one using the most incredibly effective elements of security technology to stop hackers in their tracks. Traditional cyber security allows by default and denies by exception. Anything that is not explicitly denied is implicitly allowed. That is a horrible way to manage security. We do not implicitly allow everyone through our front doors. We do the opposite. We deny by default and allow by exception. It is a much safer methodology and frees up a lot of time for security professionals to manage other areas of the network.

Social media is another avenue of concern. Your whitelist can allow social media sites as the risk of being hacked from one is low. The greater risk with these sites is the ability for employees to share company data directly onto these public platforms. Most organizations have official social media accounts managed by specific employees allowed to speak on behalf of the company. Those employees can share data and promote the company's products or positions. No one else has a legitimate need to access or use this content using the company network. It is not difficult to copy and paste information from sensitive documents directly to Facebook. One disgruntled employee with the right level of access can sink an organization very quickly on social media platforms. It is an easy thing to leave off the whitelist and employees can simply use their own smartphones if they want to access this content.

Wireless access has become as common as any other network service in today's computing environment and has been riddled with security weaknesses since the original development of Wi-Fi. The original 802.11 protocol included a rudimentary security protocol, known as wireless equivalency protocol (WEP), that could be broken in a few minutes in the right circumstance. Wi-Fi Protected Access (WPA), the update to WEP, was a little better but still allowed for an easy siphoning of encrypted credentials out of the air that could be broken offline with a password hacking application. WPA2 has similar problems, and while the latest iteration of WPA3 is better, it too includes some security challenges. The challenge with Wi-Fi is wireless connections require data to be transmitted through the air and anyone within proximity will be able to snatch packets out of the air. Those packets can turn into plaintext passwords if they are weak enough. This does not mean we should eliminate Wi-Fi. It only means passwords need to be significantly strong enough on Wi-Fi routers to shore up the weaknesses in the protocol.

A good rule of thumb is to make the password as long as reasonably possible. Unlike user passwords, Wi-Fi passwords do not need to be remembered and entered every time a connection is made, so they can be composed of a longer and stronger mix of alphanumeric and special characters. The encrypted passwords used by WPA and WPA2 can be easily grabbed out of the air in a few seconds. If that password is weak, a password cracker can break it in under one minute. It is not a difficult process when weak passwords are used. It is also not difficult to set up a stronger password which can almost completely eliminate this level of risk. Wi-Fi security is low-hanging fruit that can be easily locked down with a few steps. Filtering access based on Mac addresses used to be a common recommendation as well, but as networks have grown, this capability became more difficult to effectively implement. You really only need two steps: set a strong Wi-Fi password and force network authentication.

When using Wi-Fi in a corporate environment, all Wi-Fi users should be forced into a network authentication process before they can access the internet or any other network resource. If you have used free public Wi-Fi at a hotel, coffee shop, or airport in the past decade, you have seen how those networks redirect you to some form of login page before access is granted. Many of those are simple validation processes. In a corporate environment, Wi-Fi users can be redirected to a network login server that requires authentication with network credentials. This allows the user to log in to the same network wired users are using and access the same resources. Wi-Fi can be incredibly beneficial within an organization because it allows employees to function away from their desks and lessens the need for installing and upgrading physical network cabling throughout a building. Most users at home are strictly Wi-Fi and this is also the case in many smaller organizations. Use it to your advantage, just make sure it is locked down.

When hardening a network previously hacked, the first goal is to fix the entry point the hacker used to gain access. This can include multiple changes from closing ports, updating IDS/IPS configurations, and updating individual systems. In most instances, the fix comes in the form of a patch for the victim system. You learned about that in earlier chapters where specific hardening content for Windows and Linux was covered. For the network side of things, the common changes are configurations. A quick block of an IP address, change to a port configuration, or limiting of a protocol is typically all that is needed. The best way to routinely keep your network secure is to make updates as needed and maintain vigilance in monitoring network traffic.

Remember, hackers cannot gain access to something if they are explicitly blocked. That will always be the easiest way to keep them out of your network. Cyber security does not have to be as difficult as some believe. There are plenty of simple solutions, such as whitelisting, that can provide a high degree of security with very little work. One of your goals while managing security on a network should be to look for creative solutions to take your security to the next level. Here is one reality: hackers already know the common methodologies employed on networks. They have read some of the same books, used the same applications, and visited the same security websites as you. The experienced hackers will likely know more about security than you. They have the upper hand because, while security professionals need to be correct 100% of the time, hackers only need to get lucky once to gain access.

Practical Application – Locking Down the Network

The ability to lock down a network is determined by how many devices an organization wants to deploy and the level of allowed user access to convenient but unnecessary services. An increased number of deployed network devices will create a larger budget for hardware and employees tasked to configure and maintain, as well as those monitoring the traffic and alerts. Security is often the nemesis of convenience. Convenience can keep stronger security methods from being put in place making the job of security professionals more difficult. Do not side with convenience. This methodology will put your network in a very secure position:

1. Maintain a strong firewall at the perimeter of the network. Only open ports absolutely necessary for conducting business.
2. Locate an IDS near the perimeter to monitor all incoming and outgoing traffic.
3. Outsource email and web services to third parties effectively eliminating two major avenues of attack.
4. Encrypt all sensitive data.
5. Create an internal network segment for sensitive systems or data. Protect these segments with separate firewalls and IDSs.
6. Limit VPN access to employees.
7. Implement whitelisting or nationwide blocks to further protect open ports.
8. Use a DMZ for all public-facing servers.
9. Implement a backup plan with daily routines for all servers and critical systems.

Chapter 10: Review Questions

1. Years of training has _____ the awareness of everyday users.
   a. Heightened
   b. Lessoned
   c. Bored
   d. Eliminated

2. Which of these will stop many physical access attacks?
   a. Triple Login Requirements
   b. Host-Based Firewalls
   c. Disabling USB ports and removing other media drives
   d. Two Factor Authentication

3. _____ are the primary gatekeepers on the network.
   a. Switches
   b. Routers
   c. Firewalls
   d. VPNs

4. Initial external scans reveal what?
   a. Open ports on a firewall
   b. All Linux Systems
   c. All Windows systems
   d. All of the above

5. Which device provides a secure external connection?
   a. Router
   b. Firewall
   c. Switch
   d. VPN

6. Dividing a network into _____ provides an additional layer of _____.
   a. Virtual Systems, Obfuscation
   b. Segments, Security
   c. Layers, Security
   d. Segments, Obfuscation

7. It is impossible to hack into a network that is _____.
   a. Patched
   b. Secured
   c. Monitored
   d. Not connected to the internet

8. _____ can make mistakes that create vulnerabilities.
   a. System administrators
   b. Users
   c. Hackers
   d. All of the above

9. Rotating administrative positions creates a more _____ team.
   a. Disconnected
   b. Incapable
   c. Unhappy
   d. Well-rounded

10. _____ is when a user's access increases over time as a result of different work positions.
    a. Permission slide
    b. Permission reduction
    c. Permission creep
    d. Permission increase

11. _____ are a common target for hackers.
    a. Normal users
    b. Administrators
    c. Managers
    d. CEOs

12. Simple _____ can introduce a slew of vulnerabilities.
    a. Curiosity
    b. Paranoia
    c. Fear
    d. Weakness

13. _____ is a great avenue of attack because it does not require working around a firewall.
    a. Web servers
    b. Firewalls
    c. Media applications
    d. Email

14. Outbound connections _____ the incoming firewall rule sets.
    a. Use
    b. Check
    c. Bypass
    d. Authorize

15. A _____ can provide an attacker with long-term access.
    a. Front door
    b. Window
    c. Hole
    d. Back door
16. Which team approves changes to the network?
    a. C-level employees
    b. Configuration control board
    c. System control board
    d. Security control board
17. Which non-standard method can block 99% of all threats?
    a. Whitelisting
    b. Blacklisting
    c. Greylisting
    d. Redlisting
18. Wi-Fi access should include _____.
    a. Authorization
    b. Authentication
    c. Indoctrination
    d. Filtering
19. Hackers cannot gain access if they are explicitly _____.
    a. Invited
    b. Unauthorized
    c. Allowed
    d. Blocked
20. WPA is easily hacked when weak _____ are used.
    a. Authenticators
    b. Users
    c. Passwords
    d. Algorithms

Chapter 11
Cloud Security

The early days of computing consisted of configurations that closely mirror today's cloud construct. Large mainframe systems filled massive warehouse spaces and small terminals were used to access their capabilities. The data was stored on the mainframe. The operating system and computational power were in the mainframe. The terminals were referred to as "dumb terminals" because they only functioned as an interface to the mainframe. They had no power or capability of their own. Users would work from these terminals to issue commands for the mainframe to carry out. It functioned well for its time but also came with many limitations. The greatest limitation was that user interaction was limited to the number of available dumb terminals which often created a line of workers waiting for their turn. Scheduling time on the mainframe was very important in that era and would not work well with so many internet users today.

Technology eventually grew to the point where we could have massive computational power in the palm of our hands, and in many cases, the power in today's smartphones exceeds the capabilities of these old mainframes. The desktop computers and laptops in use today house the primary computing power and applications utilized by users. The majority of work conducted day-to-day is done on one of these systems. Users no longer need to compete for timeslots on a mainframe or wait for someone to finish working at a terminal before they can issue their own commands. The capabilities we have today far exceed what was available a few decades ago, and yet we still have this need for a mainframe style of computing providing us additional capabilities. Personal computers, as amazing as they are, sometimes need additional storage capabilities, greater processing power for incredibly complex operations, or a place to house applications many users can access simultaneously.

Google launched an experimental idea with their Chrome operating system in July 2009 based on the simple notion that most user activity is conducted online. Email is stored in an email server. Music is streamed from a remotely located platform. Internet browsing viewed content from all over the world. Office documents and spreadsheets could also be stored and edited completely online. Google's notion was that none of this content required large amounts of storage space or operating system overhead. A user could essentially purchase, what amounts to a souped-up version of the old dumb terminals and use the device for their day-to-day activities. The experiment did not fail, but it never reached a level where people completely replaced their more capable machines for this new device. It eventually became a budget system for teenagers or college students who could not afford something more powerful. It fits a niche, but that is about all it does.

Cloud computing has taken on an interesting hybrid-use style where users can access data online and still have the power of a more traditional computer at their fingertips. The ability to access data remotely has become a top priority and a big business. Almost everything has taken on a mobile perspective. We no longer need to store our entire music catalog on a computer. We can simply stream it from the internet whenever we like. And if we are going to be offline for a while, synching a local copy of the music to a computer is an easy option. The entertainment world has captured the use of cloud technology probably better than anyone else, as movies and music have moved almost completely to a cloud-based infrastructure. We now have the best of both technological capabilities with great local computing power and the ability to access non-local data from anywhere in the world. So, how do we secure this configuration?

Security needs to be considered as part of the overall construct of these technologies. Network devices and user access controls for cloud networks are largely the same as any other network. At the end of the day, the cloud is essentially made up of the same types of hardware and software used in any corporate environment. It is a collection of servers, firewalls, routers, and other applicable network devices along with systems used by administrators to keep everything functioning properly. The core network hardening methods used in any other environment can and should be used in a cloud-based infrastructure. This means the organization offering cloud services should have the same security protocols in place as any other network. Clouds are designed to provide connections to people all over the world, so by their nature, they need to allow incoming connections on the specific ports used to offer their service. This is one network infrastructure where whitelisting is not a viable option.

Cloud Technology Primer

Today's cloud technologies fall into three general categories: software as a service (SaaS), platform as a service (PaaS), and infrastructure as a service (IaaS). Each category provides a different capability for users with a little overlap in who manages each piece. The most common cloud capabilities everyday users are familiar with are in the SaaS category. SaaS gives users access to applications over the internet. Online storage capabilities such as Dropbox, OneDrive, iCloud, and Google drive all provide a software application that allows for the storing and retrieval of data. Video conferencing software, such as Zoom and WebEx, connect users from around the world with video and audio capabilities. Even email is technically in the SaaS category when using email servers located off the local network. PaaS provides an infrastructure for organizations to run their own applications on someone else's hardware. The provider handles all hardware maintenance, patching, and updates allowing the user to focus solely on their individual software needs. The Google App engine and Facebook are well-known examples of PaaS. IaaS builds on PaaS capabilities adding control over the operating system, physical or virtualized systems, depending on what the budget can handle. Amazon Web Services and Microsoft Azure are two examples of IaaS.

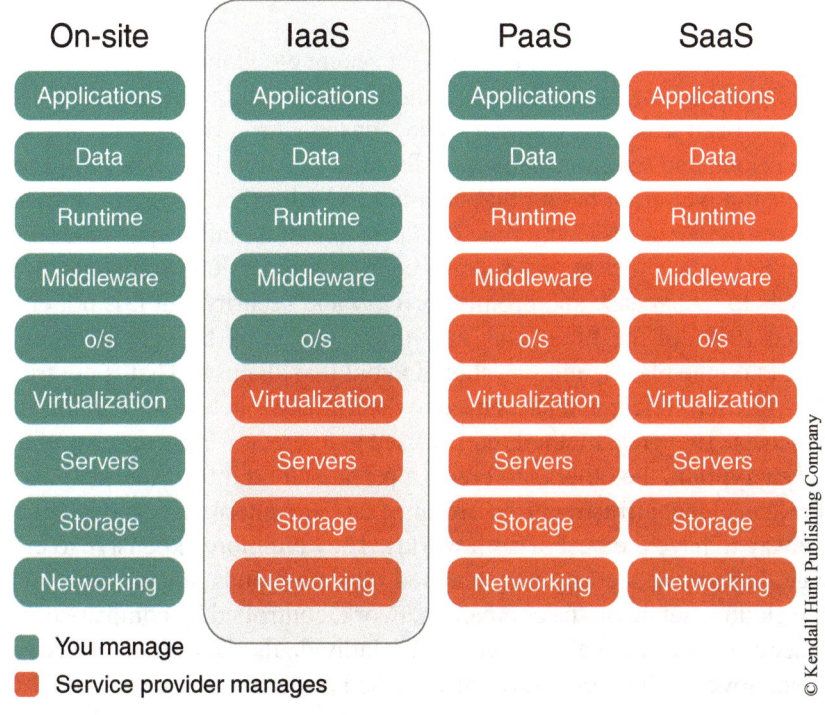

The biggest security concern – when using a public cloud service – is employees administering the cloud infrastructure. Any data stored in that infrastructure is potentially at risk of being viewed by any of the cloud company's employees. For example, if Bob's Electronics decides to open an online file storage account with Maximus Storage Solutions, they would have to be certain their data was secure from prying eyes. Any employee at Maximus could potentially access their data, provide it to competing companies, or even dump it on the internet for others to see. The challenge here is that the customer has zero control over who works for the company providing cloud services. Assurances could be made that everything will be secure, but there is no actual proof, outside of physically inspecting the facilities, that security is a top priority. This should be a concern for anyone using cloud services and servers, as a warning to never store sensitive data on a cloud infrastructure you do not have 100% control over.

In 2014 nude celebrity photos were leaked from one of Apple's cloud services that created international news as multiple female celebrities had private images plastered all over the internet. How did those images move from what was supposed to be private cloud-based accounts to public servers anyone could access? That question was never publicly answered, but one very good possibility is an employee accessed the user accounts, viewed their stored images, and made copies to share with others. It is a very likely scenario a curious employee decided to peruse the iCloud accounts of celebrities to see what type of content they were storing. They may have been surprised to find so many sensitive and compromising images, or maybe that is exactly what they were hoping to discover. And now, those pictures are available all over the internet and will never become private again. There is no taking it back. Once something goes digital online it can be copied millions of times. Even if someone was able to successfully sue websites to have these images removed, others could have already downloaded each one and shared them in other locations.

This example drives home the need for secure cloud infrastructures. In the case of the leaked photos, the celebrities endured a lot of embarrassment. But anything could have been leaked. A company's new designs for a flying car could be stolen from the cloud and sold to a competitor for millions of dollars. The only thing stopping an employee from taking that data is good ethics, or a security infrastructure greatly restricting access. Any time data is stored externally on a server outside of your control, it becomes at risk of being compromised. Cloud companies want their customers to feel at ease and promise privacy and security, but it is not effectively delivered 100% of the time. This may make you think that cloud storage is the worst idea on the planet, and you should avoid it at all costs. That is not true. It just needs to be used wisely and users need to determine what level of risk they are willing to accept. Two great methods can be used to overcome these security challenges. One is encryption, the other is to create a private cloud infrastructure.

Private cloud infrastructures are an excellent alternative and a much more secure way to have the best of both worlds. They are more expensive to create and manage, but where security is concerned, private clouds are the best solution. A private cloud is set up on the company network, controlled by company employees, and access is only available to approved individuals. Data is only accessible to those employees who would have already had access to it in a traditional network environment. This eliminates the risk of outsiders working for other companies making your data public or using it for personal gain. This does not eliminate insiders within the organization from stealing data, but other security mechanisms covered in an earlier chapter help to curb that risk. A private cloud can provide the same level of worldwide mobile access without the risk of outsourcing. It is not the best solution for organizations with smaller budgets, but great for large companies.

The use of a VPN can provide secure access to a private cloud from anywhere in the world. VPNs create encrypted tunnels extending the local network to the point of the user making a remote connection. This hardware used to be incredibly expensive and difficult to set up but is now a much more streamlined capability. Software applications can be used to set up VPN clients and servers with very little effort. Free, open-source software now exists in this space eliminating the overhead of multiple hardware devices. Though, in larger operations, a dedicated VPN device will provide a higher quality of service, especially in situations where many users need to access data regularly. Home users can even take advantage of these capabilities to access shared drives connected to their private home networks. Utilizing a private cloud requires this type of secure connection to limit access and encrypt data in transit.

Encryption is another great option if public cloud storage is the only viable solution. Cryptography will be covered more in-depth in Chapter 12. The basic concept of encryption is data can be scrambled in such a way that prying eyes will not know what it contains. If an organization must outsource its needs for cloud storage, all sensitive files should be stored in an encrypted state. This is not always the easiest thing to work with because encryption at this level is not seamlessly integrated into cloud storage solutions. For example, a database containing credit card information for all customers should be protected as much as technically

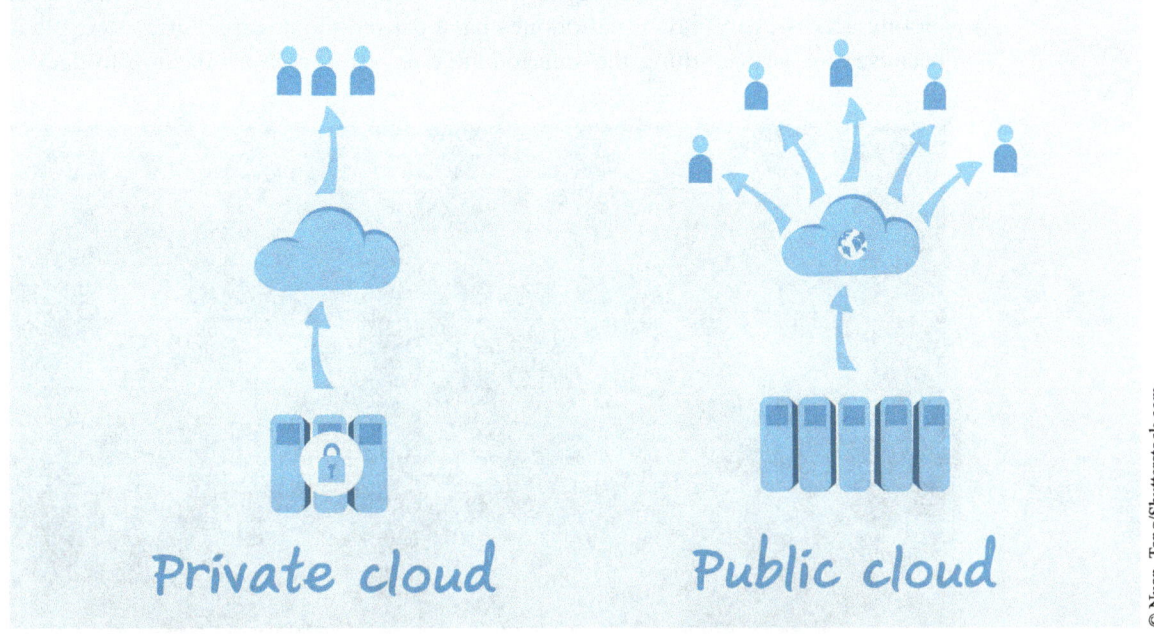

possible. The file can be encrypted before storing it in the cloud but will need to be decrypted every time it is accessed. This can become very clunky, especially if multiple users need to access the same data.

Encrypting and decrypting adds additional steps to the process, and depending on the software being used, may not be fully functional when the data is sitting on a cloud-based server. Most publicly available cloud systems do not include a function for automatically encrypting and decrypting data as it is accessed. Data could be stored within an encrypted file container on a cloud-based system and then mounted as a drive on the user's local computer when decrypted and in use. People tend to avoid encryption in these technologies because the extra steps and extra effort make it feel too difficult to implement. It is easy when a single user is involved, but thousands of users across a nation may find it more challenging to constantly encrypt and decrypt information. The advantage of encryption is clear. It provides the organization full control over the data and ensures no one else can see the encrypted contents. Even if a hacker successfully steals the encrypted contents, their chance of breaking properly configured encryption is almost impossible.

Ultimately, the wisest decision when using cloud storage solutions is to only store non-sensitive data. All sensitive data should be maintained on organizationally-controlled systems limiting access to authorized users. This is the safest way to ensure security. It may take away some remote access capabilities, but it eliminates a large risk at the same time. For example, corporate financial data should be located on the internal network and only accessible locally. Users working with this data should be required to be physically in the office and locally authenticated on the network. This eliminates a lot of risks and, in this particular example, the number of users with access to this type of data is often limited. The same is true for other categories of sensitive data stored on networks. It was mentioned earlier that the only way to be completely safe on the internet is to not be connected to the internet. The next best thing is to make sure sensitive data is not accessible on the internet.

This technology is not going anywhere. Almost everyone uses some form of mobile access every day. Smartphones have caused cloud capabilities to explode because almost everything the smartphone does requires a connection to data or

services stored in another location. This is cloud computing at its finest. Checking email from your phone? That requires connecting to an email server which is providing both a service and data. Streaming a movie from an online provider? The data is coming from the cloud. You get the point. Mobile access is the number one in-demand capability today and that demand is only going to grow. Cloud capabilities have a lot to offer and since it is not going anywhere, creating security-conscious infrastructures is the way to go. The nice thing is many of the same concepts we use to harden any network apply to clouds as well. At the end of the day, it is just another network of systems providing some type of external access to customers.

One thing we can learn from cloud computing is it gives us the capability to work from anywhere. If used correctly, cloud capabilities can save organizations a significant amount of money each year by scaling back the size of their real estate footprint and allowing employees to work remotely from their homes or other locations. This can also increase productivity by eliminating many of the distractions taking place in office environments. The available services in this arena continue to grow at an incredibly fast rate, creating a challenge for security controls tending to play catch-up. Keeping your use of cloud capabilities secure is a major piece of the puzzle. This cannot be overstated. Newer capabilities may not be ready for secure adoption so be careful navigating these waters.

Security Advantages of Clouds

Reading through this chapter may give the idea cloud computing is bad. It is not bad. It is a great technology that provides many capabilities individual users and organizations can utilize to be more productive and flexible. Not to mention the plethora of entertainment capabilities bringing streaming moves and music to devices all over the world every day. It is not a stretch to say cloud computing saved many businesses during the COVID pandemic. Many employees transferred from the office building to their own homes and continued to work on all the same products and processes as if they were sitting at a desk in a massive office building. In-person staff meetings were transferred to online meetings using web cameras and microphones that previously went unused on most computers. There was a definite learning curve to the transition, but the in-place cloud capabilities enabled companies all over the world to continue operating. Cloud computing saved the day!

Cloud communication applications have implemented encryption to protect conversations. Online meetings utilizing current software are fully encrypted! Have you ever overheard a meeting taking place in an office near your desk? Have you seen white noise generators sitting in the hallway outside of an office door when a private meeting is in session? Encrypted communications eliminate the issue of eavesdropping, purposeful or accidental, ensuring your conversation is completely private. Encryption has also been added to many text messaging applications adding a great security measure to any mobile device, even for the most benign conversations. There would not be a need to implement this level of security if regular communications were not taking place over the internet. The needs of the user eventually brought the security capabilities already in use in other areas, into the cloud computing world. Even email encryption is readily available today, though the implementation is currently a little too clunky for normal users to configure.

Another free security mechanism cloud computing provides is a level of obfuscation. Obfuscation, in the computer security world, is a methodology making it difficult for outsiders to find data or services by locating them in unusual places, making code difficult to understand, or similar methods. The goal is to insert a level of confusion. Hackers use a similar methodology when hiding data on victim systems. Obfuscation by itself is not a great security measure, but when used as one part of a larger implementation it can provide one more barrier against a successful attack. Consider this scenario: a hacker breaks into a network, gets very deep into many different servers and systems, but is unable to find any valuable data so he leaves without causing any real damage. Why was he not able to find anything he could sell on the black market or use for other personal gain? Because the data sits on a cloud provider's system he cannot access. In this scenario, the cloud once again saves the day.

Using cloud computing as a major element of operational capabilities outsources security requirements to the provider. Any service or capability you can remove from your network is one less item needing to be regularly updated and patched. It is also one less potential avenue of attack. The earlier mentioned idea of outsourcing websites to a web hosting provider is a good example. The need to keep the software up to date, leave TCP ports 80 and 443 open on the firewall, and monitor for incoming attacks against web applications completely goes away. That becomes someone else's responsibility. Outsourcing email servers to a 3rd party provider has similar results in allowing TCP ports 25, 110, 143, 465, and 993 to stay closed. This does not eliminate the threat of phishing emails since they end up on the user's system and can still give an attacker an avenue of entry. Outsourcing some capabilities frees space to focus on remaining security concerns which cannot be shifted to someone else's shoulders. The bottom line here is to ensure security is a major element of cloud capabilities, as well as any other technology in use on your network.

Cloud Providers

Many different cloud providers offer Iaas, PaaS, and SaaS services. When looking to outsource or add capabilities, make a list of all the services you need and content the provider to ensure their infrastructure can handle your requirements. Pay special attention to the security they have in place. Detailed questions in this area can help you narrow down any potential shortfalls. The following list is a good place to start:

- Do you use or sell my information? – any provider who utilizes your data to advertise other services or sells your data to other organizations should immediately be crossed off the list. Perusing your data for targeted advertising is common when using free cloud-based services as it is how those organizations generate revenue. Any service you pay for should not sell your information or use it to market new services. At the very least there should be a provision to opt-out of this practice. Selling data you store on their systems would also be a breach of contract in most situations.
- Are my data and operations stored and conducted in an encrypted environment? – quality encryption is the best way to keep data safe from prying eyes, though it can be hard to implement in some environments. A top-tier

facility should be able to provide this capability to any user willing to pay the appropriate cost. If it is not available, keep sensitive files off the cloud.
- What is your security patching process? – security patches need to be applied to cloud-based systems just as often as any other system. This needs to be a rigorous process that monitors announcements of newly discovered vulnerabilities and immediately applies patches for any affected systems. Weekly or more often is the answer you are looking for here.
- What is your incident response policy? – their policies should line up with what you learned in chapters 6-7 and include customer notifications immediately after an occurring incident has been verified. Weak policies in this area are a good sign the provider has a low interest in security measures.
- What type of activity do you actively block? – the goal here is to make sure they are actively monitoring their network and blocking threats in accordance with standard security practices. IDS devices should be in place with 24/7 monitoring capabilities, alerting analysts of any potentially nefarious activity, and policies should trigger blocking action when thresholds are met.
- What is your logon authentication process? – single-factor authentication with usernames and passwords is most common, but a two-factor approach adding an additional layer of verification is much more secure. Two-factor authentication is becoming more popular and accessible today with many sensitive accounts, such as those with banks and investment firms, requiring a secondary layer of authentication before gaining access. This provides a higher level of surety that the user is authorized.
- What is your employee vetting process? – cloud infrastructure employees may be able to access anything you store or process on their systems. They are often given privileged access as system administrators to maintain system availability and operational functions. As such, they have the ability to copy, delete, and modify data, stop and start services, and conduct any other normal system administration function. They need to be fully trusted to never access or manipulate any information you store on the cloud systems.
- How often are backups conducted? – you can certainly back up your own cloud data, but some providers have this as an additional service to save you time and hardware resources. Daily incremental backups should be expected if this service is available.
- Are backups stored offsite? – the best backup strategies store backup media in an alternate location in case the primary facility is destroyed or damaged in an accident. Storing backups in the same room as the servers is ineffective if a fire destroys the server room. Storing backups in an alternate location increases the chance of successful recovery after data loss. Security for offsite storage facilities should also be addressed to ensure unauthorized personnel cannot gain access to backup media.
- What is the average server uptime? – using someone else's equipment makes you reliant on their operational ability to maintain consistent uptime of all systems and internet connections. The industry standard is 99.999% operational availability. At this rate, there can be approximately 4 minutes of downtime every month. Determine the amount of downtime you can absorb and make sure they can meet your requirements.

Answers to these questions will help narrow down which organization's services will meet your specific needs and provide the level of security you require. It is unlikely to be perfect in all areas, so be willing to choose what is most important and find alternative workarounds for the areas lacking specific capabilities. The security provided is often dependent on the services you pay for. Renting virtual systems to run large mathematical operations may come with the caveat that you are responsible for securing the operating system, removing liability from the provider. They will have standard hardware security devices in place but leave the nuances of security up to the user allowing for complete customization. Having a securely configured pre-built virtual machine that can plug into the provider's network is best for these scenarios. A budgetary balancing act is required to determine what can be afforded and what can be conducted in-house. This will be different for every organization using cloud services, so think through it carefully before pulling the trigger.

Privacy Concerns

Apple recently announced in August 2021 they will begin scanning user devices connected to their services for child sexual abuse material to ensure the safety of children. This is a valiant effort that could help to eliminate this material from their cloud-based storage devices and similar actions are taken by other large providers such as Microsoft and Google. Apple's approach takes it a step further by placing software on the user's device allowing direct access to data before it is uploaded. Again, a valiant effort, but this implementation comes with big privacy concerns similar to internal employee data access already covered. Other personal images could easily be flagged in these operations causing legal content of a private nature to end up on an employee's screen for verification. The specifics of how this methodology is implemented may never be publicly released so it would be wise for users to be more careful with how they use their phones and know there is the possibility some of their content could be accidentally flagged for review.

All cloud providers have a term of service dictating how their services can and cannot be used. Many reputable organizations bar their systems from being used for any type of criminal activity, which makes perfect sense. A user pays for a service and is allowed to use it within the scope of the terms of service. A violation of those terms can result in termination of service. This is perfectly fair and should remain a common practice so companies can protect their interests. You have likely seen signs in stores requiring shoes and shirts for entry. During the COVID pandemic, we have also seen requirements for the wearing of masks. If you do not meet the requirements the store has in place, you cannot participate as a customer. The same exists in the digital world and companies have the right to implement rules as part of the relationship with a customer. And the customer also has the right to not use those services if the requirements are unacceptable. Security can cause user concerns ultimately leading to the cancellation of service for some and are what is perfectly acceptable to others. Choose what is best for your situation.

The average person can easily be overwhelmed when provided with a list of recommended security measures. It can appear to be a daunting task difficult to fully implement, and in some ways, seem to be overkill for what is really required. Do you really need as much security as this chapter details? Are there any hackers looking to directly target your network? Is your company so small you do not think you will ever be hacked? Many people have thought they were off the radar of an attacker because they did not have any juicy data worth stealing. And many of those people have had their systems broken into because of poor security. Maybe it is just a nuisance to clean up an attack or maybe it is something that can be completely avoided by putting a few solid measures in place.

Taking security serious requires a lot of effort, technical prowess, and vigilance to be sure the job is accomplished effectively. Just one gap is enough to allow an attacker through the front door. We do not leave our physical doors open for anyone to walk into our homes. We lock the door and set an alarm to provide a level of protection for our family and belongings. Criminals often look for weak targets because they present a much easier opportunity. We can avoid many of the insecurities of the internet with relatively easy security implementations. Configuring perimeter devices, patching vulnerabilities, and monitoring activity has become commonplace activities across the internet in virtually every sector of business. Paying for the services of a 3rd party providing cloud capabilities should come with the assurance that these security measures are part of their infrastructure. A user is not simply paying for a place to store their data. They are also paying for the peace of mind their data is stored securely and out of the reach of hackers and insiders alike. Anything less is a business relationship needing to be severed. We have the technology to keep hackers at bay and there is no good reason private networks and cloud infrastructures should not be fully secured.

Practical Application – Keep Cloud Data Secure

Your ability to securely store data on cloud-based networks is wholly dependent on the offerings of the organization and the level of control you have over the available services. Simple storage using a cloud drive is likely the least secure methodology unless you implement some form of encryption to be sure your data is unviewable by unauthorized users. Chapter 12 contains information on the technologies which can be deployed for this capability. Having complete control over a cloud infrastructure is better, but you still run the risk of cloud company employees accessing files. If cloud technologies are a major need for your organization, the best option is to keep sensitive files on internal network systems or encrypt those files when storing them in cloud mediums.

In addition, use the list of questions provided in this chapter to determine the level of service and assurances provided before entering into an agreement with a company offering cloud services. It is best to know upfront what type of security is in place, how employees are vetted, and how much control you have over the protection of your data. At the end of the day, no one will provide the same degree of protection for your data as you will. Access to many forms of data while mobile is a high priority in today's computing world. Keeping the data secure should be equally important to keep it out of the hands of nefarious actors.

Chapter 11: Review Questions

1. The early days of mainframe computing _____ cloud technologies.
    a. Were similar to
    b. Had nothing in common with
    c. Were identical to
    d. Had dumb servers
2. Smartphones _____ the power of early mainframe systems.
    a. Are slower than
    b. Exceed
    c. Are the same as
    d. None of the above
3. Google's Chrome operating system was designed to work with _____.
    a. No internet access
    b. Local USB drives
    c. Local hard drives
    d. Cloud-based services
4. Remote access capabilities have become a _____.
    a. Priority
    b. Necessity
    c. Configuration Pain
    d. Problem
5. _____ needs to be considered as part of the overall cloud design.
    a. Manageability
    b. Access
    c. Storage
    d. Security
6. SaaS provides _____.
    a. Access to applications over the internet
    b. Greater processing power for mobile applications
    c. Complete control over the operating system and all installed applications
    d. Provides infrastructure for organizations to run their own applications
7. PaaS provides _____.
    a. Access to applications over the internet
    b. Greater processing power for mobile applications
    c. Complete control over the operating system and all installed applications
    d. Provides infrastructure for organizations to run their own applications
8. 8. IaaS provides _____.
    a. Access to applications over the internet
    b. Greater processing power for mobile applications
    c. Complete control over the operating system and all installed applications
    d. Provides infrastructure for organizations to run their own applications
9. Cloud service _____ are the biggest risk in cloud storage.
    a. Speeds
    b. Hardware
    c. Software
    d. Employees
10. Apple's celebrity image leak had the marking of an _____.
    a. Insider
    b. Professional hacker
    c. Script kiddies
    d. Software malfunction
11. Storing data on a cloud service creates the potential for _____.
    a. Data loss
    b. Data corruption
    c. Information leaks
    d. Secure solutions
12. _____ are a great alternative to the current popular cloud construct.
    a. VPNs
    b. Email servers
    c. Private clouds
    d. Web servers

13. A _____ can provide encrypted connections to cloud infrastructures.
    a. Firewall
    b. VPN
    c. Router
    d. Switch
14. Never store _____ data on a public cloud.
    a. Encrypted
    b. Regular
    c. Company
    d. Sensitive
15. _____ makes cloud infrastructures much more securely viable.
    a. Partitioning
    b. Encryption
    c. User policies
    d. Automation
16. Cloud capabilities will _____.
    a. Increase
    b. Stay the same
    c. Decrease
    d. None of the above
17. Cloud computing capabilities are _____, as long as they are secure.
    a. Streamlined
    b. Negligible
    c. Bad
    d. Good
18. Online meeting applications have implemented _____ making these options much better.
    a. Error checking
    b. Encryption
    c. Parallel processors
    d. Partitioning
19. Storing data in another location can keep it out of _____ hands.
    a. Law enforcement
    b. Management's
    c. Employee's
    d. Hacker's
20. Newer _____ concerns are being raised over some cloud provider policies.
    a. Integrity
    b. Security
    c. Privacy
    d. Hacking

Cryptography

CHAPTER 12

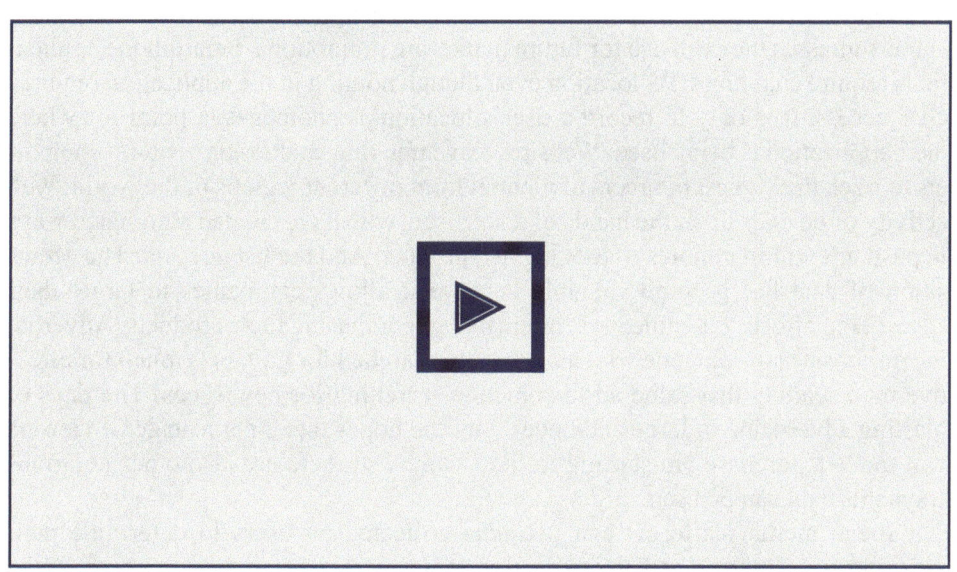

What is the best way to protect information? It can be hidden in a place no one will ever look, it can be placed in a box and buried underneath a slab of concrete, or it can be encrypted so only authorized users can view its contents. Cryptography is a method of protecting information by scrambling data to make it look like a long string of random numbers and characters. It looks like gibberish to the untrained eye, but those who understand even the most basic concepts of encryption can recognize when it is in use. The great thing about cryptography is its incredible strength when used correctly. A properly used method of encryption can remain unbroken through many years of attacks from supercomputers on the planet today. It really can be that strong! And it has been around for a very long time.

Would you be surprised to find out cryptography was used all the way back in the Roman Empire? History tells us that Julius Caesar used what is known as a substitution cyber when sending important military methods to keep the contents from being read by enemy spies. It was a simple method easily detected and broken today, but in his time, it seemed to work very well. The method was to simply replace a letter with one located a specified number of positions further up or down the alphabet. For example, if shifting 3 characters, the letter C would become F. Using this method, CAT would appear as FDW in its encrypted form. Anyone who read these letters without the knowledge of encryption would assume it was in an unreadable foreign language. The recipient of the message would only need to know how far to shift the letters to decrypt the message and reveal the real contents. We have much stronger methods available today which require computers to encrypt and decrypt using mathematical algorithms.

Data is a big business today. Everywhere you look someone is trying to collect information on someone else. Businesses offer free digital products in exchange for email addresses they can use for future marketing promotions. Smartphone applications require enabling GPS location even though nothing in the application requires GPS access. It is only to record a user's location as another data point for where their application is being used. Websites leave tracking cookies on visitors' computers to track the highest numbers of visitors from different regions of the world. Web activity often ends up in the hands of advertisers who have created automated ways to push ads within minutes of looking at a product. And the list goes on. The acquisition of data has become valuable because it allows companies to target their advertising efforts to people most interested in purchasing their products. Advertising guitar sales to someone who has recently searched for guitars is much for effective than sending that same ad to someone searching for new shoes. The days of blasting advertising to large audiences with the hopes that a percentage of viewers will make a purchase are starting to fade away. But there are also other nefarious ways this data can be used.

Social media platforms can use data collected on users to determine their viewpoints on many popular or divisive topics and use that data to control who sees the user's content. Surveys running on social media platforms asking about a person's first car, schools they attended, cities they were born in can be used to build databases full of answers to the same common questions websites use to authenticate a user before allowing a password to be reset. And some organizations collect data for the sole purpose of selling it to others. Need a list of email addresses to market your next big product? No problem, you can buy one which also includes demographics, purchase history, and interests for everyone on the list. All it takes is a little money. These practices have expanded over the past decade and will likely continue to expand as people seek to be even more connected to internet services.

There are two ways to combat this problem and protect personal data. The first is to recognize how often it is collected and stop giving it away so freely. It is easy to say no when someone wants information, to scroll past the latest survey all your friends are commenting on, and to avoid giving away personal information by joining everyone's email list. That is helpful for everyday common data people want to collect, but what about the data they really want? What about social security numbers, bank accounts, and driver's license numbers? What about the data that allows them to steal an identity or empty a bank account? That is the type of information hackers are after. Money is a great motivator and the chance to get a quick influx of cash from an unsuspecting user is difficult for an immoral person to pass up. The second way to combat this problem is to encrypt what needs to remain private. A criminal cannot do anything with a pile of encrypted data. It is worthless to them in every way. The same is true for everyone else. Keeping private data private is the easiest way to avoid many of these antics.

What you may not realize is that you already use encryption every day. Any website you visit that begins with HTTPS automatically creates an encrypted communication tunnel between your computer and the one hosting the web page using a protocol known as secure socket layer (SSL). Every bit of information sent to and from the website is encrypted inside of this tunnel, protecting the data from being viewed by anyone else who may be eavesdropping. You do not even need to log in to have this protection. The protocol in use automatically does the work for you. This allows secure transactions to be the normal mode of operation on any business-based website. Online purchases and banking are secure partially because of this technology. Obtaining a certificate to encrypt website communication used to be a laborious and expensive process, but large technology organizations have created free ways to obtain certificates to enable encryption across the entire internet. This has made the process incredibly easy, allowing anyone with a website to use encryption when communicating with every visitor. Technology companies know encryption is badly needed and have put a lot of effort into making it efficient, streamlined, and almost invisible to the end-user.

Many different encryption methodologies, known as ciphers, have been created and replaced over the years. Some have been broken as technology advanced and others continue to stand the test of time, two decades after they were designed. The basic methodology behind cryptography is relatively simple, as the Caesar cipher example highlighted. The implementation, however, can be a bit tricky even though the same simple concepts exist. A user has a set of unencrypted data, called plaintext, which needs to be protected. That data is run through a cipher using a type of secret key and the scrambled output, known as ciphertext, can then be transmitted or shared, without being read by eavesdroppers. That is a simplistic overview and there is a lot more technical detail involved, but to understand its security implications, you only need to know the basics. You do not need to be a mathematician or cryptographer to use encryption. You just need to know the types of encryptions in existence and how to implement the best ones within your networking environment.

The two most common types of encryption algorithms are symmetric and asymmetric. Symmetric key encryption uses one key to both encrypt and decrypt messages. Anyone involved in the communication stream needs to have access to the key to participate in the secure conversation. That key must remain a secret to keep the communication secure. If it becomes public, all communication using the key will no longer have an expectation of being secure. Asymmetric encryption takes a slightly different approach. It uses two keys, one public and one private, in combination to encrypt and decrypt data. The public keys are made available on a key server or website that anyone can access. A user wanting to send an encrypted message will encrypt it using the recipient's public key. Once received, the recipient will decrypt it using their private key. For example, Greg wants to send a secret message to his friend, Mark. He drafts his message, encrypts it with Mark's public key, and sends it on the way. When Mark receives it, he uses his private key to decrypt and read the message. He can respond by encrypting his message using Greg's public key, which Greg will decrypt using his own private key. The reason this works is because the public/private key pairs are generated at the same time and are mathematically connected.

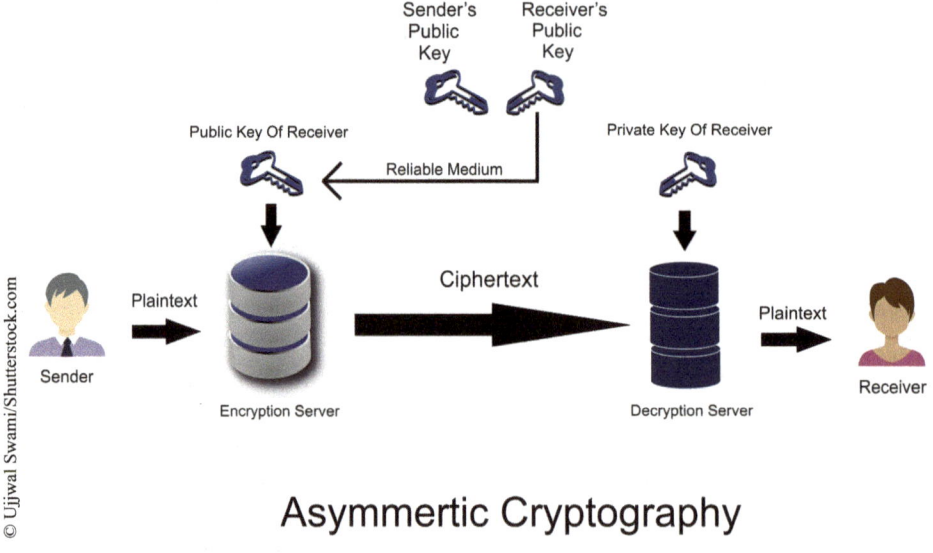

Asymmertic Cryptography

Symmetric encryption is faster than asymmetric and is most commonly used when encrypting large amounts of data such as databases and complete hard drives. It is also commonly implemented in payment applications. AES is the most widely known and used symmetric cipher today. It has been hailed as the gold standard and is at the core of many symmetric encryption operations. The biggest challenge to symmetric encryption is the management of the key. The key has to be protected to keep the data secure. Alternatively, asymmetric encryption is most commonly used in digital signatures for emails, digital currency transactions, and other applications requiring electronic signatures. And, as mentioned earlier, those secure websites you visit every day use a combination of asymmetric and symmetric encryption to make the communication stream secure. Now that you have a basic understanding of how encryption works, we can look at some practical uses where encryption can be used to provide security on a network.

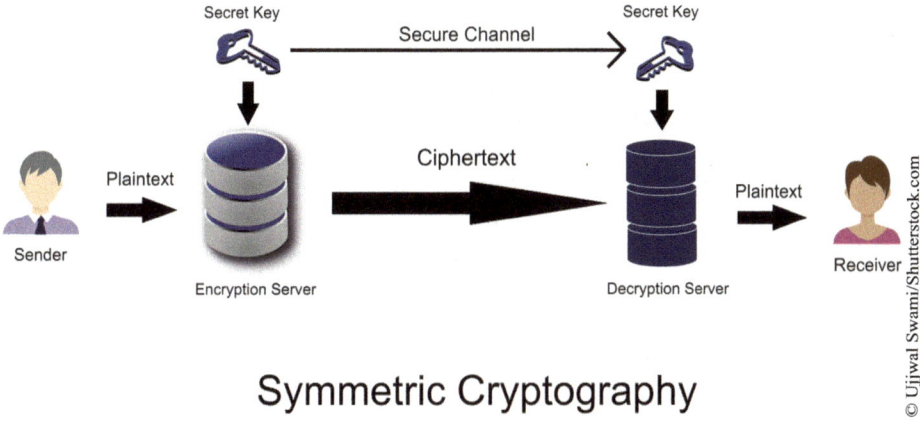

Symmetric Cryptography

Practical Uses

Any sensitive data stored on a computer should be encrypted. Hackers love to grab personal information from exploited systems because it can provide enough data to steal an identity which can lead to financial gain. Large databases full of information are an even better target and can be sold on the black market resulting in a much larger payday. If everyone followed the practice of encrypting sensitive information, this particular motive for hacking would dry up. If a hacker gains access to a network and cannot access juicy information, their goal of stealing and selling data fails. Any data containing personal information on customers or clients should be stored in an encrypted format and only be decrypted while in use. This data is usually stored within a database holding a treasure trove of information a hacker would love to get their hands on. Most modern database applications include an encryption option that keeps it secure and unreadable by anyone who does not hold the password. Taking a simple extra step can mean the difference between data exposure and keeping the database contents private.

Some text messaging apps now include the ability to encrypt conversations between users. The original form of text messaging piggybacked on telephone calls, jamming up to 160 characters into unused space in the signaling protocol. This gave phone companies an easy way to make extra money using technologies already in place. Each text message was sent in plaintext with zero security and was also displayed on phone bills each month. This was great for law enforcement looking for specific criminal activity but bad for users who wanted to protect their privacy. Newer applications were eventually written that send those same messages over the data portion of a smartphone's connection instead of using the voice signaling protocol. This solved part of the problem by making the contents of text messages less accessible to phone company employees. The next level was to provide end-to-end encryption completing obscuring the contents of a message from anyone other than the sender and recipients.

The only viable method to gain access to these messages is by accessing a phone that participated in the conversation. The same is true with full phone encryption now available on man Android and Apple smartphones. This security technology and capability is readily available and only needs to be enabled making a phone as secure as some of the devices used by intelligence agencies. Some law enforcement officers have raised a red flag over these capabilities because it limits their ability to access potential evidence located on a smartphone without a password. Suspected criminals can be compelled by courts to provide the password under threat of additional charges, but this issue has not yet fully worked its way through legal processes to establish any new laws. Time will tell if technology will be forcefully weakened with special back doors allowing law enforcement access. As for now, technology giants are keeping these practices in place and refusing to assist in attempting to unlock devices in law enforcement custody.

Email is one of the most widely used digital written communication methods in the business world. A lot of information is sent over email every day and much of it is sent without any level of security. People transmit social security numbers, bank account numbers, passwords, private details about their lives, and so much other sensitive data over this insecure medium every day. Email administrators have the ability to read every unencrypted email sitting on their servers. The legality is questionable at times, but the technical capability exists. Google even has software that scans Gmail user accounts to target advertising and offer other services a user may be interested in based on their email content. Email encryption has been in existence for over two decades but is rarely used by ordinary users because it requires some work to generate keys and configure applications for digitally signing and encrypting messages.

PGP, which stands for Pretty Good Privacy, was developed in the early 1990s and is one of the most frequently used methods to encrypt email messages. It is still secure today and uses a combination of symmetric and asymmetric ciphers to provide a high degree of protection for any data which needs to be transmitted over the internet. PGP uses the public and private key methodology described earlier allowing any user to email any other user, even if they have never met, as long as they can access their public key. Organizations that have network-wide implementation of email encryption make this much easier, as a user can simply pick someone from the address book, click the encryption button, and send off the message. That is really where email encryption becomes an easy-to-use technology, and it is something that should be a standard on any network concerned about security.

PGP is more difficult for home users to set up as the larger infrastructure does not exist and everyone involved in the conversation will have to generate their own public and private keys to be included. This makes it less common or viable for most home users. It has also become common in the media to make a copy of a reporter's public key available on the news website so anyone can send an encrypted tip. Online key repositories also exist where users can upload their public key for anyone in the world to use. Others will need to know what repository you use, and your email address and they will be able to start sending secure messages. This process takes a few extra steps to set up and configure, but it is worth the effort to eliminate the possibility of eavesdroppers reading your communications. PGP is not as popular as it used to be and does not boast a lot of users today but is still very viable and very free.

At this point, many people start to think about why they would need to encrypt everything. Some think they have nothing to hide. "It does not matter if the government knows about the shopping list I send to my spouse or my invitation to have dinner with a friend," they say. While this may be true, most users of technology use it for incredibly private information just as much as they do for meaningless drivel. People also fail to realize that collecting small pieces of information on someone over a long period of time can eventually lead to building a large personal profile of everything they like, their daily routines, the people they vote for, the names and location of their children, and many other private aspects of their lives. Again, a person who thinks they have nothing to hide may not care. Unless, of course, the information being collected falls into the wrong hands when a hacker breaks into a system, or a disgruntled employee decides to dump it all on the internet. That changes things.

In most cases, it is not illegal to collect data and many software license agreements include a clause pointing out the organization will collect some type of information from the user. Users are sometimes granted the ability to opt-out of information collecting, and other times are forced into it if they want to continue to use the service. This is less common in paid-for services and more common in those that are seemingly given away for free. Social media is a great example of the latter. If an organization wants to collect information for targeted advertising and a user wants to provide that information to receive better deals, so be it. It is their choice. The security concern here, and the reason it is important to the conversation of encryption, is the protection of the data. We have seen numerous times in the past decade where hackers have broken into systems and accessed hundreds of thousands of personnel records, user purchase transactions, and a slew of other information all made possible through a vulnerability and an unencrypted database. If the database was encrypted, even the vulnerability would have become pointless. Encrypting what needs to stay private takes away a major hacker motivation.

Private data is not only stored on databases but is also strewn across the hard drives of many computers on a network. This data must also be protected, and using a form of encryption, mentioned in Chapter 8, is the methodology best suited for the job. An organization could consider which systems process data sensitive enough to maintain it in an encrypted state and only implement full disk encryption in those particular cases. But a strong argument can also be made to have full disk encryption on all computers. From a standardization perspective, this is true. Maintaining the same configuration on all systems is a sound plan. Encryption of this magnitude is a fire-and-forget type of approach which does not need regular maintenance or updating. It does not add a regular duty to system administrators to double-check everything is working. Encryption is effective, easy to use, and should be used in all cases to maintain a higher degree of security.

Encryption can even be used for the everyday use of passwords. With the plethora of websites, smartphone applications, and computer logins, it is easy to end up with hundreds of accounts on many different systems. This can make it very difficult to keep track of which passwords go with which accounts. Some users use the same password on everything, which is a horrible idea because if one account is broken, the rest can also easily fall. It is wise to use different passwords on as many different systems as feasible. But this makes it even harder to remember how to log in. Here is a secret for you. Passwords can be stored in an encrypted file tucked away in a safe place for you to reference if you forget a password. Put it on a USB drive and toss that in a safe. It is a great backup method for when you cannot remember the password you have not used in 6 months. Some professionals do not like this idea. They think it creates a weakness with a single point of failure. This is only true if the passwords used to generate the encryption keys are weak. Otherwise, it is just as strong as the cipher protecting the login to your bank accounts.

It is important to note criminal organizations also use encryption to protect or hide their activity. Some use this as an argument for making encryption easier to bypass for law enforcement so crimes can be more easily prosecuted. This is a nice idea in theory but creates a security risk that hackers will eventually exploit. Creating a back door or skeleton key-type application that breaks through a device's encryption will only remain secret for so long. Eventually, someone will figure it out and then have the ability to gain access to the plaintext content of loads of information. No one is arguing for governments to provide a secret backdoor key for their databases to keep them honest. Yes, encryption can make it more difficult for law enforcement to do their jobs and may make it easier for a criminal to hide certain elements of information. Criminals have been attempting to hide information from the police for as long as crime has existed and will continue to do so regardless of the available technology. Making something the general public uses weaker to assist in law enforcement investigations is not a sound argument.

Just because something is used for illegal purposes does not mean the rest of the world should be limited from using that technology. If this same argument was applied to other technologies, we would have zero privacy. Bad people use phones to propagate crimes so every phone call should be recorded, monitored, and analyzed. No one would like that idea. Bad people live in homes, so the government should have the right to enter any home and look for criminal activity. That is not a good one either. To be fair, no one is asking for permission to look at the plaintext contents of every phone all the time. The goal is to have a technological capability allowing encrypted smartphones to be decrypted as part of an official investigation.

Their goal would be to use this backdoor technology in combination with a search warrant. It could be feasible and helpful in finding criminals. At the same time, it also puts every user of every device in question at risk, of having their formerly protected information made public. Even if law enforcement was granted this desire, other methods of encryption exist that could defeat any backdoor access. Users could simply encrypt data with a symmetric key before storing it on the device. Having a backdoor to the device's built-in security will not unlock other files separately encrypted. There is almost always a technical solution for attempts to weaken security. Additional methods even exist to hide data in plain sight where many people would not even realize the data is right in front of their eyes.

An older technology, known as steganography, is the method of hiding information, most commonly within digital images. It is a fascinating technology that blends data into the image by making slight modifications to certain pixels to represent the 1's and 0's of the hidden information. It is undetectable when looking at the image because the human eye by itself is unable to naturally detect the minute changes. This is not really encryption because plaintext data can be hidden within the image just as easily as something in an encrypted state. The hidden file is protected by a password and, as with other things in the digital world, the password is the key to viewing what is hidden. These modified images can be emailed to recipients or uploaded to websites to move information anywhere with most people thinking it is just a nice picture. An easy way to move data would be to prearrange the use of a particular web forum and upload a steganography-laced image as part of a conversation. A conversation including images of Jeep Wranglers could easily include images with hidden data. With the number of websites in existence, anyone who wants to pass secrets could go undetected for a lifetime. So much for hiding microfilm in the heel of a shoe.

Tools exist to help identify if some form of steganography is in use, but without the password, it is typically impossible to extract the hidden data. And which images would someone look at? Can an analyst scour the entire internet grabbing every available image to scan? That is certainly unpractical. Perhaps, in the course of an investigation, the images on a computer could be checked, but with the number of digital images on most computers, it will be a time-consuming process that may only yield evidence of existence, without any way to extract the data. Steganography has proven to be a valuable method in protecting and transmitting data and can be used by organizations looking to keep their most valuable secrets from detection. Adding a symmetric cipher to the data before inserting it into an image will provide multiple layers of protection – obfuscation and encryption combined.

Broken Algorithms

Over time, some encryption algorithms have been broken or found to have flaws. Others have become less viable due to advancements in computing technology which could more easily break the cipher using advanced computational power. They were strong in their time, but technological advancements have rendered them less useful, and they needed to be replaced by newer ciphers. The Caesar cipher mentioned earlier can easily be categorized as a broken algorithm. It is no longer effective at keeping anything secret as it is easily defeated by the computational power of modern systems. This should always be expected in cryptography. Technology can easily make older things obsolete, and since mathematical algorithms are used to provide secure storage or communication, the more powerful computers become, the more important it is to develop new algorithms. You will likely see this iteration take place several times in your lifetime.

The popular AES cipher, which maintains its status as the gold standard today was created as the result of a competition starting in 1997 and continuing for several years until the Rijndael cipher was selected as the winner and became known by the more popular name of Advanced Encryption Standard (AES). Two of the runner-ups which are widely available today were the Twofish and Serpent ciphers. Both are incredibly strong but were a bit slower in performance which allowed Rijndael to edge them out of the competition. Some cryptographic implementations today use a combination of all three ciphers, encrypting with one, and then each of the other two subsequently. This effectively encrypts data three times which is likely overkill since even one strong cipher with an adequate password is highly unlikely to ever be broken. AES is the common standard used around the world by governments, organizations, and individuals and has so far stood the test of time. The next big technology on the horizon which may challenge the effectiveness of these top-tier ciphers is quantum computing, but research has not yet made it fully viable.

Encryption is incredibly important. It provides a high degree of security for highly sensitive government documents and for an individual's personal finances. Every day people have access to some of the same levels of encryption used to secure government secrets. That should give every user of encryption a measure of surety their information is well protected. As with many other technologies, the password used to encrypt data should be incredibly strong. A weak password can cause the entire encrypted canopy to collapse leaving your data lying naked for anyone to see. No one wants that to occur. Well, no one except for the people looking to gain access to your secrets. This cannot be overstated. Take the time to develop a strong password to protect your most sensitive data.

Passwords are used to generate the keys encrypting the data. The stronger the password, the stronger the key. This is not the technology you want to skimp on with a simple 8-character password. In the interest of being extra secure, it is wise to use a much longer passphrase. Using a complete sentence as a passphrase is an easy way to reach a much longer length. A 50-character sentence with the same combination of letters, numbers, and special characters, as discussed in Chapter 8, will provide a level of protection unbreakable in a reasonable amount of time, using today's technological capabilities. This may not be true 50 years from now, but your passphrase will be changed to something different by that time.

All this content about encryption may have you thinking about the data you need to protect. That is a good thing to think about. You also may be thinking about how to implement encryption. The great news is there are many options, some free and some commercial, you can start using right away. A few are covered in the practical application section at the end of this chapter. Start making a list now of what you need to encrypt. Some of it will be organizational data, some will be personal data. Encryption should be used in both environments. Here is a good list to start with:

- Private customer data
- Financial transactions
- Corporate secrets
    - Inventions
    - Unique methodologies
- Personal finances
    - Bank records
    - Investments
    - Tax returns
- Personal identity
    - Social security numbers
    - Drivers' license numbers
    - Children's information

This is not a complete list but will get you started down the right path of what needs to be protected. In a larger environment, it is often easiest to implement full disk encryption to cover all bases. In a home environment, encrypted file containers are often easiest to utilize as they can hold specific sensitive files without encrypting every application, document, and music file. The key here is to know the technology exists to protect your information from even the strongest attacks. It is highly unlikely solid implementation of today's encryption ciphers will be broken any time soon. And when the time comes to make them stronger, a new algorithm will be developed, as has been the case in the past, to keep our secrets secret. Do not delay, start encrypting today.

Practical Application – Tools of the Trade

The great news about encryption technology is very strong algorithms, which are pretty much unbreakable when used correctly, are freely available to the public. You do not need to be a government spy or an employee of a secret cabal to gain access to, or use, highly effective encryption. As you already learned, some of these algorithms are in use throughout the internet, as many of the connections to websites use cryptography to keep information between client and server protected from prying or spying eyes. This is great! The ability to protect a network, or data, in this way is easily implemented with a few simple tools.

Full Disk Encryption

On Windows-based systems, the easiest way to configure full disk encryption is to use BitLocker, which is included in the higher modern versions of this operating system. The main feature of BitLocker is to protect against offline attacks by storing all data on the hard drive in an encrypted format. This software has not been independently verified as the source code is not publicly available, though Microsoft has stated no backdoors have been created for government agencies. These same versions of Windows also allow for the encryption of individual files and folders providing users with a free solution to many encryption options.

Encrypted File Containers

An encrypted file container is a special file configured to act like an external or network drive containing information that is only available when properly mounted. Imagine you stored all your secret files on a USB drive, and you kept that drive locked up in a safe. The only people who would have access to the secret files are those who have access to the safe. But a great criminal could break into the safe. And if they did, your USB drive would have no protection. Now, imagine the data on that same USB drive was fully encrypted. You could still store it in a safe for secondary protection, and if someone did get their hands on it, the data would be worthless to them because it would be encrypted. An encrypted file acts a lot like a USB drive, when mounted, and sits on a computer hard drive when not. It could also be saved to any other external media device a user may desire.

© Mmaxer/Shutterstock.com

One of the most well-known tools available today to create encrypted file containers is TrueCrypt. This software has been independently tested by experts and found to be safe to use and without errors in the code. One public revelation from the Snowden files also revealed NSA's inability to break into TrueCrypt volumes, which should allow anyone using this software to know their data is highly secure. The problem though is TrueCrypt mysteriously and suddenly stopped production and distribution of their software in 2014, eliminating the possibility of updates or support. Many theories exist about what happened, none of which have been verified, and fortunately for lovers of TrueCrypt, the latest version of the software is still available for download on a variety of security websites. Just be sure you check the MD5 hashes to make sure you are downloading a legitimate copy of the program. A new application, named VeraCrypt, was released not long after TrueCrypt went dark, and has many of the same features because it was built from some of TrueCrypt's original code.

Both of these tools work in a similar fashion allowing a user to create a highly secure place to store sensitive files. A user simply creates a new file, selects the encryption algorithm they want to use, and lets the software go to work. Once created, the file is mounted as a drive letter in Windows, or to a mount point in Linux, and acts like any other drive available to the system. After a user is finished working with the sensitive files, the software is used to dismount the file container, locking the data back down in an encrypted state. Encrypted file containers are incredibly easy to work with and can be an effective way to protect sensitive data on any system or network.

Chapter 12: Review Questions

1. Cryptography has been around since at least the _____ era.
   a. Germanic
   b. Aztec
   c. British
   d. Roman
2. This cipher shifted letters to the right or left.
   a. Claudius
   b. Gaius
   c. Caesar
   d. Brutus
3. _____ is a big business.
   a. Decryption
   b. Memory Analysis
   c. Data
   d. Hard drive repair
4. We can protect personal data by _____.
   a. Not giving it away
   b. Both a and c
   c. Encrypt it
   d. None of the above
5. _____ are the biggest collectors of data today.
   a. News agencies
   b. Web sites
   c. Companies
   d. Social media platforms
6. Everyone on the internet uses _____ every day.
   a. Banks
   b. Email
   c. Encryption
   d. Clouds
7. _____ encrypts communication between a user and a website.
   a. NTP
   b. RDP
   c. SSL
   d. FTP
8. Ciphertext is also known as _____.
   a. Scrambled data
   b. Plaintext
   c. Encrypted data
   d. Unencrypted data
9. Plaintext is also known as _____.
   a. Scrambled data
   b. Plaintext
   c. Encrypted data
   d. Unencrypted data
10. Symmetric encryption _____.
    a. Is insecure
    b. Is outdated
    c. Used with public and private keys
    d. Is more commonly used on large amounts of data
11. Asymmetric encryption _____.
    a. Is insecure
    b. Is outdated
    c. Used with public and private keys
    d. Is more commonly used on large amounts of data
12. All _____ data should be stored in an encrypted state.
    a. Regular
    b. Sensitive
    c. Television
    d. Computer
13. Email encryption is _____ for regular users to implement.
    a. Easy
    b. Impossible
    c. Illegal
    d. Difficult
14. _____ can be stored in encrypted files.
    a. Social Security Numbers
    b. Passwords
    c. Bank information
    d. All of the above

15. _____ also use encryption.
    a. Governments
    b. Criminals
    c. Hackers
    d. All of the above
16. Technologies used for legal and illegal purposes should be _____.
    a. Legal
    b. Illegal
    c. Limited
    d. Destroyed
17. _____ has been looking to make legal backdoors into encrypted smartphones.
    a. Companies
    b. Law enforcement
    c. Hackers
    d. Individuals
18. _____ hides data within images or other files.
    a. Stegonogra
    b. Steakanography
    c. Steganography
    d. Stegorama
19. The gold standard cipher today is _____.
    a. PGP
    b. 3DES
    c. DES
    d. AES
20. Encryption ciphers need to be _____ when technology makes them easy to _____.
    a. Replaced, break
    b. Replaced, secure
    c. Eliminated, break
    d. Eliminated, secure

Appendix One: Linux Commands

Anyone working in the cyber security field should have a basic understanding of how to navigate systems from the command line. Within the realm of penetration testing, or hacking, the attacker almost always ends up staring at a command prompt after gaining access to a victim system. GUI interfaces are sometimes available through nefarious connections, but it is most common to see a black box with a blinking cursor. Not understanding how to navigate a command line interface (CLI) will end an attack on a system before it ever gets fully underway. These basic Linux commands will help you in your cyber security work, but they are by no means an exhaustive list.

man	View the manual for a command
ls	List files in a directory
whoami	See which user you are currently logged in as
ifconfig	Display IP address information
uname -a	Display kernel version and architecture of system
mkdir	Create a new directory
touch	Create an empty file or modify the time of an existing one
cat > file	Create a new file with the text you type after
more file	View the contents of a specific file
grep	Search for patterns in a file
df or df -h	Display the current storage of mounted partitions
du	Display disk usage of a directory's contents
fdisk -l	Display information for all attached storage devices
mount and umount	Mount and unmount storage devices
tree	View the directory structure for a specified path
nano file	Open or create a file in nano text editor
vim file	Open or create a file in vim text editor
rm or rmdir	Remove a file or empty directory
rm -r	Remove a directory that is not empty

mv	Move or rename a files and directories
cp	Copy files and directories
find	Search for files or directories
adduser	Add a new user accounts
deluser	Delete a user account
usermod	Modify a user account
chmod	Change the file permissions for a files or directories
chown	Change the owner of a files or directories
chgrp	Change the group of a files or directories
groupadd	Create a new group
delgroup	Delete a group
sudo	Execute a command with root priveleges
reboot	Reboot the system
poweroff	Power down the system
tar -cf sample.tar sample_dir	Create an uncompressed tar archive
tar -xf file	Extract the contents of a tar archive
cat /etc/resolv.conf	Display DNS servers system is configured to use
ping	Send a ping to a network device
traceroute	Trace the network path taken to a device
ssh	Login to a remote device
top	Display a list of processes and resource usage
htop	A human readable version of top
free -m	Display in use and free memory information
kill or killall	Terminate a process
kill -9 or killall -9	Terminate a process with SIGKILL signal

Appendix Two: Meterpreter Commands

The Metasploit Project framework includes a built-in command line interface (CLI), which provides users with the ability to configure and launch exploits against a target system, and also includes a payload, titled Meterpreter, which provides even more advanced command line capabilities after access to a victim system has been successfully gained. The functionality of this CLI and Meterpreter payload include capabilities to use more advanced attack methodologies, erase indications of an attack, explore and infiltrate victim systems at a deeper level, access password hashes, and manipulate victim system processes and memory.

Core Commands

These core commands can be used to navigate the available commands, exploits, etc. that are available in Metasploit.

Command	Syntax	Description
? or help	?, help, or help *command_name*	lists the core commands, module commands, job commands, resource script commands, database backend commands, and credential backend commands.
info	Info *module_name*	provides information about the available payload.
show action	show action	
show advanced	show advanced	
show all	show all	lists all modules that are currently available.
show auxiliary	show auxiliary	lists all auxiliary modules that are currently available.
show encoders	show encoders	lists all encoders that are currently available.
show evasion	show evasion	
show exploits	show exploits	lists all exploits that are currently available.
show missing	show missing	
show nops	show nops	lists all nop generators that are currently available.
show options	show options	lists all options that are currently available.
show payloads	show payloads	lists all payloads that are currently available for the chosen exploit.
show plugins	show plugins	lists all plugins that are currently available.
show targets	show targets	

Exploit Configuration

These commands are used specifically for preparing the exploit before it runs by setting the necessary options, establishing the payload, and checking to see if the exploit is viable:

Command	Syntax	Description
set lhost	set lhost *IP_Address*	sets the IP address for the local host
set lport	set lport *port_number*	set the port number for the local host
set payload	set payload *payload_name*	selects the payload to be used with the exploit
set rhost	set rhost *IP_Address*	sets the IP address for the remote host
set rport	set rport *port_number*	sets the port number for the remote host
set target	set target *target_number*	selects the target number to use with the exploit
unload	unload *module_name*	unloads the exploit module from memory
unset	unset *variable1 variable2 ...*	unsets one or more variables currently set
use	use *exploit_name*	selects a particular exploit for use

Exploitation

After all the exploit options are set, the penetration tester can check on the liklihood of the exploit working, launch the exploit against the victim system, or both.

Command	Syntax	Description
check	check	checks to see if the target is vulnerable to the selected exploit
exploit	exploit	launches the attack against the target, attempts to exploit the chosen vulnerability, and run the chosen payload.

Post-Exploitation Meterpreter Commands

Exploiting a system is just the beginning, many other commands exist that can allow the penetration tester to dig deeper into the victim system, expand their foothold on the network, and continue their operation.

Command	Syntax	Description
background	background	moves your current session to the background and return you to the prompt
channel	channel	displays every active metepreter channel
close	close *channel_number*	closes the specified meterpreter channel
exit	exit	shuts down the active meterpreter session
interact	interact *channel_number*	allows you to interact with the specified channel
migrate	migrate *PID_Number*	moves the active process to a specified process ID, usually to provide stability or increase privileges

quit	quit	quits the current meterpreter session
read	read *channel_number*	reads from the specified communications channel
use	use *extension_name*	loads the meterpreter extension listed after the use command
write	write *channel_number*	writes to the specified communications channel
ipconfig	ipconfig	displays the network interfaces and configuration on the victim system
portfwd	portfwd *port_number*	sets up a port forward from the victim system to a different remote service/system
route	route	will allow you to view/modify the routing table on the victim system

Privilege Escalation

Privilege escalation commands are useful for gaining a higher level of access, typically administrator or system level, on a victim system after the initial attack is successful.

Command	Syntax	Description
getprivs	getprivs	Attempts to escalate priveleges to something higher
getsystem	getsystem	Uses 15 separate methods to attemt gaining sysadmin privileges.

Hiding Tracks

Hiding your tracks is a common element of any penetration or hacking operation to avoid detection and allow for a longer period of access to the system.

Command	Syntax	Description
clearav	clearav	will clear out the event logs on the victim system
reg	reg	allows interaction the victim system's registry

Navigating the Victim System

The ability to navigate through the victim system after gaining access is paramount to achieving the goals of the operation.

Command	Syntax	Description
cd	cd *directory_name*	changes the directory on the victim system
getlwd, lpwd, or pwd	getlwd, lpwd, or pwd	prints the local directory
getuid	getuid	displays the username that the attacker is running as on the victim system

Appendix Two: Meterpreter Commands

Command	Syntax	Description
getwd	getwd	prints the working directory
idletime	idletime	checks to see how long since the victim system has been idle
lcd	lcd *directory_name*	changes to the specified local directory
ls	ls	lists files in the current directory
screenshot	screenshot	grabs a screenshot of the meterpreter desktop
sysinfo	sysinfo	gets the details about the victim computer such as OS and name

Manipulating the Victim System

Manipulating the system allows the penetration tester to edit files, change variables, upload an download content, and modify the system as needed.

Command	Syntax	Description
cat	cat *filename*	reads and writes to standard out (stdout) the contents of the specified file
del or rm	del *filename* or rm *filename*	deletes the specified file on the victim system
download	download *filename*	downloads (copies) a file from the victim system onto the attacker system
drop token	drop token	drops a stolen token
edit	edit *filename*	will edit the specified file using vim
enumdesktops	enumdesktops	lists all accessible desktops
execute	execute *command_name*	executes a command on the victim system
getdesktop	getdesktop	gets the current meterpreter desktop
getpid	getpid	displays the current process ID
kill	kill *PID_Number*	terminates the selected process ID
keyscan start	keyscan start	starts the software keylogger when associated with a process such as Word or browser
keyscan stop	keyscan stop	stops the software keylogger
keyscan dump	keyscan dump	dumps the contents of the software keylogger
mkdir	mkdir *Directory_Name*	creates the specified directory on the victim system
ps	ps	provides a list of all currently running processes
reboot	reboot	forces the victim system to reboot
rev2self	rev2self	drops the meterpreter token and any temporary Windows token
rmdir	rmdir *Directory_Name*	removes the specified directory on the victim system
set desktop	set desktop *Desktop_Number*	changes the meterpreter desktop
shell	shell	opens a command shell on the victim machine
shutdown	shutdown	shuts down the victim's computer

steal token	steal token *PID_Number*	attempts to steal the token of a specified (PID) process
timestomp	timestomp	Manipulates the (modify, create, access) attributes of a file on the victim system.
uictl	uictl	enables control of some of the user interface components
upload	upload *filename*	uploads (copy) a file from the attack system onto the victim system

Meterpreter Scripting Environment

The Meterpreter scripting environment is one of the most powerful features of the Metasploit framework.

Command	Syntax	Description
irb	irb	puts the command line into Ruby scripting mode allowing scripting on the fly
bglist	bglist	lists all meterpreter scripts or processes running in the background on the victim system
bgkill	bgkill *script_name*	kills a meterpreter script or process running in the background on the victim system
bgrun	bgrun *script_name*	executes a command or script in the background on the victim system
run	run *script_name*	executes the meterpreter script after the run command

Appendix Three: Common Ports and Protocols

Computers operating on the internet communicate using IP addresses and port numbers to establish connections between systems. The following are a list of the most common port numbers an analyst or investigator will encounter in their work. This list is not all inclusive and does not include custom applications which may use the same official port numbers listed here. It is good to memorize or be familiar with as many of these ports as possible.

21	TCP	FTP (control)
22	TCP & UDP	SSH (Secure Shell)
23	TCP & UDP	Telnet
25	TCP & UDP	SMTP (Simple Mail Transport Protocol)
42	TCP & UDP	Host Name Server/WINS Replications
43	TCP	WHOIS protocol
53	TCP & UDP	DNS (Domain Name System)
69	UDP	TFTP (Trivial File Transfer Protocol)
80	TCP	HTTP (HyperText Transfer Protocol)
88	TCP	Kerberos - authenticating agent
102	TCP	ISO-TSAP protocol/Microsoft Exchange
110	TCP	POP3 (Post Office Protocol version 3)
111	TCP & UDP	SUNRPC protocol
115	TCP	SFTP, Simple File Transfer Protocol
118	TCP & UDP	SQL Services
119	TCP	NNTP (Network News Transfer Protocol)
123	UDP	NTP (Network Time Protocol)
135	TCP & UDP	EPMAP / Microsoft RPC Locator Service
137	TCP & UDP	NetBIOS Name Service
138	TCP & UDP	NetBIOS Datagram Service
139	TCP & UDP	NetBIOS Session Service
143	TCP & UDP	IMAP4 (Internet Message Access Protocol 4)

Port	Protocol	Service
156	TCP & UDP	SQL Service
161	TCP & UDP	SNMP (Simple Network Management Protocol)
179	TCP	BGP (Border Gateway Protocol) -
220	TCP & UDP	IMAP, Interactive Mail AccessProtocol, version 3
264	TCP & UDP	BGMP, Border Gateway Multicast Protocol
318	TCP & UDP	TSP, Time Stamp Protocol
383	TCP & UDP	HP OpenView HTTPs
366	TCP & UDP	SMTP, Simple Mail Transfer Protocol. On-Demand Mail Relay (ODMR)
387	TCP & UDP	AURP, AppleTalk Update-Based Routing Protocol
389	TCP & UDP	LDAP (Lightweight Directory Access Protocol)
443	TCP	HTTPS - HTTP Protocol over TLS/SSL
514	UDP	syslog protocol
563	TCP & UDP	NNTP protocol over TLS/SSL (NNTPS)
750	UDP	Kerberos version IV
873	TCP	Rsync - File synchronisation protocol
901	TCP	Samba Web Administration Tool (SWAT)
989	TCP & UDP	FTP Protocol (data) over TLS/SSL
990	TCP & UDP	FTP Protocol (control) over TLS/SSL
992	TCP & UDP	Telnet protocol over TLS/SSL
993	TCP	IMAP4 over SSL (encrypted transmission)
995	TCP	POP3 over SSL (encrypted transmission)
1433	TCP	SQL Server database engine
1434	TCP & UDP	SQL Server database engine
3389	TCP	Windows Remote Desktop Protocol (RDP)